Rhetoric and Death

Rhetoric and Death

The Language of Modernism and Postmodern Discourse Theory

RONALD SCHLEIFER

University of Illinois Press

Urbana and Chicago

© 1990 by the Board of Trustees of the University of Illinois
Manufactured in the United States of America
1   2   3   4   5   C   P   5   4   3   2   1

This book is printed on acid-free paper.

Library of Congress Cataloging-in-Publication Data

Schleifer, Ronald.
    Rhetoric and death : the language of modernism and
postmodern discourse theory / Ronald Schleifer.
            p.   cm.
    Includes bibliographical references.
    ISBN 0-252-01740-4 (cloth : alk. paper). —
ISBN 0-252-06138-1 (paper : alk. paper)
    1. Postmodernism (Literature)   2. Metonyms.   3. Death in
literature.   4. Discourse analysis, Literary.   I. Title.
PN98.P67S35   1990   89-77559
801.95′0904—dc20   CIP

For Nancy, Cyrus, and Benjamin
and the memory of my mother,
Helen Schleifer

Contents

Acknowledgments

This book has benefited from the advice and patience of many friends and colleagues. First I thank my wife, Nancy Mergler, and our sons, Cyrus and Benjamin, for their patience and, more important, for making my own preoccupation with rhetoric and death over the past few years engaging and, if I may say so, exhilarating. Nancy has read many versions of this manuscript and has encouraged clarity and sensibleness in the face of my penchant for circumlocution. James Comas, J. Hillis Miller, Russell Reising, and my collaborator on many other projects, Robert Con Davis, also read versions of the manuscript and helped with important suggestions, criticisms, and specific and general support. My work is better for their care.

Other friends and colleagues read and heard about substantial portions of the manuscript, and I have benefited, sometimes only much later, from their helpful comments. Karen Klein, David Gross, Laurie Finke, Cornel West, Elizabeth Hinds, Barbara Correll, Gordon Taylor, Robert Markley, Elizabeth Robinson, Richard Macksey, Gayatri Spivak, Ben Long, Patrick McGee, Elisabeth Daumer, Grant Holly, Gregory Jay, David Miller, and James Raymond all helped with comments and suggestions. Ann Lowry of the University of Illinois Press has supported this project from beginning to end so that there is hardly a page of this book that isn't better for her thoughtful care. Invitations to lecture at the University of Tulsa, Hobart and William Smith Colleges, Southern Illinois University, and Marquette University offered me forums at which I was able to present and discuss many sections of this book, and I thank these institutions for their generous invitations. I also benefited from support from the Office of Research Administration of the University of Oklahoma for a summer grant that allowed me to make substantial progress on this book, and from support from the College of Arts and Sciences and especially the dean, Robert Hemenway, whose friendship and encouragement on this project have been part of continuing help for various projects I have been engaged in here at Oklahoma. Paula Stacy, the secretary of the English Department, has gone out of her way to make my work on this book pleasant and efficient. Melanie Wright compiled the index with thoughtful attention to detail. Finally, I thank the editors of the *New Orleans Review, College English,* and *MLN* for granting permission to reprint material that in most cases has been considerably revised and rethought for its inclusion here.

1

Introduction

The Metonymy of Death and the Standing Chill of Rhetoric

In time the curtain-edges will grow light.
Till then I see what's really always there:
Unresting death. . . .

The mind blanks at the glare. Not in remorse
—The good not done, the love not given, time
Torn off unused—nor wretchedly because
An only life can take so long to climb
Clear of its wrong beginnings, and may never;
But at the total emptiness for ever,
The sure extinction that we travel to
And shall be lost in always. Not to be here,
Not to be anywhere,
And soon; nothing more terrible, nothing more true.
        . . . .
And so it stays just on the edge of vision,
A small unfocused blur, a standing chill
That slows each impulse down to indecision. . . .

                              —Philip Larkin, "Aubade"

Understanding, reading, and even the more general feeling of things
in our time, whether we call these apprehensions modern or postmodern, are inhabited by a vague, almost imperceptible sense that
things are not quite right, or at least not quite as they have been. Such
a sense is concomitant with what George Steiner has called the great
"crisis of sense" that occurred "in the concept and understanding of
language" at the turn of our century (1986: 2, 1). More recently, Steiner
has called this the "crises of the word and of meaning" in the twentieth

century (1989: 108) that have disrupted traditional Western apprehensions of the possibilities of transcendental significance in experience—significance, most specifically, in relation to God and to death. With a troubled sense of overwhelming loss—Steiner's description of Paul de Man's work as "instinct with sadness" (1989: 122) could easily describe his own understanding—Steiner narrates the crisis of Western intellectual life in a manner that is fully inhabited by what he describes as the nostalgia, pathos, and failure of consolation that constitute modernity itself.

That crisis, he argues, is the unprecedented transformation of the fecund confrontation of intelligence with "the facticity of death, a facticity wholly resistant to reason, to metaphor, to revelatory representation." In our time, that traditional confrontation has been transformed from the "statement [in aesthetic forms] of vitality, of life-presence, which distinguishes serious thought and feeling from the trivial and opportunistic" into the absence of such seriousness, into "an epistemology and ethics of spurious temporality" (1989: 140, 141, 26). For Steiner, aesthetic forms are inhabited by transcendental values—values that refer beyond the time and place of their articulations—and the crisis of our time "is the collapse, more or less complete, more or less conscious, of these hierarchized, definitional value-gradients (and can there be value without hierarchy?) which is now the major fact of our intellectual and social circumstance" (1971: 81–82). Most notable, in this collapse, is the failure to discern an intelligible order within temporal human existence. The genius of the age, Steiner argues, is the "metaphysics" of journalism—which I will describe in this book as radical metonymy. "Journalistic presentation," he says, "generates a temporality of equivalent instantaneity. . . . The journalistic vision sharpens to the point of maximum impact every event, every individual and social configuration; but the honing is uniform. Political enormity and the circus, the leaps of science and those of the athlete, apocalypse and indigestion, are given the same edge" (1989: 26–27). In an age of the instantaneous, the possibility of transcendental values seems to Steiner to be irrevocably lost; in such an age, even the "bracing acceptance of ephemerality and self-dissolution" embody "the underlying nihilistic findings of . . . in-comprehension" (1989: 132).

This collapse is marked for Steiner by a changing relationship to God and to death. In both cases, he argues, "in European, Central European and Russian culture and speculative consciousness during the decades from the 1870s to the 1930s" (1989: 93), transcendental meanings and hierarchies were replaced by a pervading sense of immanence and literality. "It is only when the question of the existence or non-existence of God will have lost all actuality," Steiner says, "it is only when, as logical positivism teaches, it will have been recognized and felt to be strictly nonsensical, that we shall inhabit a scientific-secular world. Educated opinion has, to a greater or lesser degree, entered upon this new freedom. For it, emptiness is precisely and only that" (1989: 230). Not only is emptiness precisely and only emptiness in a new "journalistic" immanence of the literal, but death itself—that great emptiness—has come, in the educated opinion of our time, to be uninhabited by any transcendental understanding that could answer its terrible facticity. The very literalness of nothingness, the emptiness of death, the absence of God that Steiner laments has become so much a part of our experience that the sadness and loss and sense of crisis he expresses (as do so many of the modernist writers born between 1870 and 1930) seem almost incomprehensible to many born at mid-century.

In this book I am attempting to describe this crisis of metaphysics and language that Steiner and others have felt to be the defining feature of modern Western culture, the sense of death that governed the discourse of modernism as it flourished in the first decades of the twentieth century and as it governs contemporary examinations of discourse in our own time. I am imagining "sense" in both of its common usages: sense as meaning and sense as feeling or sensation. In fact, one assumption of this book is that the concept of rhetoric, as it developed in the modernist era and more recently, encompasses both functions of "sense," that it creates the possibility of understanding both meaning and sensible feeling as effects of discourse. This conception of rhetoric participates in the "crisis of sense" that has generated "our present agenda for debate, which situates the problem of the nature of language at the very centre of the philosophic and applied *sciences de l'homme*" (Steiner 1986: 2). But it does so in a way that may well offer an understanding of the intellectual and affective senses of our time that is less apocalyptic and less nostalgic than Steiner describes. It offers, I think, the possibility of imagining what is almost literally unthinkable for Steiner: namely, the existence of value in a culture where hierarchies seem, to one extent or another, to be exploded.

The conception of rhetoric at the center of intellectual life in modernism and in the twentieth century more generally focuses on language as an immanent interhuman activity that is simultaneously meaningful and powerful. In this, rhetoric examines how discourse and language achieve their particular effects in particular interhuman situations. Such effects include meaning and understanding; but they also include other senses discourse communicates: desire, power, pleasure, and anxiety. One sense among these—one, I will argue, that arises for particular historical reasons at the moment of European modernism—is the felt but not always clear sense of the arbitrary and contingent nature of meaning, the sense that alongside the more or less transcendental meanings of discourse, not quite consciously apprehended as an "apocalyptic superimprinting" upon them (to use a figure Jacques Derrida develops [1978: 137]), is a sense of meaninglessness, nothingness, nonsense.

Such a sense, I believe, is linked metonymically to the sense of the overwhelming facticity of death in the modernist era. This sense, not always fully articulated, apprehends death as being without transcendental or symbolic significance, but simply as a meaningless material event. The nature of the relationship between rhetoric and death is difficult and complex, just as is the nature of metonymy itself. The complexity of the latter, as I will argue, will help define the relationship of rhetoric and death. Metonymy, of course, is the figure of speech that substitutes something that is contiguous to whatever is being figured for that thing itself: in this way, the king can be called the "crown," a presidential statement a "White House" statement. Metonymy is closely related to synecdoche, the figure of speech that substitutes a part for the whole (or the whole for a part): the royalty of Europe can be called the "crowned heads" of Europe, the narratives of particular moments in various people's lives can be called *Dubliners*. Roman Jakobson in a famous essay joins metonymy and synecdoche together under the name "metonymy" and opposes this figure to "metaphor"—the substitution of one thing for another, a "whole" for a "whole"—in the way, he argues, that Ferdinand de Saussure distinguishes between the syntagmatic axis of language and the paradigmatic axis (Jakobson 1956; see Ch. 5). Yet there is a problem in uniting metonymy and synecdoche under the name of "metonymy": such a naming is itself a synecdoche—it uses a part of the combination "metonymy and synecdoche" for the whole—which, despite its name, makes metonymy a species of synecdoche. In this understanding, metonymy always abstracts some quality that is part of the figure being described to stand for the whole. The president's speech can be figured as a White House statement only insofar as that *part* of his speech is "official"; rhetoric and death can be metonymically linked if they share in some larger whole of which they constitute parts.

In this way, metonymies have an underlying common denominator by which the link with their tenor is understood: metonymies, insofar as they make sense, present what I am calling a transcendental signification—a meaning that transcends the particular instance and example. Even the famous list of Borges with which Michel Foucault begins *The Order of Things*—the division of animals in a "certain Chinese encyclopaedia" into "(a) belonging to the Emperor, (b) embalmed, (c) tame, (d) sucking pigs, (e) sirens, (f) fabulous, (g) stray dogs, (h) included in the present classification, (i) frenzied, . . . (l) *et cetera,* (m) having just broken the water pitcher, . . ." (1970: xv)—presents the common denominator of "incongruous classification" so that each instance is a part of a whole. In other words, metonymies become synecdoches insofar as language and intelligence will find meaning *anywhere:* Saussure asserts in the *Course in General Linguistics* that "a material sign is not necessary for the expression of an idea; language is satisfied with the opposition between something and nothing" (1959: 86), so that, as Derrida says, in language even the "semantic void *signifies*" (1981: 222). For this reason Jakobson asserts that the "nature" of language is "synecdochic" (1932: 459): meaning, for Jakobson, is a whole always greater than the sum of its parts.

Still, metonymy is not always or wholly reducible to synecdoche: there is a sense in which metonymies and synecdoches are not the same thing, a sense in which, in Jakobson's discussion of Freud, the metonymic "displacement" and synecdochic "condensation" of dream work is and ought to be distinguished from one another (1956: 113). Metonymy traffics in what is accidental and random (such as the accidental color of America's presidential mansion), while synecdoche emphasizes what is necessary and essential (such as the necessity of royalty having heads to function). In more general terms, if underlying synecdoches inform metonymy, they do so by substituting the essence and depths of the meaningful whole of discourse for the surface of discourse. Yet such substitution is not the whole story. Rather, syntagmatic discourse is always metonymic even if, as Jakobson argues, the whole of meaning is always—*transcendentally*—greater than its parts. In other words, because of the *historical* existence of discourse— because discourse always arises and exists within particular contexts— the "whole" of discourse can be definite, but, in a term I borrow in Chapter 4 from Mikhail Bakhtin, it can never be wholly "finalized." For this reason, I think, Derrida asserts that "the part is always greater than the whole" (1979: 96). Most important, it is precisely the understanding of metonymy as distinct from synecdoche that allows me to link rhetoric and death. On the level of semantics, the concept of "death" exists in a relationship to "life" that is analogous to metonymy's relationship to synecdoche: "death" both is and is not a "part" of life; it is a "stage" of life (a part) and the negation of life altogether (its "other").

These two aspects of death—a "part" and an "other"—are themselves not reducible to a hierarchic (which is to say a synecdochic) relationship: death is not "essentially" a part of life or "essentially" the negation of life. Rather, both of these senses are included, non-opposably, within "death." In the same way, metonymy is not "essentially" a part of language, whose ultimate "nature" Jakobson says is "synecdochic" (1932: 459). But neither can metonymy be solely characterized in terms of the "warning" Paul de Man takes from *The Triumph of Life* "that nothing, whether deed, word, thought, or text, ever happens in relation, positive or negative, to anything that precedes, follows, or exists elsewhere, but only as a random event whose power, like the power of death, is due to the randomness of its occurrence" (1984: 122). In this, as in Borges's list, incongruity or arbitrariness becomes a negative principle of inclusion. Instead of defining metonymy by one or another of its aspects of parts—instead of defining it by abstracting its synecdochic "essence"—we can define it the same way Emile Benveniste defines the nature of the linguistic sign, as both arbitrary and motivated. "What is arbitrary," Benveniste writes, "is that one certain sign and no other is applied to a certain element of reality and not to any other," and this arbitrariness is seen from the point of view of the linguist. "For the speaker," however, "there is a complete equivalence between language and reality" in the ways language is used, and in this circumstance language is natural and "motivated" in relation to the actual social functioning of discourse (1971: 46). In just the opposite way, death is arbitrary for the subject of death, yet someone outside can take that death and make a sign of it, what Freud calls in *Beyond the Pleasure Principle* life's proper "aim of death" (1959: 71).

In this argument, I am marshaling metonymy (and the "surface" of discourse) to stand more generally, synecdochically, for the materiality of language. All discourse and meaning must take up material signifiers to articulate and communicate itself, and such materiality, like death, is both a "part" of language and the "other" of language. In other words, the "sense" of discourse is both meaningful and material, possessed of meaning that transcends (or appears to transcend) its moment of articulation, and also simply a random, material event, a moment that can and does provoke inarticulable feelings, like the blurred sense of dread on the "edge of vision" that Philip Larkin describes (and provokes) in "Aubade," or the anxiety Kafka repeatedly produces, seemingly and disturbingly unconnected to the narrated events of his novels. This, then, will be my focus in *Rhetoric and Death*: the power of discourse to create effects—of meaning, of affect, and even of an unlocatable dread linked somehow to nonsense—by means of material language in the face of an understanding of life and death as themselves contingent material events.

I am not trying to make a "theme" of death, to follow the ways that death becomes a subject, a preoccupation, something to be understood and narrated by language. In fact, in much that follows the idea of death may seem lost, on the margin, an unfocused blur, the ghostly haunting Derrida describes "which allows neither analysis nor decomposition nor dissolution into the simplicity of a perception" (1989: 62). In what follows, then, I shall examine discourse itself as a form of power and desire in modernist literature and criticism and also in contemporary discourse theory. But I am most concerned with the relationship of power and meaning with a "sense" of death that developed in the modernist era in terms of a *material* apprehension or conception, what I am calling a conception of *negative materiality*. I use this term precisely because I do not wish to make death a "theme," to make it a "substance." A. J. Greimas describes the tendency of language to transform the elements of relationships into substantives so that any discourse about meaning "is not only a signifying language, it is also substantifying, freezing all intentional dynamism into a conceptual terminology" (1970: 8). I am trying to resist this tendency to make the complexities of meaning—"death" or "metonymy" or even "rhetoric" itself—into a particular, instrumental "thing" by pursuing a rhetorical (rather than semantic) analysis focusing on the concept of "negative materiality." Such a focus, I believe, can further define the crisis of the word and of meaning in the twentieth century, a crisis that Steiner describes as "one of the very few genuine revolutions of spirit in Western history and which defines modernity itself" (1989: 93).

The conception of negative materiality, as I develop my argument in Part I of this book, hovers on the edge of "conception" to produce a sense in which death is not quite a concept or a thing but simply, negatively, "not to be here, / Not to be anywhere." Later in "Aubade" Larkin describes the negative materiality of death more fully:

> this is what we fear—no sight, no sound,
> Nor touch or taste or smell, nothing to think with,
> Nothing to love or link with,
> The anaesthetic from which none come round.
> (1988: 208)

In other words, if rhetoric describes how discourses are constructed to achieve certain effects, one such effect that traverses the discourse of modernism and the discourse of contemporary literary theory is an "anaesthetic" effect, the palpable (one might almost say "positive") effect of negativity, of blankness, a pervasive "sense," in both meanings of the word, that discourse is inhabited or haunted, metonymically, by nonsense as well as by meaning, that beyond all the eloquence of language is the "flash of insight" Marlow gets in *Heart of Darkness,* an understanding that, in the world in which he finds himself, neither speech nor silence makes much difference (Conrad 1971: 39). It is a chilling "sense," never fully articulated, of anesthesia.

In such a world—in the modern world we've inherited and, to a large degree, inhabit—there is little difference between speech or silence because, on the material surface of all eloquence—including the remarkable eloquence of Kurtz, of Yeats, of Freud, of Derrida and Barthes— stand the fact of material nonsense and, metonymically unlocatable, the dread of death. Such a representation of death—like the concomitant conception of rhetoric—is, as I argue in the next chapter, a function of the triumph and exhaustion of "positive" science in the nineteenth century, the triumph and exhaustion of what Michael Harrington, speaking of Engels, calls a "mystical" materialism that attributes "divine and providential qualities to matter itself" (1983: 80) by making a theme of matter itself. Rather than such materialism, which is fully inhabited by meaning, the negative materiality of death that I am describing here is marked by what Derrida calls "the worst violence, the violence of primitive and prelogical silence, of an unimaginable night which would not even be the opposite of day, an absolute violence which would not even be the opposite of nonviolence: nothingness or pure non-sense" (1978: 130). Such negative materiality is simply void of meaning and is the absolute absence of "sense," an absence that breaches even the binary oppositions governing significance and signification. It is linked to rhetoric, in part at least, precisely because the triumph of nineteenth-century materialist positivism saw that meaning itself—the very knowledge that Nietzsche came to question in the early modernist period—as a function of blind material forces. In this way, meaning itself seemed metonymically tinged on its "edges," as Larkin says, on its very surfaces, with material non-sense. Such materiality, as the linguists of the early modern period argue, is inscribed in discourse itself, whose material form can never fully become transparency for thought.

Throughout *Rhetoric and Death* I describe this blurred sense in discourse, the inarticulable and unlocatable feeling of its metonymic materiality, as the "resonations" of discourse. With this figure I am thinking of the material fact that through the sounding of musical notes other notes can be heard as overtones, produced by the resonations of objects encountered by the sound waves (the signifiers) of music. Moreover, while overtones help determine the natural harmonies of Western music—the first sympathetic overtones encountered are octaves, fifths, thirds, etc.—they go beyond such "nature," on and on and on, to ring disharmonies as well (sevenths, seconds, fourths, etc.). Such a material sense of music, beyond natural harmonies, presents the danger that Plato recognized in any "new style of music": "the introduction of novel fashions in music," he writes in *The Republic*, "is a thing to beware of as endangering the whole fabric of society" (1945: 115). New fashions endanger society by disrupting, metonymically, the intelligible whole of culture.

Through a similar figure Lacan describes his own difficult style and thought—difficulties, I should add, that ring throughout modernist and postmodern discourse: "It is often what appears harmonious and comprehensible," he writes, "which conceals some opacity. And conversely, it is in the antinomy, in the gap, in difficulty that we find a chance of being transparent" (cited in Tavor Bannet 1989: 42). It is through the "material" figure of resonation that I am trying to describe the modernist discovery of the material nonsense out of which signification is constructed in language and, analogous to this, a modernist recognition of death without transcendental meaning, without signification beyond itself, simply, materially, and unavoidably *there*. Such an idea of death, like the noisy system of overtones, is a form of radical metonymy: if synecdoche discovers Engels's "providential" significance in seemingly random occurrences, then metonymy articulates a world in which things happen without any touchstones of transcendental meaning, where absolutes of history and meaning and tonality take their places contingently in a world that goes on and on, where history does not stop and the contexts for meaning, like the dense underbrush of Marlow's Africa and the dense and noisy overtones of music—richly felt in oboes, felt as absence in flutes—can never be saturated.

I am arguing, then, that the advents of modernism and negative materiality and the very rhetoric I examine in this book are themselves contingent upon a complex of historical factors—an array of metonymic, decentering factors. Like the material signifiers that language assumes to make its meanings and like the particular death that ends each life, these factors could have been otherwise. The great result of these events, as I argue in Part I, is the failure of synecdoche that for centuries had allowed European civilization—which is to say the white men who possessed the inherited wealth of Europe—to imagine itself to be the culmination of human life, the measure of "humanity." This failure marks the breakdown of what Steiner perceives as the "centrality" of our "Western inheritance," which provided, until the twentieth century, "touchstones of order and of that unbroken continuum of intellectual power which had, in plain fact, made European and Anglo-Saxon man very largely master of the globe" (1971: 62). The very success of positive science in the nineteenth century conditioned this failure. This, in turn, is related (as both effect and cause) to another factor, the great development of European capital during the second half of the nineteenth century. This "second" industrial revolution replaced the wealth of landed estates with capital "wealth" and thus conditioned the destruction of the landed gentry, what I have just called "European civilization."

Another effect of the triumph of capitalism, sustaining itself as it did on wealth produced by investment and trade rather than by real estate, was the distancing of wealth and value from palpable, referential commodities. In the same way that Europe abandoned the gold standard in the early twentieth century, labor was further commodified in the second industrial revolution, cut off more than ever from the basic commodities that sustain labor in Marx's labor theory of value. (In this aspect of his work, as I argue in the next chapter, Marx himself takes his place as a pre-modern "realist.") Thus, value itself became symbolic rather than palpable, governed by relationships rather than by things. European imperialism was also (again in this metonymic array) an effect and cause of the intellectual and economic power of nineteenth-century European culture, as was what Steiner calls "the 'Thirty Years' War' from 1915 to 1945" (1971: 29). All of this contributed to the overwhelming sense that the center was somehow gone, that the transcendental symbols binding civilization together no longer held, that the traditional understanding of "the relations between time and individual death" which, as Steiner says, "is central to a true culture," no longer made sense (1971: 89).

Other effects arising metonymically alongside these contingent historical events were, as Raymond Williams has argued (1958), modernism itself—its sense of crisis, its sense of play, and its apocalyptic sense of the end of culture—and the pervasive, if usually unarticulated, sense of meaningless materialism that unobtrusively accompanied modernism. All of these helped condition the breakdown of synecdochical order in the early modern period and contributed to a sense of metonymy run amok in a world seemingly governed not by scarcity (though there was scarcity enough, even in Europe) but by meaningless plenty. In Part I, I shall examine more fully this historical moment and its relation to the rhetoric of modernism.

The relationship between these more or less historical events and the rhetoric that is my chief focus, however, is as complex as the concepts of metonymy and death. On one hand, it is clear that a particular rhetorical mode that participates in the negative materialism I describe—even if it exists half-apprehended, on the edge of vision—is a part of a historical moment, perhaps even a synecdochic part representative of that moment as a whole; on the other hand, the very crisis is a failure of coherence, an explosion of parts. Thus the materiality of rhetoric, like the materiality of death itself, both is and is not simply a "part" of modernism. One "event" of modernism (as I argue in Chapter 3) is a transformation in the very mode by which phenomena are made sense of—in the very idea of what makes sense. This is a transformation from causal explanations (understanding phenomena in terms of their causes) to functional explanations (understanding phenomena in terms of the ends they serve). Functional understanding, like the rhetorical study of discourse, is always retrospective: rather than verifying itself through the successful prediction of effects (based on causes), it attempts to account for phenomena in the way that rhetoric attempts to account for the effects of discourse. Such explanation is metonymic rather than synecdochic: it eschews the metaphysics of underlying cause, an essential depth behind the surface play of phenomena, for the sake of simply configuring phenomena relationally, discursively, phenomenologically. In it, the part is greater than the whole. That such a mode of reasoning arises in the modernist period—not only in rhetoric, but also in linguistics, psychology, philosophy, and even physics itself—is a historical "event" indeed, but an event that cannot be situated as either cause or effect of the complex historical moment in which it arises.

For this reason, I want to emphasize that my attempt to make sense out of the remarkable historical changes of the early twentieth century, like those of the modernist writers themselves, is an attempt to describe in rhetorical terms, retrospectively, the feeling and sense of that era, never fully in focus, never fully articulated, that something is wrong, out of joint—that another discourse, so to speak, is superimprinted on the discourses of knowledge and power that modernism attempts to articulate, a dull drumbeat that seems to be a kind of counter-statement to modernism's intelligence, its imperialism, its own self-conscious loss, a haunting feeling and sense that seem fully a part of modernism until one turns to focus on them and then they disappear. Such an "Other" discourse—not quite Lacan's "discourse of the Other"—seems to be figured in Larkin's description of the dread of death as "a small unfocused blur, a standing chill." Eliot offers a similar figure in *The Waste Land* as "the third who walks always beside you" (1963: 67) but who cannot be counted, focused upon, incorporated within hearing or vision or articulate awareness.

Such a level of discourse—negative, material, not precisely a "level" of discourse at all—is like the death instinct (or better, the death drive) described in *Beyond the Pleasure Principle*. The death drive, Freud writes, "though it does not contradict the pleasure principle, is nevertheless independent and seems to be more primitive than the purpose of gaining pleasure and avoiding pain" (1959: 61). Like the negative materiality of discourse I am describing, it is more primitive than "purpose" altogether. The drive to death, in Freud's description, is life's "other," not its opposite: it is "not, indeed, in *opposition* to the pleasure principle, but [works] independently of it and to some extent in disregard of it" (1959: 65). It is the limit, the boundary of life and its significance, like the dreams that obey the compulsion to repeat of the death drive in order to bind and incorporate traumatic impressions. Of such impressions Freud asks, "may not such dreams"—and, in the context of *Rhetoric and Death,* I can add, may not "death" itself— "occur *outside* analysis as well?" (1959: 62).

In the same way, the material level of discourse I am describing does not contradict the principle of "sense" in discourse. It does not stand in relation to that principle in a way that will allow it to be incorporated within sensible discourse itself, even as the opposite of sensible discourse. Rather, it is the "other" of that discourse, always there, always seemingly discernible, but never precise: an effect of discourse. Its rhetoric, however, is more muted, subtle, unobtrusive than the noisy histrionics of rhetoric as such, just as, in Freud's terms, "the life instincts have so much more contact with our internal perception— emerging as breakers of the peace and constantly producing tensions whose release is felt as pleasure—while the death instincts seem to do their work unobtrusively" (1959: 109). "The desire for death," Paul Ricoeur notes, "does not speak, as does the desire for life. Death works in silence" (1970: 294).

Yet this work, Ricoeur argues, can appear at particular historical moments, just as I am arguing that the negative materiality of death can be heard resonating in discourse since the moment of modernism. Death becomes audible—and "clamorous"—in war, Ricoeur says (1970:

305–6), especially during the great, clamorous war against the background of which Freud wrote *Beyond the Pleasure Principle*. In other ways, too, the death instinct is analogous to the materiality of discourse. "The dualism of Eros and Thanatos," Ricoeur also says, "appears as a dramatic *overlapping of roles*. In a sense, everything is death. . . . In a sense, everything is life" (1970: 292)—just as, in discourse, everything is meaning, everything is dull matter. Finally, the death instinct as Freud articulates it in *Beyond the Pleasure Principle* is, like the rhetoric I am describing in this book, metonymically plural, "an incongruous mixture: biological inertia is not pathological obsession, repetition is not destruction" (Ricoeur 1970: 314).

An examination of the details of Freud's articulation of the death instinct does not fall within the *rhetorical* study I am pursuing. But the very fact that such a description of death was formulated within the modernist era does fall within an examination of how discourses are constructed to produce certain effects. That is, *Beyond the Pleasure Principle* is important to this study because it marks the necessity of "theorizing" death within a description of human nature at a particular moment in history: the moment of the Great War, the internal combustion of European power, the explosion of Western life into what Eliot calls the "futility and anarchy which is contemporary history" (1975: 177). Freud is quite specific about this: in *Beyond the Pleasure Principle* he is attempting to make sense out of what he calls the "war neuroses" (1959: 62).

More than this, Freud is also attempting to make sense of the eruption of death into his own life: the death of his daughter Sophie—mother to the child, Ernst, who plays *fort: da* in *Beyond the Pleasure Principle*—before Freud finished writing that book, and, more strikingly, the subsequent death of that child's younger brother. Heinz was Freud's favorite grandchild, and both Freud and Heinerle (as he was called) underwent operations in 1923: for Freud, the first of thirty-three operations for mouth cancer; for Heinerle, a tonsillectomy, from the complications of which he died at age four. Heinerle, Freud said, "had stood to him for all children and grandchildren" (Jones 1961: 440); thus, as Derrida says, in his death Freud "lives the death of his entire filiation" (1987: 334). This was the only time in his life when "Freud was known to shed tears. He told me afterward," Ernest Jones notes, "that this loss had affected him in a different way from any of the others he had suffered. They had brought about sheer pain, but this one had killed something in him for good" (1961: 440). Jones speculates that the death of Heinerle is linked to Freud's own sense of mortality occasioned by his first operation, and Derrida speculates

that it is related to the death of his own younger brother, Julius, in
childhood many years before (1987: 336).

For my purposes, the deaths of Sophie and Heinerle mark, in
Freud's life, a strong, if negative, sense of futurelessness that inhabits
the discourses of modernism and postmodernism in our century, the
apocalyptic feeling that somehow the "end" of Western culture is taking
place. For Freud, as Derrida says, Heinerle's death is "the death of the
one who took the place of filiation for him, who was a kind of universal
legatee," a death that occasions the brute fact: "no more ties, no more
contracts, no more alliances, no more vows to attach him to any future,
to any descendance" (1987: 334). And more: the death of Heinerle,
standing as he did for all children and grandchildren, is the death of
synecdoche, of the transcendental ordering of parts in a whole. From
now on—as many contemporaries of Freud also imagined, having lived
through the "now" of both the second industrial revolution and the
Great War, as Steiner himself imagines when he articulates "the cat-
astrophic failure of human possibility" in our century (1971: 71)—from
now on, in Freud's language from *Beyond the Pleasure Principle,* "there
is no longer any possibility of preventing the mental apparatus [that
is, the very experience of living in the modern world] from being
flooded with large amounts of stimulus" (1959: 57), the overwhelming
"flooding" of metonymy run amok. There is no possibility, outside the
self-conscious rhetoric of art, of "arranging, deepening, enchanting
night" (Stevens 1954: 130).

Freud of *Beyond the Pleasure Principle* thus represents the complexly
metonymic relationship between rhetoric and death that I am describing throughout this study. This representation is doubled in two definitions of "representation" that I will present in the next chapter,
definitions that are synecdochic and metonymic. Representation articulates a thought or feeling by means of synecdoche, but it also presents itself as an impression or a sense in a metonymic series of impressions. In these two ways, *Beyond the Pleasure Principle* articulates a
hermetic psychoanalytic code, but it also responds to mortality and
grief simply by raising its language. In this, I think, Freud—like the
other modernist writers I examine—is modern and postmodern at the
same time. In fact, one thing that is implicit but not fully examined
in the following chapters is the relationship, in general terms, between
modernism and what I am calling "postmodern" discourse theory. It
is implicit in the metonymic linking of Freud and Steiner in the preceding paragraph, or in the repeated emergence, negative and positive,

central and marginal, modernist and contemporary, of the ghostly presence of Paul de Man throughout my argument.

A submerged but important implication of this book is the suggestion that we can understand the postmodern itself in relation to the materialism of modernism described in Part I. In this, the postmodern, which has been variously described as continuous with and as a break with the modern, can be understood as metonymically linked with its antecedent. It is inhabited with the same sense of negative materiality that modernist discourse presents, but its relationship to that materiality is not quite—not wholly—the "same." If the modern is shocked by its own language, overwhelmed by the flooding of metonymy, the drumbeat of material death within discourse and history, then for the postmodern, I believe, the shock has subsided. The postmodern is metonymically related to the modern in the complex sense of that term. It is a "part" of modernism—from one vantage point, its culmination; from another, participating, in debased form, in the essential crisis of modernism. But at the same time, it is modernism's "other," precisely as death or negative materialism is life's "other"; it presents to modernism—as death and the materiality of discourse present to life and meaning—what Shoshana Felman has called a "radical negativity" that "*escapes the negative/positive alternative*" (1983: 141), a negativity Julia Kristeva describes outside Hegelian logic that "remains heterogeneous to logic even while producing it through a movement of separation or rejection" (1984: 141).

In this complexity, the relationship between the modern and the postmodern is the translation of metaphysical elegy into "mere" rhetoric. As such, it can be likened to Derrida's rhetorical description of Nicolas Abraham's discussion of "presence, being-there (*fort/da*) or not, the presumed presence to self in self-presentation": all of these, Derrida says, are accompanied by a discussion of translation, and even translation "from one language into itself" (i.e., modern into postmodern) "with the 'same' words," Derrida says, "suddenly changing their sense, overflowing with sense or exceeding it altogether, and nevertheless impassive, imperturbable, identical to themselves, allowing you still to read in the new code of this anasemic translation what belonged to the other word, the same one, before psychoanalysis" (1979a: 4–5). In other words, the "loss" and "crisis" of the modern are still there, still loss and crisis in the postmodern, but they are anemic, anasemic, like the absence of God that Steiner describes as still available to us, but without its *mysterium tremendum* (1986: 23–24). In these terms, the negative materiality of modernity is what *is* for the postmodern, but the ways in which it unobtrusively undermines value and meaning and "Europe" altogether is hardly news, nothing to write home about, simply, like death and love and the promise of meaning I describe in the final chapter of this book, an "ordinary" event. Cornel West (1988) has argued that both modernism and the postmodern mark the end of Europe by responding to the crisis of the breakup of European imperialist hegemony and the great decolonization of the world since 1945, but for ourselves and our contemporaries that breakup is the world we have always known. For us, that breakup is hardly the occasion for despair that it is for Forster or Eliot or even Steiner and de Man. In West's argument, the crisis of modernism is "completed" in the postmodern, but such "completion," like death itself, is both a culmination and a negation.

This relationship between modernism and postmodernism is implicit within the structure of this book. *Rhetoric and Death* is divided into two parts. The first, "Modernism, Metonymy, and Death," attempts to define the "negative materiality" of death as it inhabits, discursively, the historical and intellectual moment of modernism. To that end, it examines the complex historical factors that contribute to a modernist sensibility and rhetoric, and it attempts to describe that rhetoric itself, both the assertion of synecdoche and the configurations of metonymy in the face of the breakdown of hierarchical values. It does so not in terms of the traditional logic of causal explanation, but (to borrow an expression from Perry Anderson) by means of a "dense description" of the configuration or constellation of forces in the modern world. Chapter 2 attempts such a metonymic-descriptive understanding in terms of historical events. Chapter 3 attempts it in terms of ideology (including this transformation in modes of understanding), and Chapter 4 attempts it in terms of rhetoric and discourse. In these chapters there is a good deal of overlap, just as metonymy itself presents the "impurity" of overlapping understandings of the "same" words in different contexts. In Chapter 4, for instance, de Man and Bakhtin are opposed to one another in relation to the failure of synecdoche. But that opposition is itself presented in terms of the "incompatibility," as Derrida describes it, between the logic "of lack and that of alterity" (1989: 49). De Man presents the "privation" of synecdoche—its absence in the modern world. Bakhtin describes that "same" privation not in terms of what is lost, but within another contextual framework in which de Man's terms (haunted, privatively, with traditional hierarchies of value that Steiner articulates) both exceed their sense and are identical to themselves.

The second part of *Rhetoric and Death,* "Modernist Postmodern Rhetoric," continues the dense, overlapping description of rhetoric by examining particular writers whose work focuses on discourse and rhetoric: Roman Jakobson, Roland Barthes, Jacques Lacan, and Jacques Derrida. The language of each is examined in conjunction with that of a particular Anglo-American modernist writer: Jakobson in relation to Yeats, Barthes in relation to Lawrence, Lacan in relation to Conrad, and Derrida in relation to Stevens. I do not historicize these writers in the way I attempt to historicize modernism in Part I. Instead, I narrow my focus to discourse and rhetoric, the postmodern translation of metaphysics to rhetoric. Such a narrowing can be seen in modernism itself, represented here in the imperial, synecdochic modernism of Jakobson and Yeats. It can be seen also in the overlapping discussions of modernist and postmodern writers in these chapters. I also narrow my focus because of my sense that the forces—historical, ideological, rhetorical—conditioning postmodern culture are in important ways the "same" forces described in Part I. This reasoning is more fully articulated by Eve Tavor Bannet in *Structuralism and the Logic of Dissent*. Tavor Bannet suggests that the "concrete and immediate" conditions of "French cultural and historical circumstances" after World War II (1989: 42, 225), like the interwar period in eastern Europe for Jakobson, repeated the great transition between landed "real" wealth and symbolic capital wealth that governed, in part, the phenomenon of modernism. "The rapid changes introduced in France after the Second World War," Tavor Bannet writes, ". . . converted what had been a predominantly rural and agricultural society into a modern, industrialised, 'americanised' 'technological civilisation' in the course of about twenty years" (1989: 231; see also 43).

The writers I treat here lived through this change and responded to it in discourses inhabited by a material rhetoric that is, I believe, illuminated in relation to that earlier European modernism. If the early modernists discovered themselves, like Marlow (or even Eliot in London) in a world that is uncanny (the *unheimlich* of which Freud and Heidegger speak), then the writers treated here, including perhaps most notably Jakobson, are homeless, displaced, exiles within Europe. Steiner notes "the tensed overlap between [modernism] and the tragic destiny of European Judaism," mentioning Jakobson, Freud, Wittgenstein, Kafka, Benjamin, Lévi-Strauss, Derrida, and others (1986: 5), and to this list of displaced persons can be added the repeated alienations of Lacan from his psychoanalytic associations and what Tavor Bannet calls the "plural marginality" of Barthes' Protestantism in Catholic France, his atheism, his homosexuality, and his fall from the *grande bourgeoisie* because of his father's early death (1989: 84). Cornel West (1988) describes Derrida as a marginalized Algerian Jew in Paris, for twenty-two years an assistant professor whose work transgressed the thought of a European, Eurocentric empire that no longer exists. In this, he may well be situating the homelessness of the modern/ postmodern European subject haunted by the sense of the loss and death, just on the edge of vision, of some remembered/imagined patrimony. In this, like Steiner (though to very difference purpose), he is imagining a metonymic wholeness to twentieth-century experience.

The mention of lost patrimony, wholly governing modernism and to some extent governing the postmodern as well, brings up the relative absence of women writers from my study, both in terms of women figures of modernism and the postmodern articulation of feminism within the framework of rhetoric and discourse theory that has become so powerful recently. Andreas Huyssen has argued in an important essay that "woman" was "modernism's other," that women were significantly excluded from the "real, authentic culture" of men, and that a "powerful masculinist and misogynist current within the trajectory of modernism" produced "the art-life dichotomy so frequently found at the turn of the century, with its inscription of art on the side of death and masculinity and its evaluation of life as inferior and feminine" (1986: 47, 49, 54). In the first volume of *No Man's Land* Sandra Gilbert and Susan Gubar more fully describe the situation of "embattled masculinity" of early modernism attempting "to construct *his* story of a literary history in which women play no part" (1988: 145, 154). Indeed, they argue that the remarkably powerful misogyny perceptible throughout modernism "may arise from the fact that, as much as the industrial revolution and the fall of God, the rise of the female imagination was a central problem for the twentieth-century male imagination" (1988: 156). The exclusion of women from modernism— like the absolute silence of Africans in *Heart of Darkness* (see Achebe 1988: 255); or the "nasty" description of working people in *The Waste Land,* whom Eliot, remarkably, describes as "the low on whom assurance sits / As a silk hat on a Bradford millionaire" (see Craig 1974: 201–2); or the unremarkable, hardly noticed racism throughout Stevens's poetry—is part of the dialectic of modernism that I describe in the next chapter. Huyssen calls it the fact that "warding something off, protecting against something out there seems indeed to be a basic gesture of the modernist aesthetic, from Flaubert to Roland Barthes and other poststructuralists" (1986: 47).

If warding off its "other" is the gesture of modernism, it is, I think, hardly the gesture of postmodernism. Derrida, unlike Barthes and Lacan, rhetorizes this "otherness" of women in his discourse—with terms like "invagination," the "hymen," and the extended examination of Father Logos in *Dissemination*. Moreover, throughout her work Julia Kristeva recontextualizes Jakobson, Barthes, and Lacan within a discourse that incorporates, rather than wards off, female sexuality. Nevertheless, Kristeva's discourse does not emphasize the aspect of rhetoric on which I am focusing in *Rhetoric and Death*, and a few words about why it does not might more fully introduce the discussions which follow. Gilbert and Gubar end the first volume of *No Man's Land* with an examination of differences between male and female "linguistic fantasies" (1988: 262). Male fantasies, they argue, attempt to recover a "father-language"—what they call, following Walter Ong, a *patrius sermo*—from the "ordinary" *materna lingua,* our mother tongue. "To mystify the (mother) tongue that one must speak," they say, "is, of course, the simplest way of defending oneself against that tongue's linguistic contamination; it is to say that, 'ordinary' as 'ordinary language' appears, a privileged speaker can perceive that it is not ordinary" (1988: 254). In this way, the "privileged" discourse of the male fantasy of a *patrius sermo* attempts to recover what D. H. Lawrence calls "dead speech" within discourse (cited in Gilbert and Gubar 1988: 258), the "lost" patrimonic, patriarchal speech of dead fathers. It attempts, as Eliot says of Lancelot Andrewes, to achieve an "ecstasy of assent" by taking a word and deriving the world from it, "squeezing and squeezing the word until it yields a full juice of meaning which we should never have supposed any word to possess" (1975: 184), and discovering within it, as he says elsewhere, "our common patrimony of culture" (1975: 305). (Steiner also discusses the "masculine nature" of the arts [1989: 206–8].)

Gilbert and Gubar argue that the recovery of such a hermetic discourse, what they call "the last lost quackings of a father tongue" (1988: 257), transforms the "comments" of ordinary language into a linguistic "charm," a "spell of power" specifically over women (1988: 257). But at the same time it also marks a sense of male belatedness in relation to language and life itself in its spell of power over the intuition of a "maternal primacy" in language and "the primal verbal fertility of the mother" (1988: 262–63). In this case, the hermetic male discourse, which I am examining here as the rhetoric of death as it inhabits the discourses of modernism and Jakobson, Barthes, and Lacan, would be a kind of "reaction-formation against the linguistic (as well as the biological) primacy of the mother." "If," Gilbert and Gubar write, "as language acquisition researchers have demonstrated, and as most mothers know, it is in many cultures the mother who feeds the child words even as she furnishes her or him with food, then, as Freud himself observed (in his analysis of a child's creation and use of symbols to cope with maternal separation), the birth into language delivers the child from helplessness at the goings and the comings, the 'oo' and the 'ah,' the 'Fort' and the 'Da,' of the mother" (1988: 264). If this is true, then at least some aspect of the materiality of rhetoric in the language of modernism and postmodernism is itself an occult "charm" aimed at "mourning and waking a lost *patrius sermo,* [through which] all these male modernists and postmodernists transform the maternal vernacular into a new morning of patriarchy in which they can wake the old powers of the 'Allfather's Word' " (1988: 261). Moreover, this "transformation of the *materna lingua* into a new *patrius sermo*—the occulting of common language, the transformation of the comment into the charm—seems to offer a definitive cure of the male linguistic wound" (1988: 258).

Such a wound suggests "otherness" inscribed within language itself, an "otherness" I am describing in this book under the figure of "death," "negative materiality," even "rhetoric." "There used to be no house," Walter Benjamin asserts in a remarkable essay that attempts to describe the rhetorical power of storytelling,

> hardly a room, in which someone had not once died. . . . Today people live in rooms that have never been touched by death. . . . It is, however, characteristic that not only a man's knowledge or wisdom, but above all his real life—and this is the stuff that stories are made of—first assumes transmissible form at the moment of his death. Just as a sequence of images is set in motion inside a man as his life comes to an end—unfolding the views of himself under which he has encountered himself without being aware of it—suddenly in his expressions and looks the unforgettable emerges and imparts to everything that concerned him that authority which even the poorest wretch in dying possesses for the living around him. This authority is at the very source of the story. (1969: 94)

The "sequence of images" Benjamin mentions constitutes the elegy of modernism as I describe it in the early part of this book, a sense held by the men of Europe that they were at the end of a history, a culture, a way of living, and that that end could be heard resonating in the very language of their discourse. "The unforgettable" is the hermetic sign embedded in this discourse, available to those who can apprehend, to those who can hear within the noisy and natural death of even the poorest wretch a "secret," a pervading vision that changes everything even as it leaves everything the same.

Benjamin's rhetoric also signifies a kind of bondage to death in its very discourse, its very "charm." But its "secret" remains on the very surface of its language. That is, even this rhetoric is embodied in the mother tongue and so remains "different" from itself, ordinary, ongoing, the babble of the vernacular. For if there used to be no house or room in which someone had not died, there also used to be no house or room in which someone had not been born and mothered, in which, nonapocalyptically, someone had not lived. It is precisely this ordinariness, including "ordinary" language, that Gilbert and Gubar focus upon when they focus on Ernst's "creation of symbols" rather than on the death drive in reading Freud's *Beyond the Pleasure Principle*. (For an extended discussion of this theme, see Schleifer 1985a.) To remember this ordinariness is to see that the articulation of a hermetic discourse is, as Kristeva says, imprisoning. Twice in the last few centuries, she writes, "wishing to escape, [Western reason] turned toward and became haunted by childhood. Witness Rousseau and Freud—two crises of classical and positivist rationality." At these moments

> Reason was thus transcended by a *heterogeneous element* (biology: life) and by a *third party* (*I/you* communication is displaced by *it*: the child). These challenge the speaker with the fact that he is not whole, but they do so in a manner altogether different from that in which the obsessed person's wretched consciousness ceaselessly signifies his bondage to death. For if death is the Other, life is a third party; and as this signification, asserted by the child, is disquieting, it might well unsettle the speaker's paranoid enclosure. (1980: 271)

There is a sense in which the material death and mortality I am examining—occulted, hermetic, charmed—describes the "paranoid enclosure" of modernism and perhaps even the postmodern discourses I examine in the last chapters of this book. If this is true—if what I call, following Derrida, the "nonreserve" of discourse remains, despite the fact that it describes "an expenditure and a negativity *without reserve*" (Derrida 1978: 259), within an enclosure and preserve of reason, of patriarchal history, of material "death" itself—then there is good reason for the absence of women as the subjects of discourse and rhetoric in this book.

But there is another sense in which the material death and mortality I am examining is not only or simply the hermetic, masculinist absence of women, a sense in which "absence" is not an opposition, not absolute, and (like the negative materiality of death and the radical metonymy of rhetoric) not fully *here*. For the death that inhabits language (perhaps seen most clearly in the rhetoric of mourning in the final chapter) exists on the babbling surface of discourse as well as in its hermetic depths; it is ordinary as well as extraordinary, as ordinary as the affection and faith and promise that are realized in birthbeds, if no longer in deathbeds. If modernism attempts to erase women and children from its history as fully as Yeats attempts to erase women and children from "Among School Children," replacing their plural voices with the philosophical, masculine austerity of Plato, Aristotle, and Pythagoras, the nuns and mothers and female children nevertheless remain in that poem, even as they are more fully and insistently heard in the discourses of postmodernism.

In his reading of *Beyond the Pleasure Principle,* Derrida offers this speculation that traverses his and all the rhetorics I am examining here. "All speculation, as we said above," he writes, "implies the terrifying possibility of this *usteron proteron* [the "preceding falsehood" of a fallacious argument; here Derrida means the parent outliving the child] of the generations. When the face without face, name without name, of the mother returns, in the end, one has what I called in *Glas* the logic of obsequence. The mother buries all her own. She assists whoever calls herself her mother, and follows all burials" (1987: 333). All speculation confuses generations because it makes the metonymic ongoingness of time and generation into a hierarchy of precedence and tradition. In this it confuses death and life, and Derrida here (like Barthes in his play and Lacan in his enunciations, like the rhetoric of this book) faces death with life. He does so by translating Freud's "death instinct" as "life death"—just as, throughout his discourse, he confuses the hermetic and the ordinary.

In a way—the way of Yeats's poem and Jakobson's modernist readings of Yeats's chthonic power—Freud's book is a mother's book, an attempt to narrate the presence and absence of motherhood, *fort: da,* without remembering motherhood itself. Such mothering, unremembered (and not Benjamin's hermetic "unforgettable"), unfocused, never quite articulated, exists on the very surface babble of *Beyond the Pleasure Principle.* That is, the babble of *fort: da* as a metonymic representation resonates in Freud's discourse along with death itself, just as it resonates in the fallacious temporality governing Jakobson's linguistic poetics, in Barthes' erotics of textuality, in Lacan's curacy of mortality, and in Derrida's rhetoric of mourning. If Freud's death drive is to be understood as "life death," then my focus on death and on hermetic terror rather than human pity—even though, as I imagine, it is inhabited by life—is a focus on Benjamin's dying man rather than on Kristeva's birthing woman. Still, I would say that this book, as I said of Freud's, remains a mother's book as well, a kind of mourning that attempts to articulate, even in its hermetic language, the living vernacular of our time.

Part One

Modernism, Metonymy, and Death

2

Historicizing Modernist Rhetoric

Modernism, Materialism, and the End of Europe

[Looking through the X-ray machine,] Hans Castorp saw, precisely what he must have expected, but what it is hardly permitted man to see, and what he had never thought it would be vouchsafed him to see: he looked into his own grave. The process of decay was forestalled by the powers of the light-ray, the flesh in which he walked disintegrated, annihilated, dissolved in vacant mist, and there within it was the finely turned skeleton of his own hand, the seal ring he had inherited from his grandfather hanging loose and black on the joint of his ring-finger—a hard material object, with which man adorns the body that is fated to melt away beneath it, when it passes on to another flesh that can wear it for yet a little while. . . . He gazed at this familiar part of his own body, and for the first time in his life he understood that he would die.

> —Thomas Mann,
> *The Magic Mountain*

At the end of *A Passage to India,* which was effectively the end of E. M. Forster's novelistic career, the material landscape of modern India rises up against the characters in the novel and cuts them off from one another; it denies the recovered sense of solidarity they seem to achieve at the end of the novel. "Why can't we be friends now?" Fielding asks his friend Aziz; "It's what I want. It's what you want."

But the horses didn't want it—they swerved apart; the earth didn't want it, sending up rocks through which riders must pass single file; the temples, the tank, the jail, the palace, the

> birds, the carrion, the Guest House, that came into view as
> they issued from the gap and saw Mau beneath: they didn't
> want it, they said in their hundred voices, "No, not yet," and
> the sky said, "No, not there." (1952: 322)

Disrupting the intentions of characters and novelist is a world of things
speaking in a cacophony of voices that cannot be reduced to harmony.
Instead, Forster narrates the disruption of human relationships by an
aggregation of things that resist, to one degree or another, those human
meanings that comprise our world.

Such disruptions, like the modernism that articulates them, are
fully historically determined. They inhabit literary discourse at a historical moment that witnessed one of the great transformations of
Western culture, what Steiner calls "one of the very few genuine revolutions of spirit in Western history" (1989: 93). The triumph of capitalism in the late nineteenth century and the concomitant second
industrial revolution at the beginning of the modernist era created, as
Fredric Jameson describes it,

> one of the most active periods in human history, with all the
> smoke and conveyance inherent in new living conditions and
> in the rapid development of business and industry, with the
> experimental triumphs of positivistic science and its conquest
> of the university system, with all the bustling parliamentary
> and bureaucratic activity of the new middle-class regimes, the
> spread of the press, the diffusion of literacy and the rise of
> mass culture, the ready accessibility of the newly mass-pro-
> duced commodities of an increasingly consumer-orientated
> civilization. (1981: 251)

This is the triumph, as Franco Moretti argues, of the bourgeois ideology
of the "self-regulating market" of the nineteenth century, "the realization of the idea that society can function in a rational and coherent
way due to the existence of a *purely economic* mechanism . . . free from
any restriction issuing from *symbolic* and *cultural* values" (1983: 212).

Paradoxically, in just such a period, when the human seems to
triumph over the natural, the kinds of resistances that disrupt and end
Forster's novel and his career seem to take on remarkable power. Thus
Jameson goes on to describe the anomaly that

> it is only in the most completely humanized environment, the
> one most fully and obviously the end product of human labor,
> production, and transformation, that life becomes meaning-
> less, and that existential despair first appears as such in direct

proportion to the elimination of nature, the non- or antihuman, to the increasing rollback of everything that threatens human life and the prospect of a well-nigh limitless control over the external universe. The most interesting artists and thinkers of such a period are those who cling to the experience of meaninglessness itself as to some ultimate reality, some ultimate bedrock of existence of which they do not wish to be cheated by illusions. . . . (1981: 251–52)

This phenomenon, Jameson suggests, is a function of "the virtual obliteration of all value by a universal process of instrumentalization" (1981: 251) that is part and parcel of the capitalist commodification of labor. To make human activity—which can be taken, as Marx takes it in the labor theory of value, as the *standard* of value—a commodity transforms values inherent in human life into some *thing,* like a tool or a machine, that can be bought and sold. Even aesthetic experience in the modern period, Theodor Adorno has argued, functions like a commodity so that art is transformed to phantasmagoria, "the absolute reality of the unreal [which] is nothing but the reality of a phenomenon that . . . strives unceasingly to spirit away its own origins in human labor" (cited in Huyssen 1986: 39–40; see also Moretti 1983: 197).

In this instrumentalization, I think, we can see the *materialization* of value. This is not the concept of "materialism" held by the nineteenth- and twentieth-century positivists, who conceived of all truth as "sense data" reducible to physical experience and observation to one extent or another (see Janik and Toulmin 1973: 208–12). In fact, such instrumentalization is not a "concept" at all; it assumes, unconsciously, ideologically, that all human "goods" and values are inhabited by a materiality that ultimately *resists* intelligence, just as in *A Passage to India* the things of the world—not only *natural* things such as the rocks and carrion and sky, but also *human* artifacts, "the tank, the jail, the palace, . . . the Guest House"—resist the human. Here in Forster and throughout modernist discourse, material things are divorced from their possible signification, from their human meanings. In an almost completely humanized environment, where all things serve positive human needs, such instrumental "things" are seemingly, materially, divorced from human significance; in this environment matter resists meaning.

The extreme instance of such resistance and disruption is death itself. Western philosophy—especially nineteenth-century philosophy, which offers "a conspiracy of silence about the literal and figurative 'skeleton in the closet' " (Charon 1963: 268)—has always attempted to

incorporate death within a system or vision of human values by conceiving of it, in Herbert Marcuse's words, as "an essential as well as
biological fact, ontological as well as empirical," so that life is "transcended" and "man's empirical existence, his material and contingent
life, is . . . defined in terms of and redeemed by something other than
itself" (1965: 65). In the almost "completely humanized environment"
of the turn of the twentieth century that Jameson describes, however,
the positive "fact" of death is not transformed by its transcendental
meaning, just as the imperialism Conrad describes in *Heart of Darkness*
is not "redeemed" by an "idea" (Conrad 1971: 7). Instead, like the
strange, almost Borgesian list with which Forster ends his novelistic
career, it takes its place within a seemingly random and contingent
aggregate of "things" that are, as Marcuse says, "*essentially* external"
to meaning or truth (1965: 64). In this way death, in Hillis Miller's
words, becomes a kind of "betrayal" that we are always subject to in
our relations with others (1985: 21)—and, I might add, in our relationship to the world and to the discourses that articulate the world.
A Passage to India is a novel whose plot—like the imperialism it describes—hinges on betrayal even as it contemplates, in a tradition I will
argue is not quite modernist, the possibility of keeping faith. But in
any case, its final passage articulates betrayal by narrating the voices
of the world in a kind of cacophony of *material* things.

Such cacophony, as I will argue in this chapter and the next, characterizes the rhetoric of modernism, even if many of the early modernist
writers self-consciously resisted the naive materialism of nineteenth-
century positivism. The difference between these two conceptions of
materialism—roughly speaking, that of realism and modernism—is the
difference between a positive and negative conception of materiality.
For the positivism of the nineteenth and twentieth centuries, all truth
was material and could be measured and mapped (Hynes 1968: 133).
In this way positivism was anti-metaphysical and "held out scientific
knowledge as the model of what rational men should believe" (Janik
and Toulmin 1973: 208). As Paul Engelmann has put it in describing
Ludwig Wittgenstein's work, "positivism holds—and this is its essence—that what we can speak about is all that matters in life. *Whereas
Wittgenstein passionately believes that all that really matters in human
life is precisely what, in his view, we must be silent about*" (cited in
Janik and Toulmin 1973: 191). The materialism of modernism—and
especially of modernist rhetoric—is not comprised of "positive" facts
that could be "spoken" in language. Rather, modernist materialism is
the resonance in language and consciousness of a "negative materi-

ality," unintelligible materiality; it is the always present possibility, as Engelmann says of Wittgenstein, of catching or glimpsing what *could not* be spoken. What cannot be spoken is not simply the ethical and nonmaterial values that Wittgenstein says are the important part of the *Tractatus* that he, nevertheless, *cannot* articulate (cited in Janik and Toulmin 1973: 192; Steiner 1989: 103 concurs). Rather, it is materiality itself, nonhuman, brute, unintelligible, literally unspeakable: what Jacques Derrida calls the "nothingness and pure non-sense" (1978: 130) that inhabit discourse and meaning. If nineteenth-century positivism ratified, above all, the positive nature of material objects, then the materialism I will be examining is a negative materialism resonating in discourse.

Jean Baudrillard describes this opposition between nineteenth- and twentieth-century materialism in *L'Echange symbolique et la mort* when he describes the difference between orders of simulation. *"Production,"* he says, "is the dominant scheme of the industrial era," while *"Simulation* is the reigning scheme of the current phase that is controlled by the code" (1983: 83). The scheme of production is the scheme of the "same": the industrial era creates, positively, the possibility of *identical* objects. "The fact alone," Baudrillard writes, "that anything might be simply reproduced, as such, in two copies, is already a revolution; you only have to consider the shock of the African native seeing, for the very first time, two identical books" (1983: 99). The order of the code, on the other hand, is that of difference: it is "the structural law of value" (1983: 83) in which "cybernetic operationality, the genetic code, the random order of mutations, the principle of uncertainty, and so on: all of these replace a determinist and objectivist science, a dialectical vision of history and consciousness" (1988: 122). In this, he goes on, *"referential value is nullified, giving advantage to the structural play of value.* The structural dimension, in other words, gains autonomy, to the exclusion of the referential dimension, establishing itself on the death of the latter. Gone are the referentials of production, signification, affect, substance, history, and the whole equation of 'real' contents that gave the sign weight by anchoring it with a kind of burden of utility—in short, its form as representative equivalent" (1988: 125). The effacement of the referential force of discourse that Baudrillard is describing is at the heart of Steiner's view of the crisis of meaning in our century, the revolution in spirit he describes. For him what marks the modern as a unique epoch within Western culture is "the break of the covenant between word and world" (1989: 93). By the "transcendental" force of language Steiner means largely its *referential* force, the fact that traditional Western culture presupposes the "real presence" of that to which language referred: "until the crisis of the meaning of meaning which began in the late nineteenth century," he argues, "even the most astringent scepticism, even the most subversive of anti-rhetorics, remained committed to language. It knew itself to be 'in trust' to language" (1989: 92).

For Baudrillard the transformation from referential value to structural play—which marks the transformation of synecdochical hierarchy to metonymic interplay (or the "superimposition" of one upon the other)—not only takes place in language and art; it takes place as well in the meaning that inhabits all human activity. Most notably, he argues, the same transformation of value can be seen in labor power: production comes to function like a code rather than a base, and this permits even the monetary system "to escape in indefinite speculation, beyond any reference to the real, or even to a gold standard" (1988: 126). Such escape is possible because the "code" Baudrillard describes is inhabited by what I am calling "negative" materialism. The code governs "a universe of structures and binary oppositions"; "digitality is its metaphysical principle" (1988: 139).

Such a principle is based upon the fact, first articulated by Ferdinand de Saussure in the early modernist period, that language (the code) will use *anything*—any material thing—to articulate its structures. And more: as Saussure notes in the *Course in General Linguistics,* "a material sign is not necessary for the expression of an idea; language is satisfied with the opposition between something and nothing" (1959: 86). That is, the code is inhabited by a "negative" materialism in the very fact that it does not distinguish between "positive" and "negative" materiality, "something" and "nothing." Phonology, for instance—a science whose possibility Saussure was the first to understand—distinguishes between phonemes in relation to the category of voiced and voiceless (the difference between /d/ and /t/ in English) so that the *absence* of voicing, the very "nothing" of that absence, functions the same way as its *presence,* the engagement of the vocal chords. In discourse, also, as Derrida says, even the "semantic void *signifies*" (1981: 222). Signifying through absence as well as presence, making the absence of a material signifier function in the same way that a present signifier functions, the code marks its own "nonsimplicity" and "nonidentity" with itself (Derrida 1982: 13; Todorov 1982: 36).

Moreover, it marks the nothingness of materiality itself, very different from Engels's mystical materiality, the radical *otherness* from human comprehension and from inclusion within a system of intelligibility. In this, the code marks materiality by circumscribing it as a form of radicalized unconsciousness, just as, Baudrillard suggests,

Freud's death instinct radicalizes Freud against himself by simultaneously (metonymically) perfecting and destroying Freudian psychoanalysis. "Such is the fatality," writes Baudrillard,

> of every system devoted through its own logic to total perfection, and thus total defectiveness. . . . At the peak of value, ambivalence intensifies; and at the height of their coherence, the redoubled signs of the code are haunted by the abyss of reversal. . . . There is only one word to designate the finality of death that is internal to the system, the one that is everywhere inscribed in its operational logic, and the radical counter-finality, ex-scribed from the system as such, but which everywhere haunts it: the same term of death, and only it can manifest itself on either side. The ambiguity can already be seen in the Freudian death instinct. It is *not an ambiguity*. It simply translates the proximity of realized perfection and the immediate defection of the system. (1988: 123)

As in Derrida, here the "same" word, "death," suddenly changes its sense, overflowing with sense or exceeding it, synecdochic kernel or metonymic other of Freud's systematic intelligence and of Western culture more generally. That is, within the code is inscribed its "outside" so that the "same" term—"death," "materiality," "otherness"— is also its "other." "Mauss must be turned against Mauss, Saussure against Saussure, Freud against Freud," Baudrillard says; "we must oppose the Saussure of the *Anagrams* against that of the linguistics" (1988: 120), which is to say, we must apprehend within the systematic transcendental intelligibility of language its random, contingent, arbitrary and material immanence. In this way, signification becomes the "similacra" of a system "fluctuating in indeterminacy, all of reality absorbed by the hyperreality of the code and of simulation" and escapes in "indefinite speculation, beyond any reference to the real, or even to a gold standard" (1988: 126, 120).

Despite his rhetoric, Baudrillard, like Steiner, is attempting to describe a remarkable *historic* transformation of apprehension and understanding in the West. Jean-Joseph Goux makes the similarity of Steiner and Baudrillard (modern and postmodern) much clearer by describing the historical nature of the opposition between "production" and "simulation" and the emergence of the order of the code in his examination of the functioning of the gold standard in Western culture at the turn of the century. Goux does not acknowledge the fact that the gold standard operated only for a short time at the height of liberal capitalism and philosophical positivism: it effectively existed between

1880 and 1914. As Frank Tipton and Robert Aldrich write, "the system which in retrospect appears so natural and stable . . . operated for at most 34 years" (1987: 43). Still, *Les Monnayeurs du langage* examines the relationship between the functioning of money and that of more general systems of exchange at the moment of the transformation Baudrillard and Steiner describe. Goux focuses on André Gide's novel, *The Counterfeiters,* and argues that "the structural homology between money and language, which articulates itself within literary fiction in a coherent play of metaphors, marks a historical break" (1984: 10). This break is, again, the transformation of referential signification (best exemplified by the "convertibility" of banknotes to *identical* gold or silver coins and ingots) into a mode of signification in which convertibility *cannot* take place (best exemplified by the fact that soon after World War I Western European currencies could no longer be exchanged for gold). In this second, nonreferential mode of signification "contemporary questions concerning the nature of the sign are over-determined by a socio-symbolic system in which the logic of the 'token' as an elemental agent predominates" (1984: 173; see also 55). In this "logic," instead of standing for a "material object" whose value is intrinsic to it, currency functions without regard to its "natural" qualities. Like other elements in the almost completely humanized world Jameson describes, the value of money is humanized and socialized to pure instrument: it is transformed from value based on more or less "natural" needs (i.e., "use value" possessed by gold as the "shiny yellow metal" in Goux's repeated description) to value based on circulation (i.e., "exchange value" indifferent to whether the token is paper or metal). "The circulation of pure tokens, without a cash reserve or a standard of measure" became dominant in the modern era. Now, Goux continues, "the illusion of an intrinsic value of the monetary commodity is no longer sustained, but rather one of the possibility of a *complete autonomy of pure symbolism*" (1984: 197).

This analysis marks, in historically specific ways, the transformation of a sign-system related to the production of identical objects to a sign-system based on simulation in which no natural referential original exists for its simulated "copies." In such a system, Goux suggests, the transcendental value of material objects is erased: "at this stage of the historical development of the signifier," he writes, the non-convertibility of currency into species (i.e., the non-convertibility of the signifier into the signified) "is a challenge to all transcendental meaning [*signifié transcendental*]" (1984: 183–84). Here again, in historically specific terms, the nature of material objects is divorced from their positive meaning: Goux notes that in Gide's description of the funeral for Gontran's father in *The Counterfeiters*

> a fundamental *resonance* is absent. It is as if a meaning, a value, a numinous intensity which ought to have expressed itself here and opened onto a dimension of transcendence (toward the beyond, toward the suprasensible, toward ethereal and sublime regions) remained without effect. An immemorial power, which ought to have deployed here all the wealth of its overwhelming meaning to reveal the pure magnificence of its treasure, its metaphysical significance, remains unemployed, fallow, untranslated, like this indifferent cadaver, and failed to evoke for the attending son the infinite echoes which are attached to the dead ancestor. (1984: 63)

Within the dispensation Goux describes—within the modernist discourse of "simulation," rather than the referential realism of an earlier age—death itself loses its traditional power of meaning and is transformed to a kind of material indifference resonating within social and discursive life. "At roughly the historical turning point where Western culture gave up looking systematically beyond death for religious meaning," observes Garrett Stewart, literature, and especially the novel, began to evaluate "death as an end in itself" (1984: 8).

This deathly rhetoric of materialism inhabits modernist discourse unspeakably, unconsciously. Moreover, in the opposition between production and simulation, between realism and modernism, between the same and difference are embedded two conceptions of rhetoric that traditionally have been synecdochically related, with one or the other taking precedence. One of these conceptions is that of rhetoric as *persuasion,* in which discourse is used to modify the "ideas" of its interlocutor; the other is the conception of rhetoric as *trope,* in which discourse helps to shape the world itself by positing (simulating) meaningful distinctions. In the first conception, rhetoric aims at identity; it aims at the listener *identifying* with the speaker in an overt social activity. In the second conception, rhetoric aims at difference, at making distinctions and articulating minute discriminations. In these two conceptions are embedded two ways of conceiving of discourse: discourse as *communication*—the transference of the same ideas from speaker to listener—and discourse as *signification*—the discrimination of meanings.

In the modernist era the possibility of a hierarchical relationship between communication and signification breaks down. At the end of

A Passage to India, Forster still maintains a tenuous hierarchy in which
the language of communication remains in the service of the representations of signification, even when that signification represents the
breakdown of communication itself. In other words, the novel does
not enact its meaning: the very language that communicates the failure
of communication remains transparently communicative. But in Gide
such a hierarchy is breached: for example, by means of powerful metonymy, he enacts the incompatibility of communication and signification when he describes Gontran beside his dead father without tears,
looking "at the dead man's bloodless hands and [wondering] for how
much longer the nails will go on growing" (1931: 40). In Gide the
materiality of life, like the materiality of signification, is indifferent to
its possible transcendental, referential significance. The wonder at the
dead man's nails—its very difference from the transcendental feelings
that the "sign" of a dead body traditionally communicates—creates an
uneasy, unlocatable sense. Forster's hierarchical discourse allows for
a more definite, more communicable sense, even while this definiteness
remains tenuous. Things, identifying with people, raise their material
voices, but they do so to disrupt the world, to forestall the possible
identification between Indian and Englishman—the very identification
that the ideology of industrial-era imperialism attempted to effect. In
India, as in Ireland and elsewhere, the British claimed to be developing
the native populations into good English citizens.

The difference between these two rhetorics—and, more important,
the possibility of their incompatibility—is perhaps best articulated in
the two German words for "representation," *Vorstellung* and *Darstellung.* At the turn of the century, these terms distinguished between
"sensory" or "perceptual" representations and "public" or "linguistic"
representations: "on the whole," Janik and Toulmin write in *Wittgenstein's Vienna,* "the 'sensory' use was associated with the German word
Vorstellung, and the 'public' use with the word *Darstellung;* the former
word is, for instance, the standard German translation for the Lockean
term 'idea' " (1973: 132–33). Gayatri Spivak uses this distinction in
examining the nature of English imperialism in India in her essay "Can
the Subaltern Speak?" There, reading Marx, Spivak notes that

> the event of representation as *Vertretung* (in the constellation
> of rhetoric-as-persuasion) behaves like a *Darstellung* (or rhet-
> oric-as-trope), taking its place in the gap between the formation
> of a (descriptive) class and the nonformation of a (transfor-
> mative) class: "In so far as millions of families live under
> economic conditions of existence that separate their mode of

life ... *they form a class.* In so far as ... the identity of their
interests fails to produce a feeling of community ... *they do
not form a class.*" The complicity of *Vertreten* and *Darstellen,*
their identity-in-difference as the place of practice—since this
complicity is precisely what Marxists must expose, as Marx
does in *The Eighteenth Brumaire*—can only be appreciated if
they are not conflated by a sleight of word. (1988: 277)

In this analysis, these "rhetorics" participate in the complexity of metonymy I described in the preceding chapter. *Vorstellung* and *Darstellung* complement one another in a traditional constellation of part and
whole (whether that whole is understood as essentially one or another
of the terms, or as the general term of "rhetoric" in which both are
parts). But in both Marx and Spivak, the sense of contradiction and
complicity also suggests that they are "other," rather than complementary to one another. This complexity is underlined in Spivak's
attempt here (and elsewhere) to bring a rhetorical analysis to bear on
questions of social practice, an effort that is part of her larger project,
as a "postcolonial intellectual," to map the function of discourse within
practices of European power. In the essay just quoted, Spivak examines
the ways in which contemporary discourse theory—specifically, the
theories of Michel Foucault and Gilles Deleuze—attempt, synecdochically, "to conserve the subject of the West, or the West as Subject"
(1988: 271).

Such attempts, as Cornel West has recently argued, take their place
within the overall modernist response to the "decentering" of the West
that Steiner and others have described. They are manifestations of the
reaction to the "end" of Europe as the center of political, economic
and military hegemony over the world and, equally important, the end
of "Europe" as a self-identical entity. This ending is first articulated,
West argues (1988), in Matthew Arnold's recognition that the traditional ideology of the West—and especially the religious ideology that
sustained the great centering of Europe from 1492 until the triumph
of liberal capitalism in the nineteenth century—is no longer relevant
to the material instrumentalization at the base of European power (see
Lunn 1982: 38). The year 1492 marks the beginning of European imperialism, with Columbus's discovery of a world that is "New" only
to the men of Europe. Equally important, it is the year in which Spain
defined "Europe" against its "other" by expelling the Jews. In this way,
the Age of Europe—450 years during which European capitalism and
imperialism shaped the world—is defined *against* non-European peo-
ples and, within Europe, *against* workers, women, and people of color.

But by the time of the Great War, as I shall argue, the West as subject has become a problem: it has fragmented into the warring classes that Arnold hopes to unite in an idea of "culture," and the "nightmare of history" that Joyce describes in *Ulysses*. Eliot hopes to overcome the problem of the fragmentation of European culture by articulating what never had to be explicitly articulated in the age of the European centering of the world, the idea of a great Western "tradition" that comprised "the mind of Europe" (1975: 39; see West 1988, Harrington 1983: esp. 12–13; and Steiner 1971). Thus, as Andrew Ross notes, "at the moment in literary history when the very idea of literary history is in question, this overriding interest in 'tradition' comes as a placebo, a way of sublimating the traumatic knowledge that history is not rational" (1986: 59–60).

Spivak situates contemporary discourse theory in this broad historical context—the context, I am arguing, of European modernism. The end of the Age of Europe, as West describes it, is most clearly seen when what had been felt to be a universal human problem (and articulated as such in the synecdochic discourse of modernism) comes to be seen as a European problem. This is why Spivak prefers Jacques Derrida's "critique of European ethnocentrism in the constitution of the 'Other' " to the more generalizing discourses of Foucault and Deleuze. "As a postcolonial intellectual," Spivak writes, "I am not troubled that [Derrida] does not *lead* me (as Europeans inevitably seem to do) to the specific [political] path that such a critique makes necessary. It is more important to me that as a European philosopher, he articulates the *European* Subject's tendency to constitute the Other as marginal to ethnocentrism and locates *that* as the problem with all logocentric . . . endeavors. *Not* a general problem, but a *European* problem" (1988: 293). In the same way, modernism is a particular *European* response to the felt breakup and breakdown of the nineteenth-century cultural hegemony of the landed gentry. In Anglo-American modernism, at least, the modernist response to this breakup was overwhelmingly male, Protestant, politically and culturally conservative (even though forms of continental modernism, as Peter Burger argues, were more progressive [1984; Huyssen 1986: 7–8]). Within that cultural hegemony people outside the ruling class—workers, women, "non-Europeans"—could not speak. Their silent presence, like that of the violence at the base of European power, or the terrible *fact* of personal mortality, or the voiceless, seemingly nonmaterial phoneme of Saussure's linguistic code, could be overlooked, literally rendered *immaterial,* amid the cluttered material triumph of nineteenth-century capitalism that Jameson and Marx described (see Berman 1982: 87–131).

But by the turn of the century, such negative materiality—in public and private life and in the codes of signification—came to be felt as brute materiality that was associated with but could not be incorporated within the "mind" of Europe, just as discourse could not incorporate communication and signification into a single understanding of itself. Instead, negative materiality became the "death," as Baudrillard calls it, of the "mind" of Europe, its material other, resonating, unconsciously, within the discourse of that "mind" itself.

Such a resonance rang sympathetically as an overtone of the breakup and breakdown of what West calls the "last years of the Age of Europe" (1988). This historical crisis was governed by a complex of forces that undermined the universal and transcendental truths that had, as West and Steiner note, centered post-Enlightenment Western civilization, sustaining what Oswald Spengler calls in *The Decline of the West* the "current West European scheme of history, in which the great Cultures are made to follow orbits round us as the presumed centre of all world-happenings, ... the *Ptolemaic system* of history" (1962: 13). The late nineteenth century was the age of imperialism—between 1835 and the Great War, European powers came to control over 85 percent of the world's population—and it was founded, as Alan Bullock has said, "not only on the material superiority but, as the great majority believed without a shadow of doubt, on the cultural and racial superiority of the white races of European stock" (1976: 60; see also Steiner 1971: 61–62. Harrington describes the link between European imperialist "centering" and the discipline of anthropology [1983: 130–32]).

Already in Nietzsche, however, the faltering of this ideology of a self-identical Europe at the center of the world is articulated. In his notebooks in the 1880s he historicizes the idea of Europe to find, at a particular historical moment (the first decades of the nineteenth century), the conception of "Europe as a political unit" in Napoleon and the image of "a European culture that would harvest the full inheritance of *attained* humanity" in Goethe (1968: 66). The faltering of such a conception, Nietzsche saw, was a function of the breakup of landed property and power during the nineteenth century. "The former means for obtaining homogeneous, enduring characters for long generations," he wrote, is "unalienable landed property, honoring the old." "Now," he continues, "the breaking up of landed property belongs to the opposite tendency: newspapers (in place of daily prayers), railway, telegraph" (1968: 44). Steiner has argued that "we cannot determine the deep-lying forces which brought on the crisis of the word" in the twentieth century (1989: 94), but here Nietzsche is suggesting at least one force that helped condition the metonymic "metaphysics" of journalism that Steiner laments in our culture.

In the breakup of the power of landed property Nietzsche saw the destruction of the authority of originality altogether and the positivist *transhistorical* sense of the nineteenth century that grounded phenomena in their causes—in which, in Baudrillard's analysis, phenomena are somehow *identical* with their causes. In this context, Derek Attridge's observation that the "transhistorical viewpoint" of nineteenth-century philological etymology drains language "of its heterogeneity and materiality" (1988: 103–4) is quite relevant. Thus, in the *Genealogy of Morals* (1887) Nietzsche writes, "there is for historiography of any kind no more important proposition than the one ... which really *ought to be* established now: the cause of the origin of a thing and its eventual utility, its actual employment and place in a system of purposes, lie worlds apart; whatever exists, having somehow come into being, is again and again reinterpreted to new ends, taken over, transformed" (1967: 77). In this mode of understanding, as in Spengler, the West is radically *historicized*. Its significance becomes a function of historical rather than transhistorical events, metonymic configurations rather than synecdochical causes. Moreover, "modernism" as a cultural movement responds precisely to this historical sense, to the negative materialism embedded in the implicit contingency of historical events which do not seem "necessary," but "somehow come into being." Such historicization paradoxically destroys the idea of history as a self-identical continuous ("transhistorical") force; it exhausts and replaces that idea of history with disruption, fragmentation, negative materiality (Ross 1986: 58–59). One response to such metonymic fragmentation is the ahistorical conservatism of modernism that attempts to discern "mythical" synecdochic essences in the welter of experience—what I describe in Chapter 5 as "imperial" modernism, represented by Jakobson. But embedded in even that "ahistorical" response, as I argue in the next chapter, are the resonations of the material and heterogeneous experience of modern historical existence, the "end" of Europe.

In this way, the historical breakup of landed property—of "tradition" in Eliot's magisterial sense, of the Protestant aristocracy in Ireland as Yeats describes it more specifically, of the "real presence" inhabiting art and language that George Steiner describes and laments—was a major condition of the rise of modernism and its discourse. It was, to one extent or another, the historical crisis to which modernism in all its forms responded. Chief among the forces conditioning this breakup, as I have already implied, is the movement of the concentration of European capital from industry to finance. At the beginning of the nineteenth century, banks were more or less individual (i.e., family-held) institutions that served more or less individual entrepreneurs. By the end of the century banks had become impersonal corporations accumulating the huge amounts of capital necessary for financing large corporations. A new form of capitalism developed, "characterized by the emergence of banker control, increased monopolization and growing state regulation of the economy" (see Rudolf Hilferding, *Finance Capital* [1910] cited in Hansen 1985: 51; see also Tipton and Aldrich 1987: 15; and Harrington 1983: 29). In England, for instance, the number of corporations rose from 700 in 1855 to 7,900 in 1883 (Edwards 1938: 29).

"In the field of financial organization" before the Great War, George Edwards notes, "the most important trend was the amalgamation of the commercial banks which welded them into a few institutions. These banks departed more and more from strictly commercial operations and engaged in security [finance] operations to a greater extent than in the past. There was a complete reversal in the relation of the demand for and the supply of capital with the increase in the relative demand for capital as compared with the supply" (1938: 45). This increased demand was a function of the increased accumulation of capital—especially the unconsumable capital tools of the early nineteenth century, the "first" industrial revolution. During that time individual capitalists produced basic necessities (food, shelter, clothing) and accumulated the capital that gave rise to the "second" industrial revolution at the end of the nineteenth century—the triumphant capitalism that Jameson describes. In the first stage of capitalization, landed wealth could and did coexist and compete with the wealth of industry: throughout Europe the landed aristocracy of the Old Regime continued to rule up to 1914 (Anderson 1988: 324). But by the time of the capital accumulation in the late nineteenth century, neither family bankers nor individual entrepreneurs nor landed aristocrats could command the vast social wealth needed to finance the second industrial revolution.

The transformation of industrial capitalism to finance capital ensured the breakup of the unalienable landed property, the destruction of "tradition," and, as Stephen Kern describes it, the transformation of the "essential foundations of experience" (1983: 5). The wealth of "real" estate—referential wealth literally founded upon land—paled before the vast capital wealth of investment and trade; no longer was land the basis of political and economic power in Europe. In this context it seems clear that Marx's analysis of capitalism, in some ways at least, was a product of the first rather than the second industrial revolution. That is, the labor theory of value that Marx inherited from Ricardo and others and upon which he establishes the creation of surplus value and the accumulation of capital—a theory that measures value in relation to "real" human needs, specifically in reference to the food, clothing, and shelter that sustain labor—is transformed in the modern era, as Baudrillard says, to "the flotation of labor itself." "Marx and Saussure," Baudrillard continues in a remarkable conjunction, "never foresaw this indeterminacy, this commutability of every kind of term, which accompanies such unlimited speculation and inflation" (1988: 126; see also Shell 1982, and Newman 1985).

The second industrial revolution transformed the very nature of consumption by transforming the nature of commodified wealth. Now commodities answered more than basic needs for food, shelter, clothing—the great products of the first industrial revolution in England, which created, above all, textile and furniture industries and transportation systems for foodstuff (see Anderson 1988: 324–25). Now commodities also "created" needs—the rise of the advertising industry with canvassers like Leopold Bloom attests to this. This transformation of the nature of wealth is both cause and effect of the remarkable technological achievement of the second industrial revolution, which transformed and widened industrial production to include a host of products beyond the "basic" consumer needs. The negative side of this transformation is the economic crisis of *laissez faire* capitalism manifested in the great depression of 1873–96 and the concomitant rise of militant labor and socialist movements throughout Europe. Furthermore, the second industrial revolution—in communication, transportation, production, finance, and the general commodification of "things" for mass consumption—created the felt experience of the demise of the landed aristocracy, the modernist experience, as Stephen Spender describes it (in terms close to those of Steiner), of "the swan song, the end of our culture, enclosed in a doomed civilization" (1965: 253).

Perry Anderson situates the rise of modernism at a particular moment in European social and economic history, "at the intersection between a semi-aristocratic ruling order, a semi-industrialized capitalist economy, and a semi-emergent, or semi-insurgent, labor movement" (1988: 326). In this situation, Anderson argues, the modernist artists of the turn of the century faced cultural values *against which* art could measure itself, and also *in terms of which* they could articulate themselves within "a set of available codes and resources from which the ravages of the market as an organizing principle of culture and society—uniformly detested by every species of modernism—could also be resisted" (1988: 325). Anderson is correct in this analysis, but he fails to take into account the products as well as the structure of social and economic history and to notice that the technology of the second industrial revolution transformed the material base of value in European society.

That technology changed the very products of capitalism from the basic commodities by which Marx measured the labor theory of value to commodities that not only created their own demand, but whose "use value" became progressively more distant from such basic human needs. With this change, "value" was less directly related to "positive" material goods—food, clothing, shelter—and more fully related to "values" which were "negatively" exchangeable. The metonymic interchangeability of goods affected life and art and understanding as much as did the synecdochical "organizing principle" of political and economic power that Anderson describes. The telephone and the radio, for instance, served different human needs, but, as Edward Bellamy suggests in *Looking Backwards* (1888) when he has the utopian society he describes "broadcast" symphonic music through the telephones, these new products can replace one another far more easily than they can fulfill the basic need for food or clothing. Similarly, smokeless gunpowder, part of the great revolution in chemistry of the second industrial revolution (which included plastics and film [Tipton and Aldrich 1987: 13]), made the trench warfare of the Great War possible by allowing the soldiers to see what was going on far better than the American Civil War soldiers can see what is going on in the smoky battles described in Stephen Crane's *The Red Badge of Courage* (1895). But in making trench warfare possible, the effect of smokeless gunpowder was to render the activity of soldiering indifferent to which particular soldiers use the smokeless machine guns. Here soldiers function like the material tokens of a signifying system that Goux describes. In the second industrial revolution production, rather than serving a "basic" need, called for more technology and production (such as the tanks and airplanes that ended trench warfare) and more, and still more, on and on and on.

Such differences stand to reason, since what makes particular products "basic" is precisely the way in which they serve universal human needs. In the nineteenth century, the minute differences in standardized "identical" basic consumer products were ignored: Richard Sennett notes in one striking instance that a member of the Jockey Club said "one could always recognize gentlemanly dress because the buttons on the sleeves of a gentleman's coat actually buttoned and unbuttoned," even though a gentleman would keep the buttons "scrupulously fastened, so that his sleeves never called attention to this fact" (1976: 165). But in the modern era, it is precisely the difference between identical products—such as washing detergent and breakfast cereals, invented around the turn of the twentieth century—that launched the mass advertising industry (as depicted in H. G. Wells's *Tono Bungay* [1908]). Finally, "it was not until the late nineteenth century," as Eugene Lunn notes, "that the full implications of the new market situation" affected art "production." Artists came to emphasize their differences from others and, as in the case of Ezra Pound, make art "new" with different slogans ("Imagism" vs. "Vorticism," for instance) in order to find an audience and a market (Lunn 1982: 41–42; see also Kenner 1971).

This complex of revolutionary financial and technological changes conditioned the crises of the early modern period. The intellectual crisis of the exhaustion of nineteenth-century positive science, perhaps best represented in the success of diachronic (etymological) linguistics in accounting for European languages in causal and historical terms, or the fulfillment of Newtonian physics by Planck and others, can be understood in relation to the undermining of the authority of the landed gentry; so can the breakdown of individual-centered understandings of culture, represented in Freud's development of psychoanalysis and articulated in Spengler's Nietzschean description of the decline of the West. The breakup of European world hegemony manifested in the rise and fall of nineteenth-century imperialism is likewise related to the destruction of the landed cultural base of Europe. Imperialism, as both J. A. Hobson and Lenin argued before the war, is a function of international finance capital (see Heilbroner 1953: 187–91; Tipton and Aldrich 1987: 49). Finally, the dizzying pace of change in the face of the second industrial revolution presented a crisis in itself (see Kern's powerfully documented study of the change in the textured experience of life at this time, *The Culture of Time and Space, 1880–1918*).

The relationship between these historical events and the rhetoric of modernism can be best understood in relation to negative materialism—in relation to metonymy and death. Such an understanding encompasses the material conditions that govern the production of meaning. In these terms, Baudrillard's distinction between "production" and "simulation" describes the effects of the great economic change in the last half of the nineteenth century from industrial to finance capitalism that Goux examines in relation to currency. As Goux notes, "the subordination of industry to the banking apparatus (the greater and greater domination of the industrial sector by the financial establishment) . . . not only dominated monetary exchange more than anything else did, it also played a primary role in the production of merchandise for the market" (1984: 36). This complex of the mode of financial-industrial production and the products that system creates knelled the end of the aristocratic class to which many modernist writers—especially the more or less marginal and exiled Anglo-American writers I will examine in this book—looked for their sense of cultural value.

As I have already suggested, products were as important as production as part of the world to which modernism responded; the particular material objects with which people lived were as important as the abstract social formations that produced them. (In the same way, I shall argue in a later chapter, the metonymic enunciations of language are as much a part of the meanings and power of rhetoric as the synecdochic linguistic system that makes them possible.) The amazing array of new commodities utterly transformed modes of life in Europe and America: the telephone, the airplane, electrical power, the radio, inexpensive iron smelting, the automobile, plastics, the X-ray machine, synthetic chemicals, even our sprawling cities, all were newly invented. These inventions created a "crisis of abundance": the "essential foundations of experience," as Stephen Kern describes them, were radically altered in the face of technological innovations (1983: 9, 5; see also Tipton and Aldrich 1987). Such technological achievements led Henry Adams to imagine in 1900 that the world is *futureless,* without relation, positive or negative, to anything that precedes or follows it. "Satisfied that the sequence of men led to nothing and that the sequence of their society could lead no further," Adams wrote, "while the mere sequence of time was artificial, and the sequence of thought was chaos, he turned at last to the sequence of force; and thus it happened that, after ten years' pursuit, he found himself lying in the Gallery of Machines at the Great Exhibition of 1900, his historical neck broken by the sudden irruption of forces totally new" (1931: 382). These forces overwhelmed the repetitions of production, the conception and unformulated feeling that different things are the "same" that allow transhistorical continuity and the idea of history to appear and remain effective.

More generally, Walter Benjamin describes a modern sense of the fact that, in the face of this technology,

> experience has fallen in value. And it looks as if it is continuing to fall into bottomlessness. . . . For never has experience been contradicted more thoroughly than strategic experience by tactical warfare, economic experience by inflation, bodily expe-

rience by mechanical warfare, moral experience by those in power. A generation that had gone to school on a horse-drawn streetcar now stood under the open sky in a countryside in which nothing remained unchanged but the clouds, and beneath these clouds, in a field of force of destructive torrents and explosions, was the tiny, fragile human body. (1969: 83–84)

The telephone can stand as a less dramatic example than the Great War of the changes Benjamin describes and how they affected the ways people lived and conceived of themselves. A phone call, Kern argues, is both more immediate and more unpredictable than a letter.

It is a surprise and therefore more disruptive, demanding immediate attention. The active mode is heightened for the caller who can make things happen immediately without enduring the delay of written communication, while the intrusive effect of the ringing augments the expectant mode for the person called. . . . Indeed, waiting for the telephone to ring became a symbol of loneliness and helplessness . . . more tormenting than waiting for a letter, because the call may or may not come at any time. (1983: 91)

Two literary examples might clarify the disruptiveness the telephone created. In *Remembrance of Things Past* Proust describes a telephone call to his dying grandmother in terms of its "sorcery"

for which a few moments are enough to bring before us, invisible but present, the person to whom we have been wishing to speak and who, while still sitting at his table, in the town in which he lives (in my grandmother's case, Paris) under another sky than ours, in weather that is not necessarily the same, in the midst of circumstances and worries of which we know nothing, but of which he is going to inform us, finds himself suddenly transported hundreds of miles (he and all the surroundings in which he remains immured) within reach of our ear, at the precise moment which our fancy has ordained. (1934: 809)

Here Proust is describing the remarkable historicity the telephone creates, the very sense of difference within the "same," of a world that is unknown and other existing simultaneously with our own. It is precisely this *otherness* that the phone reveals to Marcel, a real presence indeed that voice so near—in actual separation. But a premonition also of an eternal separation! Over and again, as I listened in this way, without seeing her who spoke to me from so far away, it has seemed to me that the voice was crying to me from depths out of which one does not rise again, and I have known the anxiety that was one day to wring my heart when a voice should thus return (alone, and attached no longer to a body which I was never more to see), to murmur, in my ear, words I would fain have kissed as they issued from lips for ever turned to dust. (1934: 810)

The phone call Marcel describes does not take place. Instead, he narrates the evocation of mortality provoked by the very technology that, seemingly like magic, traverses unheard of distances. (Kern describes the instrumentality of the telephone in fueling the rush to war in the last weeks of July 1914: "Proust had a vision of death when he first spoke to his grandmother over the telephone; perhaps the Kaiser and the Tsar heard a death rattle of diplomacy in the clicking of the telegraph key" [1983: 268].)

Proust figures both the magic of the telephone and the materiality it invokes metaphorically: he describes "the ever infuriated servants of the Mystery, the umbrageous priestesses of the Invisible, the Young Ladies of the Telephone" (1934: 810). In *The Castle* Kafka describes the materiality of the telephone metonymically, in the static heard on the line. K. is told that the continual telephoning that takes place in the Castle is heard "in our telephones down here as a humming and singing. ... Now, this humming and singing transmitted by our telephones is the only real and reliable thing you'll hear, everything else is deceptive" (1974: 93–94). In Kafka, the *noise* of the telephone, its materiality as a mode of transmission, conveys its significance. In this, as Benjamin notes, is a sign of the materiality of modern life, "For just as K. lives in the village on Castle Hill, modern man lives in his body; the body slips away from him, is hostile toward him. It may happen that a man wakes up one day and finds himself transformed into vermin" (1969: 126).

In these examples we can discern a kind of material modernist rhetoric. As in Baudrillard's "simulation," it is difference that conveys meaning. For Proust, the difference is between the "real presence" of voice and the figured absence of "actual separation" and, more strikingly, the fact that the meditation takes place precisely because the phone call failed to take place. For Kafka, the difference is between noise and meaning, a kind of constant metonymy of materiality that signifies the material absence of meaning altogether. In both is inscribed a sense of bodily existence that is not quite the object of discourse, but that inhabits it the way these writers felt it to inhabit the technological, discursive innovation of the telephone itself. Here, as in the economic and political history of the early modern era, within the "mind" of Europe is inscribed its possible material "other," within the discourse of modernism the resonating noise of death.

Perhaps the most striking contemporaneous expression of the other within the "mind" of Europe was Oswald Spengler's *The Decline of the West,* written before the war and published in 1919. Spengler describes different periods governing history, now conceived not as continuous—not participating in the "same"—but as separate and distinct *moments* of human existence that can be figured in terms of life and death, with beginnings, middles, and ends. "Every new Culture," he writes, "comes into existence with a new view of the world, that is, a sudden glimpse of death as the secret of the perceivable world" (1962: 89–90). Such a glimpse, Spengler argues, is the great "world-fear," the dread borne of a past that seems, as it did to his contemporaries throughout the first decades of the twentieth century, irretrievably past (see Spender 1965: esp. 209). "In the present," Spengler writes,

> we feel a trickling away, the past implies a passing. Here is the root of our eternal dread of the irrevocable, the attained, the final—our dread of mortality, of the world itself as a thing-become, where death is set as a frontier like birth—our dread of the moment when the possible is actualized, the life is inwardly fulfilled and consciousness stands at its goal. It is the deep world-fear of the child—which never leaves the higher man, the believer, the poet, the artist—that makes him so infinitely lonely in the presence of the alien powers that loom, threatening in the dawn, behind the screen of sense-phenomena. . . . It is something beyond comprehension, this transformation of future into past, and thus time, in its contrast with space, has always a queer, baffling, oppressive ambiguity from which no serious man can wholly protect himself. (1962: 59)

Spengler is here articulating the sense of mortality and material death that inhabits modernism. Such a sense, I think, is implicit in the work of Spengler's teacher, Nietzsche, who described European civilization in 1884 as similarly futureless: "disintegration characterizes this time, and thus uncertainty: nothing stands firmly on its feet or on a hard faith in itself; one lives for tomorrow, as the day after tomorrow is dubious" (1968: 41). This futurelessness is, as Paul de Man has argued in relation to Nietzsche's discourse, a function of conceiving of representation as *Darstellung* rather than *Vorstellung,* of conceiving of the sign—whether it be of economic or other "value"—as being arbitrary rather than motivated, based not on goods but on structural distinctions. Implicit in this argument is the complex conception of rhetoric I have described, the complex metonymic relationship between *Vorstellung* and *Darstellung* in which one cannot be fully incorporated within the other, so that, within a sign system, the *materiality* of the signifier cannot be wholly erased.

This leads Spengler, as it does Baudrillard in his different way, to characterize a particular rhetoric of modernism. "World-fear," Spengler asserts,

> is assuredly the most *creative* of all prime feelings. . . . Like a secret melody that not every ear can perceive, it runs through the form-language of every true art-work, every inward philosophy, every important deed. . . . Only the spiritually dead man of the autumnal cities—Hammurabi's Babylon, Ptolemaic Alexandria, Islamic Baghdad, Paris and Berlin today—only the pure intellectual, the sophist, the sensualist, the Darwinian, loses it or is able to evade it by setting up a secretless "scientific world-view" between himself and the alien. (1962: 59–60)

Here Spengler is articulating the anti-positivism of his time—and of modernism more generally. At the same time he is describing the "materiality of thought" that Michel Foucault describes in modernism, "in that region where death prowls, where thought is extinguished, where the promise of the origin interminably recedes" (1970: 383). It is in this space, Foucault goes on, that modernist literature "posited itself as experience: as experience of death (and in the element of death), of unthinkable thought (and in its inaccessible presence), of repetition (of original innocence, always there at the nearest and yet always the most distant limit of language); as experience of finitude (trapped in the opening and the tyranny of that finitude)" (1970: 384). Such a conception of modernism can be heard in Arthur Symons's description of Jules Laforgue in 1899, a description that can stand, synecdochically, for the "end" of Europe more generally. "Laforgue died at twenty-seven," Symons writes in *The Symbolist Movement in Literature;* "he had been a dying man all his life, and his work has the fatal evasiveness of those who shrink from remembering the one thing which they are unable to forget" (1958: 61). The whole of European modernism, I suspect, resides in the *evasion* of the materiality of thought that cannot quite be forgotten, but haunts its discourse like a secret melody.

The sense of a modernist rhetoric of death that I am trying to describe, a rhetoric that acts on the interplay of the same and difference, that inscribes within its own discourse a non-positivist idea of materiality, haunts discourse that is postmodern as well. This is perhaps captured best in a passage from Maurice Blanchot's *Writing of the Disaster* (to which I will return in the last chapter) tentatively entitled "A primal scene?" Blanchot describes a scene in which a child looks out a window:

> What he sees: the garden, the wintry trees, the wall of a house. Though he sees, no doubt in a child's way, his play space, he grows weary and slowly looks up toward the ordinary sky, with clouds, grey light—pallid daylight without depth.
>
> What happens then: the sky, the *same* sky, suddenly open, absolutely black and absolutely empty, revealing (as though the pane had broken) such an absence that all has since always and forevermore been lost therein—so lost that therein is affirmed and dissolved the vertiginous knowledge that nothing is what there is, and first of all nothing beyond. (1986: 72)

In a language capturing nothingness, Blanchot's discourse can stand as a heterogeneous example of the rhetoric of modernism inhabited by a secret and material melody. What makes it "material," as I shall argue in Chapter 4, are its metonymic "representations" that do not encompass synecdochical hierarchies but oppose them, even while they articulate them, complicitly, as other.

What is more important here, however, is the *quality* of modernism inhabiting this passage. As Stephen Melville has argued, modernism both "is and is not an event"; rather, it "transforms the terms in which we can construe history—so that history appears as a continuity that is traversed at every point by discontinuity and disruption, permanent revolution" (1986: 31). In the same way that Blanchot describes the "transformation" of vision that reveals absence and otherness within the same, his discourse explicitly narrates what the rhetoric of modernism implicitly presents: the deathly traversing of the real by *another* sense of its existence, absolutely black and absolutely empty. Such a revelation of the other in the same is the secret melody of death and materialism that Spengler describes in the traversing counterpoint of modernism; it is a revelation of *negative* materialism. It makes the accidents of existence, including the material "accidental" formation of codes of signification, and including contingency and death, resonate in art. Such a negative understanding can be heard, for example, in Paul Klee's description of the "meaning" of his modern art: "Formerly we used to represent things visible on earth, things we either liked to look at or would have liked to see. Today . . . things appear to assume a broader and more diversified meaning, often seemingly contradicting the rational experience of yesterday. There is a striving to emphasize the essential character of the accidental" (cited in Bradbury and McFarlane 1976: 48). Such striving emphasizes the material medium as well as the subject of art and what is at least their partial incompatibility. It emphasizes the ways in which the canvas and pigment of painting and the rhetoric of modernist discourse, which I examine in the next chapter, counterpoint and disrupt the visions and meanings they articulate.

3

Negative Materiality
and the Surface of Things

The Rhetoric of Modernism

Is it possible that despite discoveries and progress, despite culture, religion and world-wisdom, one has remained on the surface of life? Is it possible that one has even covered this surface, which might still have been something, with an incredibly uninteresting stuff which makes it look like the drawing-room furniture during summer holidays?

Yes, it is possible.

Is it possible that the whole history of the world has been misunderstood? Is it possible that the past is false, because one has always spoken of its masses just as though one were telling of a coming together of many human beings, instead of speaking of the individual around whom they stood because he was a stranger and was dying?

Yes, it is possible.

—Rainer Maria Rilke, *The Notebooks*
of Malte Laurids Brigge

One aspect of the breaking up of European hegemony and European culture at the end of the nineteenth century—the great and terrifying changes to which "modernism" responded—was the breaking up of the concept and functioning of discourse. As I mentioned in the last chapter, language and discourse can be understood to be forms of signification and of communication, and many of the great modernist writers use language in a way that implies that these two purposes are incompatible. The breaking apart of signification and communication in discourse gave rise to phenomenology as a philosophical movement and a psychology at the end of the nineteenth century. Phenomenology, as A. J. Greimas says of the linguistic phenomenology that developed into the structuralist movement in the early twentieth century (see Schleifer 1987: 44–82), is a science of "perception and not of expression" (1962: 57). As such, it is concerned with signification (with how language *articulates* experience) rather than with communication (with how it expresses preexisting phenomena).

This emphasis on perception rather than expression is directly related to the issue of the phenomenally felt presence of materiality and death in discourse and the rhetorical strategies that allow this negative materiality to be articulated within language. The recognition that the material nature of discourse—the material vehicle for the communication of meaning, the signifier—always bears meanings beyond those that are "intended" is a form of the breakdown of hierarchical subordination between meaning and communication. Such "excessive" meaning, in Maurice Blanchot's terms, "impoverishes all experience, withdraws from experience all authenticity" (1986: 51). When Blanchot says in his "primal scene" that "the sky, the *same* sky, suddenly open, absolutely black and absolutely empty," reveals absence within the fullness of experience (1986: 72), he is presenting explicitly what the discourse of modernism presents implicitly within its rhetoric: difference within the same, the breakdown of a culture, the death of authority. As he observes elsewhere in *The Writing of the Disaster,* the "sovereignty of the accidental causes us to acknowledge that forgetfulness is not negative or that the negative does not come after affirmation (affirmation negated), but exists in relation to the most ancient, to what would seem to come from furthest back in time immemorial without ever having been given" (1986: 3–4).

Throughout *The Writing of the Disaster,* Blanchot figures this as *material* death, "the dying which, though unsharable, I have in common with all," "the way one dies: without purpose, without power, without unity, and precisely, without 'the way,' " "*what remains without remains* (the fragmentary)" (1986: 23, 39, 33). Hillis Miller alludes to this quality in Blanchot's writing when he attempts to describe the feeling "of terror or dread readers may experience when they confront a text which seems irreducibly strange, inexplicable, perhaps even mad" (1985: 20). Such experiences inform the reading and writing of the early modernist writers. In the next chapter I examine this in more technical rhetorical terms as the failure of synecdoche, and in the chapter following I will examine the modernist attempt to recuperate such experience to synecdochical meaning in the work of Jakobson and Yeats.

Here, however, I want to trace the ways in which modernism articulates or circumscribes such experience, how it inhabits modernist discourses, often despite the express intentions of those discourses. In Blanchot, Miller continues, this experience of the disruption of cultural coherence

> is properly religious, metaphysical, ontological, though hardly in a traditional or conventional way. To borrow a mode of locution familiar to readers of Blanchot it is an ontology without ontology. Nor is it to be defined simply as a species of negative theology. Blanchot gives to this "something" that enters into the words or between the words the names, among others, of it [*il*]; the thing [*la chose*]; dying [*mourir*]; the neutral [*le neutre*]; the non-presence of the eternal return [*le retour éternel*]; writing [*écrire*]; the thought [*la pensée*]; the truth [*la verité*]; the other of the other [*l'autre de l'autre*] meaning something encountered in our relations to other people, especially relations involving love, betrayal, and that ultimate betrayal by the other of our love for him or her, the death of the other. (1985: 21)

Here Miller, like Blanchot himself, is attempting to articulate some phenomenal quality of rhetoric—something that enters words or the relation between words—that carries what I called in the preceding chapter the resonance of materiality and death.

Perhaps I can make this clearer if I return to *A Passage to India*. Like his contemporaries, E. M. Forster articulates a sense of failure of civilization in his work; in all his novels he describes a sense of the world that is vastly changed, that will never be the same. Doing so, he creates, as the great modernist writers do, a sustained elegy for a world that seems forever lost. But unlike the modernist writers, he does not *present* this crisis within the very discourse he offers us; his understanding of what is gone from the world is not *enacted* in his language. Rather, the "death" of a civilization is the theme of his work, but his language, his rhetoric, never quite rings with this theme. Instead, he constantly subordinates the communicative function of language to the significative, so that whatever his theme, his discourse presents a hierarchical order of meaning and communication. In the style of the great humanist writers of the Victorian era, he enacts what Fredric Jameson calls "the instrumental subordination of narrative language to narrative representation" (1979: 7) so that the "accidents" of discourse are in no way taken to be "essential" or "sovereign."

In *A Passage to India,* for instance, Forster comes close to narrating "negative materialism" in the terrifying experience of Mrs. Moore in the Marabar caves. Yet although he even creates an almost palpable and material sense of betrayal and death in the world, his theme never quite resonates in his language. Rather, the materialism of meaning seems always to signify: the "boum" Mrs. Moore hears is almost immediately "translated" to meaning so that it seems "to murmur, 'Pathos, piety, courage—they exist, but are identical, and so is filth . . .' " (1952: 149). Less melodramatically, the narrator thematizes the "boredom" of colonial life so that it is easily recuperated to meaning (1952: 132–33), just as the temples, tank, jail, carrion, the earth itself at the end of the novel can easily translate the resistance and betrayal of material things into a promised future (see Fleishman 1978: 149–62). Forster's significance—his intentional meanings, which, by virtue of being intentional, are future oriented—are hierarchically superior to the communicative function of his discourse: we know what he "means" by the "Boum," even if Mrs. Moore doesn't.

Forster's difference from the modernists—or at least from the *metonymic* modernism I am describing here—should become clear. Modernism has usually been characterized in relation to the past, and to some extent I followed this mode of characterization in the preceding chapter. As Paul de Man has noted in an influential essay, "Literary History and Literary Modernism," "modernity exists in the form of a desire to wipe out whatever came earlier, in the hope of reaching at last a point that could be called a true present, a point of origin that marks a new departure" (1971: 148). Such a characterization is based on the opposition between the essential and the accidental, the "true" and the "false"—based, in other words, on synecdochic understanding. (In Chapter 5 I examine such desire embodied in synecdochic, "imperial" modernism.) But there is another way to understand modernism that will allow us to see its self-conscious temporal understanding of itself as "a true present" in relation to the negative materiality of its rhetoric and its historical situation. In this understanding, modernism, sometimes self-consciously but most often unconsciously, conceives of itself as a moment cut off from the future as well as from the past. This "situation" of rhetoric characterizes postwar continental criticism and literary theory, the "postmodern" moment within modernism.

If Forster attempts to find rhetoric and voice for material things in order to make a future possible, modernism is faced with the materialism of both culture and rhetoric which forecloses the future. Rhetoric characterizes language—is essential to language—insofar as language can be conceived of as the locus of the future, the only "place" in which the contrary-to-fact status of the future can be realized. Rhetoric defined as persuasion is a way of understanding discourse as the condition for a future; and even the more radical sense of rhetoric as trope, as the foundation for knowledge and the *possibility* of knowledge, also conditions the future. When rhetoric and meaning are understood in material terms—when language, as Derrida shows, can be said to be the "materialism" of the idea (1981a: 64–66)—then the *theme* of the death of meaning and the *function* of rhetoric that Forster articulates in a hierarchy of meaning and communication cancel one another out, and the negative anxiety of materialism Blanchot describes and communicates appears to inhabit discourse. "If spirit is always active," Blanchot writes, "then patience is already nonspirit: the body in its suffering passivity—cadaverous, exposed, flattened, sheer surface. Patience is the cry beneath the word: not the spirit; the letter. And in this sense life itself, as the shade of life, the gift or living expenditure even unto dying" (1986: 40).

The materialism of the physical cry beneath the word finds its most precise and most disturbing articulation, as Baudrillard suggests, in Saussure's description of the foundation of meaning as the arbitrary nature of the sign. Modernism takes that arbitrariness very seriously as a starting place for giving the world a shape and significance, even when it pursues that beginning into all sorts of nonmaterial "ideas." More than Forster—who found that the modern world was not possible for art ("not yet, not there")—modernism is haunted as much by the loss of the future as by the loss of the past in relation to its own overwhelming material moment, the *sheer surface* of that moment. Perhaps the most precise articulation of this haunting is found in T. S. Eliot. In Eliot the past in the form of the "tradition" of the landed gentry is the locus of the attempt to "solve," as Franco Moretti describes it, "the short circuit between 'meaning' and 'value' " (1983: 188, 214). Such an attempt at a "solution" to the historical crisis of Europe can be seen in Eliot's attempt, a year before Forster's novel was published, to tame and comprehend the present by discovering in *Ulysses*—and, implicitly, in his own work—a "mythical method" in discourse. "In using the myth," Eliot writes,

> in manipulating a continuous parallel between contemporaneity and antiquity, Mr. Joyce is pursuing a method which others must pursue after him. . . . It is simply a way of controlling, of ordering, of giving a shape and a significance to the immense

panorama of futility and anarchy which is contemporary history. It is a method already adumbrated by Mr. Yeats, and of the need for which I believe Mr. Yeats to have been the first contemporary to be conscious. . . . It is, I seriously believe, a step toward making the modern world possible for art. . . . (1975: 177–78)

What concerns me here is less Eliot's understanding of Joyce's achievement than his description of the "panorama" of contemporary life. That panorama, for Eliot, as for Forster and for many of their contemporaries, is a vast chaos, what Wallace Stevens describes as the old chaos of the sun. Such chaos was not so mythically (and *synecdochically*) old as Stevens (or Eliot) imagined it. Both writers invented a past, as did the modernists in general. But they did so not so much to legitimate or account for or even excoriate the present—usual motives, I believe, in discursive-artistic inventions of the past. Rather, the chaos that modernism addresses with its versions of the past is the chaos of *not* imagining a future, the chaos of the end of Europe. In Yeats, in Eliot, in Conrad, even in Freud can be heard the plaintive cry Yeats remembers in *A Vision* after recoiling in horror from Paul Valéry's rejoicing that "human life must pass": "O Lord, let something remain" (1966: 220).

Implicit in the examination of contemporary literary criticism and theory in Part II of this book is the assumption that the rhetoric of Jakobson, Barthes, Lacan, and Derrida attempts in one way or another, as modernism itself does, to create an imaginable and sufficient future in the face of the negative materiality of death. Jakobson's work most fully participates in the side of modernism that attempts to recuperate transcendental meanings in the face of the twentieth-century crisis of Western culture. But even those others who, to one degree or another, attempt to reimagine "culture" metonymically rather than synecdochically are responding to this crisis. In *Howards End,* in a remarkably nostalgic moment, Forster has Helen Schlegel assert that "Death destroys a man: the idea of Death saves him" (1908: 239). Yet the great "discovery" of modernism—not only in literature, but also in the revolution of spirit articulated by Nietzsche, Freud, Marx, and Saussure, and even, as in Eliot, when modernism denies it—is the *materiality* of signification, the materiality of the "idea" (everything that comes under the category of the "spiritual"), so that the possibility of salvation that Helen Schlegel envisions becomes as accidental and contingent as death itself.

Four years after *Howards End,* D. H. Lawrence narrates a different idea of death in "Odour of Chrysanthemums"—what he calls there the "naive dignity of death"—in a rhetoric that approaches the inarticulate before the physical fact of death. Elizabeth Bates is suddenly confronted with the sheer physical presence of her husband's body in death: "Who am I?" she asks; "What have I been doing? I have been fighting a husband who did not exist. *He* existed all the time" (1961: 300). Against her "idea" of her husband is his physical existence, the physical presence of the *same* man that Lawrence can only reveal in the moment of death and signify here in the material gesture of italics. The story ends with Elizabeth dressing the dead body while "a terrible dread gripped her all the while: that he could be so heavy and utterly inert, unresponsive, apart. . . . She knew she submitted to life, which was her immediate master. But from death, her ultimate master, she winced with fear and shame" (1961: 302). In Lawrence, as in the other Anglo-American modernists, is the tacit—and sometimes more than tacit—acknowledgment of the anarchy of inert materiality and the struggle to make sense of it. This is the import of Nietzsche's proclamation that "God is Dead" (an enunciation that governs Yeats's prayer in *A Vision* and even Eliot's positing of a "mythical method" of art): all things are possible now because there is no future beyond the materiality of the present, beyond the materiality of the imagination. Meanings, Saussure teaches, are *effects* of language, subject to material accountability; beliefs and values, Marx argues, are institutional *effects* of the material conditions of social life; metaphysics, Nietzsche asserts, are *effects* of the materiality of power relations; passion, piety, and affection, Freud tells us, are *effects* of the materiality of psychic life.

Such materiality is the mark of death in the world, the "flavour of mortality" that Marlow, in *Heart of Darkness*, finds most hateful. It reduces or seems to reduce whatever is valuable in life—whatever a great realist such as Chekhov could describe, without irony, as "everything that was important, interesting, essential, everything about which he was sincere and never deceived himself, everything that composed the kernel of his life" (1979: 233)—to simple effects, contingent material accidents that could easily be imagined to be otherwise. The modernist response to this, as Mikhail Bakhtin has noted, is irony. Irony is the rhetorical trope that figures death: like the idea of death—like the very "ideas" language gives rise to—irony is a material (linguistic) fact that creates "immaterial" effects. As Kierkegaard says, it "both is and is not," the figure of a present moment radically conceived as cut off from past and future (see Schleifer 1984: 184–200). Thus it is no accident that Stephen Melville characterizes modernism in a verbal formulation similar to Kierkegaard's description of irony, as both an event and not an event (1986: 31). "Irony," Bakhtin has noted, "has penetrated all languages of modern times (especially French); it has penetrated into all words and forms. . . . Irony is everywhere—from the minimal and imperceptible, to the loud, which borders on laughter. Modern man does not proclaim; he speaks. That is, he speaks with reservations" (1986: 132).

If irony has penetrated contemporary discourses—especially that of the Frenchmen upon whom the last three chapters of this book focus—it has done so because the modern world does not provide its inhabitants an imaginable and sufficient future (which is to say, an "idea" of a future). One character in Conrad's *Under Western Eyes* mentions that "women, children, and revolutionists hate irony" (1963: 235; see Schleifer 1977a), and they do so in Conrad's understanding because they all live for and symbolize possibilities of a future, an idea of a future.

Irony itself, the most protean of figures, is not simple or reducible. Like all meanings governed by the contingent material signifiers that effect them, it is, in Derrida's phrase, "irreducibly nonsimple" (1982: 13). By saying one thing and "meaning" another, irony speaks without material signifiers, but it does so precisely because it *always* situates its discourse against the material and historical situation out of which it arises. It can only convey something "other" than what it says by situating its discourse so that its language contradicts the situation out of which it grows. To say "Great!" in response to disappointment articulates meanings fully situated in the disappointment that occasions speech; it makes the negativity of disappointment as fully, materially *there* as the absence of voice in a particular phoneme. For Kierkegaard, the negative, contradictory nature of irony is radical: irony suggests "depths" of meaning and at the same time suggests that there are no "depths" at all, only the phenomenal "surface" of reality. Such a sense of irony characterizes contemporary literary theory: it is the non-simplicity of contemporary critical responses to the material world/word that joins the rhetoric of criticism to the languages of Anglo-American modernism.

In an ironizing reading, then, I imagine that the mythical parallel Eliot describes in Joyce is, in fact, precisely what he explicitly denies that it is in his review—simply a kind of scaffolding Joyce uses, something to be discarded after the futility and anarchy of contemporary history rise up and are represented in language. In *Ulysses* what is scaffolded is an "absence of internal order and of hierarchies," the "reproduction of a form of consciousness which is subjugated to the principle of the *equivalence of commodities*" and in which "use-values . . . are by now

perceived as secondary" (Moretti 1983: 197). As Moretti says, Joyce
is the opposite of Eliot (1983: 192). If Eliot wants to "save" the mind
of Europe and recuperate the "tradition," then Joyce offers it "only
the hideous caricature of itself and its world" (1983: 188). Still, Eliot's
review brings together these two conceptions of the modern world,
synecdochic myth and metonymic chaos. It brings them together metonymically, not hierarchically, despite Eliot's hierarchic aims. That
is, "scaffold" is a fine figure for a *material,* metonymic understanding
of rhetoric: like the relationship between modern and postmodern that
I discussed in Chapter 1, the relationship between a scaffold and what
it supports is irreducibly complex: scaffold is both "part" and "other"
to what it supports. With such a complex figure, Eliot's review explicitly
articulates the problem of the nature of linguistic representation—the
loss of a clear hierarchical relationship between the depth of meaning
and the linguistic surface of that meaning. That loss is, more or less
consciously, the felt crisis of literary modernism.

In this uncertainty concerning hierarchical relationships lies the
problem of the "scaffold" of rhetoric, whose two seemingly incompatible (i.e., nonhierarchical) senses I am exploring in this book: rhetoric as strategies to achieve linguistic and extralinguistic ends, and
rhetoric as the examination of the particular, concrete material manifestations of language. (In Chapter 6, following Roland Barthes, I
describe these as the "tactical" and "tactile" aspects of rhetoric.) Rhetoric is the study of the surface of language; it studies the effects language
creates both within and beyond the control of its users. Language creates interpersonal effects, the forms of persuasion, and rhetoric studies
language to describe what its users wish to say, what could have been
said differently. But language also creates the effects of meaning themselves, the felt, "given," sense of meanings it cannot wholly control.
In this understanding rhetoric studies the ground of meaning as a
linguistic effect, meaning that is as immediately, as phenomenally apprehended as a smell or a touch. These understandings of rhetoric are
issues of great urgency for modernism and the contemporary literary
criticism that participates in modernism because they suggest two ways
of reading. We can choose to understand literature and our world in
terms of the causation, as Eliot says, of a controlling order analyzed
in depth, where "depth" itself does not call for rhetorical analysis, the
analysis of what Derrida has called "the rhetoricity of rhetoric" (1986:
109). Or, as Joyce suggests, we can stay on the surface of things to
discover scaffolded topographies and configurations of textual play to
situate our understanding—including our understanding of the "effect
of depth" to which language gives rise—in terms of rhetoric.

For what is scaffolded in modernist literature after all is a kind of depthlessness that reduces meaning to material effects: the play of voices Forster describes at the end of *A Passage to India*; or the "grain" of voices, as Barthes describes it, clearly marked in Eliot's original title for *The Waste Land* (cited from *Our Mutual Friend*), "he do the police in different voices." Goux describes such depthlessness in monetary terms in describing the words of the Pastor Vedel in *The Counterfeiters* as "only *tokens* which do not correspond to any wealth in the treasury of the interior life" (1984: 66). The rhetoric of such depthlessness is most apparent in relation to the chilly materiality of death itself. Kenneth Burke has argued that the representation of death in literature serves to reveal immaterial "essence": "the poet could define the essence of a motive narratively or dramatically (in terms of a *history*) by showing how that motive *ended*: the maturity or fulfillment of a motive, its 'perfection' or 'finishedness,' if translated into the terms of tragic outcome, would entail the identifying of that motive with a narrative figure whose acts led to some fitting form of *death*" (1969: 14; see also Stewart 1984: Ch. 1). Death in literature "fits" precisely because it fulfills and reveals the cause behind the action, the depth below the surface. As Chekhov asserts in the passage from "The Lady with the Dog" that I quoted, "everything that was important, interesting, essential . . . went on in secret, while everything that was false in him, everything that composed the husk in which he hid himself and the truth which was in him . . . was on the surface" (1979: 233).

For modernism, the hierarchical opposition between surface and depth, between truth and lie, between kernel and husk—what Steiner calls the compact between word and world—is no longer convincing. While the essence or "kernel" of Walter Bate's life in "Odour of Chrysanthemums" is revealed in the *material* fact of his death, that essence is negative, "accidental," a material "fact" without past or future. In the same way Joyce describes death in *Ulysses* by means of an irony that literalizes its figures:

—*I am the resurrection and the life.* That touches a man's inmost heart.

—It does, Mr Bloom said.

Your heart perhaps but what price the fellow in the six feet by two with his toes in the daisies? No touching that. Seat of the affections. Broken heart. A pump after all, pumping thousands of gallons of blood every day. One fine day it gets bunged up and there you are. Lot of them lying around here: lungs, hearts, livers. Old rusty pumps: damn the thing else. The res-

urrection and the life. Once you are dead you are dead. That
last day idea. Knocking them all up out of their graves. Come
forth, Lazarus! And he came fifth and lost the job. (1961: 105)

Here, as Burke says, an "essence" is revealed in the representation of
death, but that essence for modernism is, ironically, the contingency
of material accident, the mechanical operation of the spirit. Joyce emphasizes this in his pun grounded in the *accident* that, in English, the
material sounds of "fourth" and "forth" coincide while the immaterial
meanings do not.

In this way literary modernism articulated, at least in part, the
"panorama" of history not in terms of human intentions, hidden or
"parallel" orders of shape and significance, harmonies of voice and
base—not in terms of secret and originary causes—but in terms of
palpable material effects, rhetorical effects, such as the voices and futility with which Forster ends his novel. The phenomenal panorama
of history is fragmented and rendered incoherent in the same way that
the simulacra of finance capitalism and the second industrial revolution—the "end" of Europe—rendered Western civilization incoherent.
Joyce, in Moretti's description, "has managed to break down the connection between 'possibility' and 'anxiety' ": adultery, the great signifier for the "treasure" of another possible life in nineteenth-century
fiction, becomes in *Ulysses* "a harmless pastime" (1988: 343) with no
significance beyond the present moment.

This lack of an assured awareness of the continuity and power of
the past—a lack of a sense of history, of a future as well as of the past—
characterizes modernism. It leads Eliot to figure the present as inhabited, at some deep level, by the past. It leads Joyce to present Bloom
as wholly on the surface, living a day that is interchangeable with all
his other days. "Joyce concedes him a genealogy," Moretti notes, "but
no male descendant" so that "Bloom's life is suspended between these
two deaths [of his father and his son]: by now, he is an accident, a
historical relic" (1983: 199). In this suspension we can see Gramsci's
description of the crisis of Western civilization between the world wars:
"the crisis consists precisely in the fact that the old is dying and the
new cannot be born" (cited in Anderson 1988: 332). In it we can see
Jameson's more specific assertion that "the thematics of 'death' and
the rhetoric of mortality" in modernism are "but a disguise for the
sharper pain of exclusion by history" (1981: 238). History is exhausted
as much by its fulfillment as by its demise, what Ernest Becker calls
in *The Denial of Death* "the overproduction of truth that cannot be
consumed" (1973: 10). It is exhausted by the reification of experience,

which is Jameson's constant theme (1979: 14; 1981: 249–52), by the
clutter of material things divorced from value.

Such clutter situates consciousness on the material surface of experience and replaces, in Baudrillard's description, "the old illusions of
relief, perspective, and spatial and psychological depth linked to the
perception of the object" with "an optics functioning on the surface
of things, as if the gaze had become the molecular code of the object"
(1988: 145). This, in any case, is where contemporary continental literary theory draws our attention: to the *surface* of things, to what
Richard Rorty calls "textualism" rather than "idealism," the pragmatics of asking how things work, what effects they have, rather than
what they mean. "Pragmatism," Rorty writes, "is the philosophical
counterpart of literary modernism, a kind of literature which prides
itself on its autonomy and novelty rather than its truthfulness to experience or its discovery of pre-existing significance. Strong textualism," he concludes, "draws the moral of modernist literature and thus
creates genuinely modernist criticism" (1982: 153). In another essay
Rorty contrasts pragmatism to an earlier tradition that "thinks of truth
as a vertical relationship between representations and what is represented." Pragmatism, on the other hand, "thinks of truth horizontally. . . . This tradition does not ask how representations are related
to nonrepresentations, but how representations can be seen as hanging
together" (1982: 92), as pragmatically functioning.

   Such a conception of "pragmatism" is marked in a host of modernist approaches to experience contemporaneous with Eliot, Joyce,
and Forster, including the structuralist revolution in linguistic science
following in the wake of Saussure's work. As we will see in Chapter
5, structuralism simply assumes synecdochical hierarchies, yet it does
so (as does the conservative modernism of Eliot, Yeats, and others in
the Anglo-American tradition) in response to the metonymic chaos of
contemporary culture. Like modernism, structuralism resonates with
the negative materiality to which it responds. In 1929 Jakobson coined
the term "structuralism" in a definition that is very close to Rorty's
definition of the pragmatics of modernism. "Were we to comprise the
leading idea of present-day science in its most various manifestations,"
Jakobson wrote, "we could hardly find a more appropriate designation
than *structuralism*. Any set of phenomena examined by contemporary
science is treated not as a mechanical agglomeration but as a structural
whole. . . . What appears to be the focus of scientific preoccupations
is no longer the outer stimulus, but the internal premises of the development; now the mechanical conception of processes yields to the

question of their functions" (1929: 711). In this conception, cause gives way to effect as the mode of explanation; how phenomena work, how they are *configured* (that is, their rhetoric, how they hang together) rather than their secret cause, is the nature of explanation.

In *The Decline of the West* Oswald Spengler calls for a similar treatment of history, "entirely free from the methods of Darwinism—that is of systematic natural science based on causality." "The great problem set for the twentieth century to solve," he writes, is "to explore carefully the inner structure of the organic units through and in which world-history fulfills itself, to separate the morphologically necessary from the accidental, and, by seizing the *purport* of events, to ascertain the language in which they speak" (1962: 72–73). Jakobson's and Spengler's language of inner premises and morphological structures (as opposed to outer stimuli), like Eliot's anxious need to find a grounding method in the chaos of Joyce's and his own world, seems to present the tension between the old conception of meaning and the new conception of function, a metonymic incompatibility that generates much of the power of modernist thought. But the transformation from cause to effect, from causal to functional explanation—or, in Saussure's terms, from a mode of understanding based upon the diachronic discovery of the origin to a mode of understanding based upon a synchronic apprehension of relationships between and among phenomenal data—is at the heart of modernist thought.

The same opposition is at the heart of postmodern literary theory. At the beginning of *Structural Semantics,* A. J. Greimas describes what he calls the "epistemological attitude" of "the human sciences in the twentieth century in general" (1983: 7). That attitude, he argues, eschews the depths of metaphysical constructs for a sense of the palpable surfaces of things and the "play" of those surfaces. Although Greimas cites only one "particularly striking" example of this attitude—"we have seen," he writes, "the psychology of manners and behavior substituted for the psychology of 'faculties' and introspection" (1983: 7)—this attitude of replacing the causal explanation of faculties with the functional (or rhetorical) description of behavior can be seen throughout twentieth-century thought. Perhaps the most striking example, again from psychology, is Jacques Lacan's rereading of Freud's so-called depth psychology (see Chapter 7). Whatever the unconscious is for Freud—and Peter Brooks has argued persuasively that it is a kind of secret cause behind psychological phenomena (1976: 202)—for Lacan the unconscious resides on the surface of things. For Lacan, as Colin MacCabe has argued, "the unconscious is the result of the fact that, as we speak, what we say always escapes us—that as I (the ego) say one thing, it (the id) says something else" (1979: 7). In Baudrillard's terms, Lacan here is radicalizing Freud against himself. For Lacan, the unconscious is on the surface of discourse, the difference between what I mean and what the language I use conveys—the difference between what Gabriel Conroy in "The Dead," for instance, says about himself and what his language reveals about him. Both "messages" are on the surface of discourse, phenomenally *there,* playing together or, as Rorty says, hanging together horizontally.

The transformation from cause to effect as a mode of explanation is essentially the *materialization* of understanding, the transformation of more or less occult relationships between events to a phenomeno-logical accounting of the configuration of those relationships. Perry Anderson, working from a realist rather than a modernist conception of "explanation," argues that this is hardly a form of explanation at all. The transformation of "the explanatory power of modern science . . . to the classificatory magic of totemism," he writes, is a mode of understanding "whose effect depends on its density of description rather than force of explanation" (1984: 49, 50). In this mode of un-derstanding, causes do not "produce" effects in the mode of Anderson's Marxist notion of "production" or the "mystical estate" of paternal propriety that Stephen describes in *Ulysses.* Rather, this mode of un-derstanding examines events "no longer in terms of cause and effect, but of the serial and the unpredictable" (Anderson 1984: 51)—in short, in terms of metonymy—in order to account for effects without assuming logic or order or "essential" origins. By reducing the past to an "agency" that exists only on the surface of the present, an agency that simply creates the phenomenal "effect" of causality that can only be *retrospectively* discerned, it reduces the future to an accident that can-not be predicted. In this transformation of the mode of understanding is embodied the historically determined sense of futurelessness I de-scribed in the last chapter. Thus at the end of *Reveries Over Childhood and Youth* after his own accounting of the early part of his life, Yeats defines life, "weighed in the scales of my own life," to be "a preparation for something that never happens" (1965: 71). What never happens is a final summing up, a judgment such as Marlow imagines he hears Kurtz make (and which, I shall argue in Chapter 7, can itself be seen as a rhetorical effect on Marlow accountable in terms of material sig-nification).

This mode of understanding—which is thoroughly rhetorical—does not conceive of death as an idea, a summing up and a judgment, as Marlow conceives of Kurtz's death, or as a revelation of essential causes, as Burke conceives of the representation of death in literature

more generally. Unlike Chekhov's realism, such a modernist conception does not assume that life is based upon deep and secret truths
(even if it sometimes asserts, with a good deal more anxiety than
Chekhov displays, that it is). Rather, this modernist conception assumes there is no cause to be synecdochically summed up; only the
accidental metonymic phenomenal data of experience to be recon-
structed linguistically and rhetorically. In this, death is a simulacrum,
phantasmagoric, yet absolutely *there,* black and empty: it both is and
is not. In this is the resonance of negative materialism.

The literary aspect of what I am calling the phenomenal data of experience is rhetoric in the complex sense I am presenting, the metonymic voices of literature, the competing and simultaneous voices
heard throughout modern texts, voices that both express and articulate
the panorama of contemporary history Eliot describes. Literature has
always imitated voices, of course, but such imitation has been or-
chestrated—that is, synecdochically organized—by the presiding genius
behind the work. George Eliot explains what her characters mean, what
their words and actions signify; Keats speaks in his own double voice
about the curious relationship between pleasure and pain, fulfillment
and loss. Swift and, less successfully, Defoe simply assume that their
readers can hear the difference between what the narrators say about
children and dissenters and what the author must mean—must "wish
to say," as the French define "meaning." But in Joyce, for instance,
the orchestration of voices is no longer reducible to authorial intention.
Does Joyce intend to define Gabriel Conroy as "a nervous well-meaning
sentimentalist, orating to vulgarians and idealising his own clownish
lusts" (1976: 219–20)? Or does he intend to describe the transformation
of Gabriel in an epiphanic moment? At the end of "Clay" is he mocking
the drunken sentimentality of the Dubliners? Or is he sympathizing
with their capacity to feel, despite the sordidness of their environment
and the poverty of the vehicles for their emotion? Has Eveline missed
her one chance at happiness through the paralysis Joyce describes at
the end of that story? Or is her lover, "Frank," in fact handing her a
bill of goods?

Joyce's style—what Hugh Kenner has called Joyce's voices (1978)—
authorizes no particular understanding of the stories he tells. Rather,
he writes without authorization in what Bakhtin/Voloshinov describes
as quasi-direct discourse (1986a: 136). This is the significance, I think,
of the lack of quotation marks in his work. There is no privileged point
of view in Joyce, no narrator outside the quoted discourse of the characters to tell us what the language "really" means. Instead, all we have

is rhetoric, the play of voices: Eveline sitting by the window like Madame Bovary, two gallants strolling through Dublin like characters out of Maupassant, Gabriel rehearsing not only what he will say to his wife when they are alone, but also how she will respond.

Joyce makes the modern world possible for art not through the scaffold of hidden meaning but through the rhetorical play of elements on the surface of his text. Bakhtin describes this rhetoric in terms diametrically opposed to my description of the thematized rhetoric with which Forster ends *A Passage to India.* "This stage in the vicissitudes of the word in present-day bourgeois Europe and here in the Soviet Union," Bakhtin/Voloshinov wrote in 1929, ". . . can be characterized as the stage of *transformation of the word into a thing, the stage of depression in the thematic value of the word*" (1986a: 159). In other words, Joyce's modernist rhetoric effects the materialization of the idea. From one vantage point (that of Eliot?), the materialization of Joyce's rhetoric effects, as E. R. Curtius wrote in 1929, "the destruction of the world. . . . This entire wealth of philosophical and theological knowledge, this power of psychological and aesthetic analysis, this culture of the mind educated in all the literatures of the world, this ratiocination which is so far above all positivistic platitudes—all this is finally nullified" (cited in Moretti 1983: 204; Steiner expresses the same sense of loss in *Real Presences*). From another vantage point, however, the materialization of rhetoric effects the kind of frantic energy of Baudrillard or, as we shall see in the next chapter, the play of Bakhtin's dialogics, what Derrida describes in another context as "a new relation to language and tradition, a new *affirmation,* and new ways of taking responsibility" (1983: 15).

Take the description of the man Maria meets on the tram in "Clay," for instance:

> Maria thought he was a colonel-looking gentleman and she reflected how much more polite he was than the young men who simply stared straight before them. The gentleman began to chat with her about Hallow Eve and the rainy weather. He supposed the bag was full of good things for the little ones and said it was only right that the youngsters should enjoy themselves while they were young. Maria agreed with him and favoured him with demure nods and hems. He was very nice with her, and when she was getting out at the Canal Bridge she thanked him and bowed, and he bowed to her and raised his hat and smiled agreeably; and while she was going up along the terrace, bending her tiny head under the rain, she thought

how easy it was to know a gentleman even when he had a drop
taken. (1976: 103)

The sentences here move along, subject-verb-predicate, without any
privileging of their elements. There is no syntactic hierarchy, and consequently little semantic hierarchy. Joyce, or rather this text, does not
call attention to any element as crucial to interpretation. The attentive
reader might notice the use of Maria's favorite term in the story, the
word "nice"—which recurs eleven times in seven pages—but only if the
word is apprehended not as an idea, but as a thing, a characteristic of
Maria (like the way she laughs). Here is effected the materialization of
the word. We can recognize on the first page of *Dubliners,* as Thomas
Staley notes, "that 'simony' and 'paralysis' when run together, as they
are nearly so in the boy's mind [in "The Sisters"], suggest the word
'syphilis' and broaden the associative power of the corruption . . .
throughout *Dubliners*" (1980: 132–33). Such broadening is a form of
the resonance of materiality I discussed in the preceding chapter. The
historically situated Irish reader would certainly likewise be aware that
Maria's "colonel-looking" interlocutor is Protestant; but that awareness would be only peripheral, as Maria herself is "aware" of it, so
close to unconscious that it need not be mentioned. The "meaning"
of this term functions like a material attribute, like the physical sounds
of words heard and ignored at the same time.

The narrative itself doesn't make these connections, nor does it
establish the semantic hierarchy they imply. It doesn't attempt to posit
any causal relationship between the drunkenness of the gentleman and
his conversation with Maria. Rather, the narrative offers a metonymic
constellation of details, of things, none more or less important than
any of the other details of this discourse. It is up to the reader to make
sense of this chaos, to make it "hang together," as Rorty says, rather
than to discover its hidden meaning. Instead of simultaneously con-
cealing and revealing the secret cause of the discourse, its meaning and
significance, details in Joyce are there to be interpreted, to occasion
and create rhetorical effects. They are there, as Saussure says in a
different context, as seeming accidents on the surface of things for the
mind to seize upon and attach value to. They are there, as André Breton
says, to prompt the spirit "to seize the faintest rapport that exists
between two objects selected by chance" (cited in Lunn 1982: 56). We
will never be able to decide if June 16, 1904, mattered to the lives of
Leopold and Molly Bloom, if the party and the story of Michael Fury
mattered to Gabriel Conroy, if the Hallow Eve party made a difference
in Maria's life. All of these are narratives without a future, preparing
for something that never happens.

These are all possible effects of the text, rather than its hidden cause and meaning. Even the constant disputes over these matters, the "professors" Joyce describes as "busy for centuries arguing over what I meant" (cited by Ellmann 1959: 535), are literary, rhetorical effects. The "future" of each of these narratives is so situated that one can never be sure these narratives will produce—will *cause*—particular results. In Joyce, the future is never part of the narrative, never realized—this is why he can have so much fun with the professors (Schleifer and Velie 1987: 1143–49). The closest he comes to articulating or defining a future is in the titles of "Clay" and "The Dead," which give the narratives the authority—the causal authorization—that the narratives themselves deny. But in these stories the authoritative interpretation articulated in the titles describes a material and accidental conception of death. Death resonates within "Clay"—as it does within Gabriel's story—as an unspoken negative material future for Maria; it is a possible understanding of the significance of the title, a retrospective interpretation of the "soft, wet substance" that Maria touches but does not comprehend (1976: 105). "Clay" invokes the material fact of death without naming it—without presenting it as an idea. Even when Joyce does name death, as when Leopold Bloom describes the material workings of the heart-pump by denying its traditional "immaterial" signification, he finds a strangely literal rhetoric adequate to his vision, just as in "Easter 1916" Yeats corrects himself when he figures death: "What is it but nightfall? / No, no, not night but death" (1956: 179).

Another text that can demonstrate my contention about the rhetorical play of the surface in modernist discourse is the last chapter of Saussure's *Course in General Linguistics* as it was compiled, retrospectively, by his students and colleagues. In this chapter Saussure is arguing against a causal explanation of descriptive linguistics and in favor of a kind of Darwinian chaos and accident, the purely accidental nature of any particular language form. That is, he is arguing that the differences between and within language groups are arbitrary. Rather than necessary cause-and-effect relationships between earlier and later language forms, there are, in language families, simply phenomenal relationships. Such relationships are something like what Wittgenstein calls "family resemblances" that can be recognized as relational only retrospectively, just as Maria's "nice," or the gentleman's drinking in "Clay," can be made part of an interpretation only retrospectively. "No characteristic" of language, Saussure writes, "has a right to permanent existence; it persists only through sheer luck" (1959: 229).

By way of example Saussure describes the characteristics of the Proto-Indo-European language and notes that "it is clear that none of the foregoing traits has been retained in its original form in the different [living] Indo-European languages, and that several of [these traits] . . . no longer appear in any member of the group" (1959: 229). At the end he compares the changing Indo-European characteristics with seemingly permanent characteristics of the Semitic languages. Saussure goes on to argue that even these apparent counter-examples to his thesis of the arbitrary nature of language are themselves accidental rather than necessary, the result of "sheer luck": "mere phonetic modifications," he writes, "which are due to blind evolution, result in alternations. The mind seizes upon the alternations, attaches grammatical values to them, and spreads them, using the analogical models which chance phonetic developments provide" (1959: 231). Here again, the mind seizes on phonetic accidents retrospectively, in order to make them function linguistically.

More striking, however, is the rhetoric strategy Saussure uses in his argument. The Semitic example he uses—more specifically, the Hebrew example—is not simply used to prove a point. As Hillis Miller notes in *The Ethics of Reading,* "the choice of examples, moreover, and their ordering, are never innocent" (1986: 11). As linguistic phenomena and linguistic strategies—the two descriptions of rhetoric embodied in *Darstellung* and *Vorstellung*—examples create signifying effects, what linguists call "meaning-effects." Moreover, they create these meaning-effects even when they appear to be simply a transparent medium for expressing underlying truths. The choice of Hebrew as an example of the non-permanence of linguistic characteristics and its ordering as the final example of Saussure's *Course* cannot be innocent precisely because throughout Western history Hebrew was understood to be the sacred language, the language of Adam and of the Old Testament, the oldest, purest, least "accidental" language. For its permanence to be a function of "sheer luck," simply phonetic accidents inhabiting the surface of things which the mind seizes in order to make function in a particular way, toward particular ends, would transform the world from one in which God is the necessary first cause to one in which pragmatic results, functions, and effects—not causes—rule. For Saussure, the accidental permanence of Semitic linguistic characteristics functions in the same way Joyce's reader may seize upon the adjectival detail of the gentleman's "colonel-lookingness" to effect a particular interpretation. Such emphasis on the essential character of the accidental transforms the world into events as random and accidental as death, sheer phenomena hanging together and, perhaps, even pleasing—what Stevens calls the pleasure of merely circulating—but not a world of symbols pointing elsewhere. It makes rhetoric and rhetorical studies of crucial importance.

Moretti correctly opposes Eliot to Joyce in his attempt to "heal" the cultural crisis of Europe (1983: 220) and reachieve what Cornel West calls the "order, authority, and stability" of Europe as the synecdochical "center" of the world (1988). Yet even Eliot takes pleasure in merely circulating, in rhetoric, and can write in what is perhaps his most overtly religious poem, *Ash Wednesday*, of the circulating word:

> If the lost word is lost, if the spent word is spent
> If the unheard, unspoken
> Word is unspoken, unheard;
> Still is the unspoken word, the Word unheard,
> The Word without a word, the Word within
> The world and for the world;
> And the light shone in darkness and
> Against the Word the unstilled world still whirled
> About the centre of the silent Word. (1963: 92)

Here, as in *Prufrock, The Waste Land,* and other poems—as in Joyce's puns—the circulation of sound is as important as the conveyance of meaning. As Kenner notes, "Eliot deals in effects, not ideas; and the effects are in an odd way wholly verbal, seemingly endemic to language" (1959: 4). In this way, religion and materiality are metonymically situated in *Ash Wednesday*, "each living in the other's death and dying in the other's life." (This is a phrase of Heraclitus's that Yeats repeatedly cites [see Schleifer 1979: 224–29].)

Other so-called mythical modernists, including D. H. Lawrence as well as Yeats (whom Eliot explicitly cites in describing the mythical method), traffic most powerfully in rhetorical effects along with ideas, in surface phenomena along with—metonymically *against*—what Yeats calls "the deeps of the mind." The most striking moment in Lawrence, I think, occurs in *The Rainbow* when the narrator disrupts his narrative to respond in his first-person voice to the Brangwen Christmas he describes: "Why," he asks, "when Mary says: Rabboni, shall I not take her in my arms and kiss her?" (1976: 281). And throughout Yeats's poetry, adjacent to the scaffolding of his myths and vision, is the sheer phenomenal power of his poetry hanging together, discovering coherence in what he calls "the Path of the Chameleon," the bewildering incoherence of his experience. More important than the aesthetic questions at the end of "Among School Children" is the "order" of love the mind finally seizes upon (its shape and significance). Yeats artic-

ulates that order in his poem in the configuration of the accidents of
his experience, the nuns, mothers, and lovers imagined in the classroom, transformed, female to male, into Plato, Aristotle, Pythagoras.

Just as "Clay" narrates a story that avoids at all cost the "end"
toward which it is moving—the material death it configures in the very
resonations of its avoidance—"Among School Children" is occasioned
by the poet's aging and, as Yeats noted in his diary, "the old thought
that life prepares for what never happens" (cited in Parkinson 1964:
93). It is occasioned, that is, by the sense of the impossibility of a
meaningful future that the material decay of aging produces. Yeats
answers this "old thought" with his transcendental and "timeless"
vision. In this, like Leopold Bloom before him, Yeats translates the
situated female discourse of nun, mother, lover into a male philosophic
voice. He reduces the gendered materiality of the experience related
in the poem—experience and poem wholly inhabited by schoolgirls,
nuns, Maude, and remembered mothers—to the philosophical depths
of symbolized, immaterial "Presences." That is, he makes the surface
of his experience, like the surface discolorations of the lapis lazuli he
writes about elsewhere, function to create his rhetorical effects (see
Schleifer 1990).

In the material occasion and the aesthetic response of Yeats's poem
we can see two forces in modernism, the metonymic chaos and the
synecdochic myth I mentioned in relation to Eliot. Both play in modernism, even if the latter is the theme Anglo-American modernism
emphasizes most. Postmodernism emphasizes metonymic chaos, not
simply as "theme"—theme itself is a synecdochic ordering—but in its
style and "take" on the world. Its emphasis is not wholly the negation
of modernism, just as Anglo-American modernism does not simply
thematize its experience (as Forster attempts to do). Rather, like metonymy itself, like rhetoric, like the simultaneously occult and linguistic
relationship between cause and effect, these are two ways of understanding the "same" phenomena: the rupture of word and world that
Steiner describes, the transformed sense of materiality and death that
I am describing, the realization of the rhetoricity of rhetoric.

"History is necessity," Yeats wrote in a late diary entry, "until it
takes fire in someone's head and becomes virtue or freedom" (1962:
336). The great historical necessity Yeats never quite describes in his
poetry is the "end" of Europe that Cornel West describes. In Yeats
and in modernism more generally, this nightmare hovers behind the
"vision," just as Stephen's nightmare of his mother's deathbed hovers
behind his day in *Ulysses* (even if he transforms that literal nightmare
into a metaphor for "history" from which he is "trying to awake"

[1961: 34]). It is barely figured as a kind of blurred vision of the night-mare of a fully material death, the "superficiality" of the negative materiality of death. In this turning from the periphery—from death, from women, from the contingency of value—Yeats's aim, like that of much of modernism, is to make a virtue of necessity and to create at least the illusion of coherence. It is to create at least the illusory (aesthetic) freedom of a future.

At the same time, in response to such a material world, modernism both eschews depths for surfaces and thinks of truth rhetorically, playfully, phenomenally. That is, it conceives of the future negatively, as a material effect of language whose ghostly haunting presence—whose deathly presence—can be accounted for, after its accidental fact, by rhetoric. As Stevens says in "To an Old Philosopher in Rome" in a counterstatement to the "primal scene" Blanchot describes, "It is a kind of total grandeur at the end / With every visible thing enlarged and yet / No more than a bed, a chair and moving nuns ... Total grandeur of a total edifice" (1954: 510). Like Yeats's nun—and like the "veiled sister" Eliot invokes in *Ash Wednesday* or Clarissa Dalloway or even Maria herself in "Clay," who Joyce makes clear is a kind of secular nun—Stevens's nun takes her place within a topology of figures, an edifice of surfaces that constitutes modernism as much as its transcendental posturings. What I have done in invoking these disparate nuns is to read the surface rhetorically, in the manner that Joyce and Saussure (and even Eliot and Lawrence) have taught us and have taught postmodernism, as a configuration, a way of making, not finding, sense in the world of philosophy, of history, of literature and language. *Ash Wednesday* itself defines this material historicity in its religious renunciation of anything else:

> Because I know that time is always time
> And place is always and only place
> And what is actual is actual only for one time
> And only for one place
> I rejoice that things are as they are and
> I renounce the blessed face
> And renounce the voice
> Because I cannot hope to turn again
> Consequently I rejoice, having to construct something
> Upon which to rejoice (1963: 85)

This is a far cry from the promise at the end of *A Passage to India,* "not yet, not there." Rhetoric like Forster's creates the illusion—the "meaning-effect"—of a future, not yet, not there, but articulable and

consequently imaginable. Eliot does not quite renounce such a future—
"Teach us to care and not to care," *Ash Wednesday* prays—but he
situates his enunciation fully and materially in a world reduced to
seeming random events, the fragmented "end" of Europe. In this way,
the focus on surfaces and rhetoric is a focus on the literal present—
"always and only" its own time, its own place—that necessitates the
construction of meaning itself.

As the evidence of modern literature suggests, such a focus is on
language itself, on the *phenomena* of representation, which is a chief
concern of contemporary literary theory. In this book, then, I am not
so much focusing on modern texts as attempting to use and describe
how those texts have taught us to read, the ways in which they share
in our reading. I examine the discourses of linguistics, philosophy,
pedagogy, and psychoanalysis as well as literary writers in an attempt
to come to an understanding of their rhetorical practices. Such a focus
on rhetoric, I believe, is a commitment to the surface and texture of
texts themselves, a commitment that is particularly "modernist." It
includes a sense of the configured textuality of discourse and of the
ways in which such configurations constitute shape and significance
and may, in fact, make the modern world possible for art. Before I
turn to particular readers and readings in Part II, in the next chapter
I turn again to the materiality of modernist rhetoric and read it in
more explicitly rhetorical terms, through the opposition implicit in
this chapter between Joyce and Eliot, in the work of Paul de Man and
Mikhail Bakhtin.

4

The Failure of Synecdoche

The Power of Death and the Situation of Enunciation

No poet, no artist of any art, has his complete meaning alone.
His significance, his appreciation is the appreciation of his relation
to the dead poets and artists. You cannot value him alone; you
must set him, for contrast and comparison, among the dead. . . .
The existing monuments form an ideal order among themselves,
which is modified by the introduction of the new (the really new)
work of art among them. The existing order is complete before the
new work arrives; for order to persist after the supervention of
novelty, the *whole* existing order must be, if ever so slightly,
altered. . . .

—T. S. Eliot, "Tradition and the
Individual Talent"

If he had smiled why would he have smiled?
To reflect that each one who enters imagines himself to be the
first to enter whereas he is always the last term of a preceding series
even if the first term of a succeeding one, each imagining himself to
be first, last, only and alone, whereas he is neither first nor last nor
only nor alone in a series originating in and repeated to infinity.

—James Joyce, *Ulysses*

When Emma Bovary kills herself at the end of *Madame Bovary,*
Flaubert describes the poison she takes as having "the frightful taste
of ink" (1965: 230). Such a curious and suggestive detail in the midst
of the extended realistic description of Emma's suicide is just the self-
conscious rhetorical detail that contemporary literary criticism focuses
upon. Emma is a reader, not a writer, and while one could understand

the progress of her final illness—culminating in her vision of the blind singer as the devil himself—as an extended metaphorical conceit, the novel itself hardly ratifies such a reading. Nevertheless, modernism has taught us to read in just that way and to note the detail that does not fit. It has taught us, as the historical crisis that conditioned its own appearance had taught it, to attend to the failure of coherence and structure, the failure of hierarchy and synecdoche. "In the first decades of the century," Franco Moretti writes, "society no longer seems endowed with an intrinsic rationality; it is no longer an organic system of relations capable of holding all its elements together" (1983: 183). In such a society, as Jean Baudrillard says, "operationality, the genetic code, the random order of mutations, the principle of uncertainty, and so on . . . replace a determinist and objectivist science, a dialectical vision of history and consciousness" (1988: 122). That is, modernism has taught us to see metonymic fragmentation as the proper vehicle for expressing experience. It has taught us to conceive of ink not as a part of the whole of discourse, but as its material other, a kind of poison that halts life and figures death, like the meaningless but viscerally horrifying dream of the blind singer resonating with an absolutely incomprehensible experience that Emma, on her deathbed, fails to comprehend.

In this is another, more radical version of Klee's description of the modernist "striving to emphasize the essential character of the accidental" (cited in Bradbury and McFarlane 1976: 48), with the accidental understood as "essential" in precisely its contingency. The metonymic nature of contingency provokes responses without understanding, anxiety without an object. Such anxiety can be found in T. S. Eliot's *The Waste Land,* whose fragmentation, I believe, functions to bewilder and lose its readers more than anything else. Its aim is to "essentialize" the experience of incoherence—the meaningless affect of its free-floating anxiety—that, for Eliot, *is* the modern world. In Eliot we get the dissociation of feeling and meaning, the breakdown of the relationship between the significatory and communicatory functions of language and rhetoric. In "A Game of Chess," for instance, in a passage for which Vivien Eliot praised her husband, *The Waste Land* presents affect without meaning, details which call for coherent interpretation but ratify none:

'What is that noise now? What is the wind doing?'
    Nothing again nothing.
                                        'Do
'You know nothing? Do you see nothing? Do you remember

'Nothing?'
    I remember
Those are pearls that were his eyes. (1963: 57)

In this passage, as in *The Waste Land* as a whole, discourse crowds upon discourse without order, in fragments shored against ruin.

Modern literature has taught us to read *Madame Bovary* the same way. What is striking in Emma's dream and in a modernist reading of it is the physical response to which discourse gives rise, the dread that Hillis Miller, following Blanchot, describes in reading. Shoshana Felman has called such responses the scandal of the speaking body (1983): this is the *power* of rhetoric, the fact that discourse, which aims at signification, also communicates phenomenal effects which are, in Lévi-Strauss's description, as palpable as a taste or a smell (1975: 14). Flaubert's metaphor of ink attempts to create and represent such power (*Darstellung* and *Vorstellung*). Or rather, my focus upon this heterogeneous figure attempts to seize the text retrospectively—modernistically—and to understand its meanings and power as linguistic effects susceptible to rhetorical analysis. I am reading Flaubert's 1857 text in a manner tutored by the strategies of reading that modernism demands of us; contemporary criticism has learned to read all manners of text in much the same way.

For instance, in *The Genesis of Secrecy* Frank Kermode presents an extended discussion of the nature of narrative by focusing on the sacred text of the Gospel of Mark. He introduces his study with a short reading of a mysterious stranger in Henry Green's *Party Going* as a kind of rhetorical figure or allegory to make sense of the interpretations of Mark that follow. The stranger in *Party Going* functions, as Kermode understands him, in many of the ways we can understand the blind stranger and the metaphor of ink in *Madame Bovary*. As Kermode says, this figure is conditioned by the "vast panorama of futility" Eliot describes in the modern world that leads us, as readers, to seek "junctures of the occult and the representable" (1979: 10). Herbert Schneidau has called this the "sacramentalism" in modernist writing, which allows "representation of divine things only if, paradoxically, the signifying figures are sufficiently humble and unremarkable" (1977: 438). This should be understood *negatively*: it points to the fact that literary modernism has taught us to attend to ghostly hauntings in language, the simultaneous (and incompatible) presence and figuration of death: the power of the *random* materiality (of language, of death itself) and the figured meanings of that presence.

Modernism may tutor this reading, or it may simply participate in its larger social manifestation. In any case, it offers texts that present or call for two seemingly incompatible conceptions of rhetoric: the study of the language of persuasion, and the study of the tropological configurations of meanings and meaning-effects of language. Modernism offers us texts in which there is a competition between art and life, between the attention to configured rhetorical detail and the "unattended" felt sense of narrative progression. The ink before us calls for a figurative reading so that rhetoric itself seems both the locus of occult narrative intentions and a kind of material poison that disrupts narrative.

In such a conception both art and life are haunted by an arbitrary and accidental conception—a *material* conception—of the world, of death, of "meaning" that cannot be recuperated within a body of belief or "explanation." This conception can only be densely described, in a term I have already used, as the situation of enunciation. As Paul de Man says in one of the most chilling readings in contemporary literary study, "*The Triumph of Life* warns us that nothing, whether deed, word, thought, or text, ever happens in relation, positive or negative, to anything that precedes, follows, or exists elsewhere, but only as a random event whose power, like the power of death, is due to the randomness of its occurrence" (1984: 122). Such a conception of life and meaning as fully and darkly arbitrary touches on the *power* of rhetoric, especially the modernist rhetoric of fragmentation, the force enlisted in language to persuade and to delimit worlds of meaning, deed, thought, and texts. But de Man's assertion fails to demonstrate the conditions of such discourse, which Fredric Jameson describes as the "reification" and "commodification" of experience at the turn of the century that led to the "fragmentation and commodification of the psyche as [the] basic precondition" of modernism (1979: 13–14).

Moreover, de Man's description fails to demonstrate how such rhetoric works, specifically how, within such a random and material world, it creates the effect of relationship—and especially the relationship of "sameness" that governs rhetoric and language altogether and creates its global effect of *representation*: the felt sense of narrative progression, of visceral horror, and understandings of connectedness, relationships, and apprehended meaning. In other words, de Man's vision of the random and arbitrary nature of signification does not allow for a conception of discourse that links the unique and seemingly random enunciation of acoustic events to the larger social life of language that makes the accidental situation of enunciation effectively, even if contingently, meaningful. If language creates the possibility of a future—of promise, of the friendship, memory, and love Derrida describes in mourning de Man's death (see Chapter 8)—then de Man allows for the power of these things, but not for their recuperation in meaning. His is an extreme articulation of the blank "future" of modernism that I described in the preceding chapters, an articulation governed by a conception of the random materiality of life and death.

Modernism and contemporary criticism—even de Man's criticism—make room for both "knowledge" and "power," to use Yeats's recurrent terms (what de Man calls "symbol" and "image" in his study of Yeats [1984: 145–238]). They do so precisely by eschewing the kind of negative metaphysics that inhabits de Man's discourse. In this chapter I shall explore more fully a materialist conception of rhetoric that can account for the effects of sameness and global signification in a world that can be understood, as de Man understands it, as inhabited solely by random events. In other words, I want to describe how rhetoric can situate enunciatory events to account for the powerful effects of meaning that modernism affords us, even in the face of death.

Contemporary literary criticism is intimately bound up with literary modernism, and the form of that bond is the enunciation of rhetoric. By focusing upon metonymic enunciation, criticism and modernism foreground the destabilizing work of language and understanding: they emphasize the *power* in language beyond both its significatory function and its practical or communicative function. Language not only communicates or configures meaning; it also communicates and configures powerful feelings. This is the engine of persuasion, but it is more than this. It is also the possibility, inherent in discourse, of communicating or creating laughter or dread—what Aristotle calls pity and terror. The "chill" of de Man's discourse, the opposition between the pathos of its vision and the impersonality of its expression, is an example of this (see Schleifer 1985), as is the free-floating anxiety created by the juxtaposition of images and discourses in *The Waste Land*. But other critics (such as Mikhail Bakhtin) communicate in their discourse the pity, laughter, and "carnival" that the power of "randomness" de Man describes also provokes, as does Joyce in the many-voiced comedy of *Ulysses*.

The emphasis of such power, as Kingsley Widmer notes, characterizes modernism as the "somewhat ambiguous post-Enlightenment humanistic inventions to destabilize the social and moral order, even to break it" (1980: 1). Here Widmer, like so many students of modernism, is asserting cause where there is only contiguity: modernism, as I argued in Chapter 2, is a metonymic element in the destabilization of the social and moral order that I am calling the "end" of Europe. Nevertheless, the "otherness" of modernism and of contemporary discourse theory has destabilized, if not broken up, traditional ways of reading. Postmodern criticism, following literary modernism, reads in a self-conscious rhetorical way: it reads literature as if it were, in some ways, materially *against* life and meaning, or, more positively, against the habitual, non-reflective, unconscious, cliché-ridden lives we lead. Instead of "discovering" in literature what Hugh Kenner has called "the authority of the Ancients, doughty men whom we had been accustomed to treating . . . with the familiarity we accord living eminences" (1973: 17), it reads literature as the tracings of the absence of such authority, as irreversibly *textual,* as the materialism of the idea. Certainly criticism in the last twenty-five years has participated in the self-conscious focus on rhetoric that literary modernism demands in order to be understood, its own *enunciated* break with the past, its extremes (as opposed to earlier literature's humanistic reconciliations), its overwhelming anti-mimetic impulse, its foregrounding of the materiality of language, its simultaneous freedom and despair.

As I suggested in the last chapter, at the heart of modernism lies a felt sense of contradiction between material accident and seeming transcendental ("mythic") truth. The contradiction cannot be resolved. It is not simply confusion, or passions to be cured, or fear to be overcome, or ignorance; at its heart is a kind of poison that denies what Sartre calls the "idealistic humanism" that E. M. Forster expresses in *A Passage to India* and throughout his work. "Chateaubriand Oradour, the Rue de Saussaies, Tulle, Dachau, and Auschwitz," Sartre writes,

> have all demonstrated to us that Evil is not an appearance, that knowing its cause does not dispel it, that it is not opposed to Good as a confused idea is to a clear one, that it is not the effects of passions which might be cured, of a fear which might be overcome, of a passing aberration which might be excused, of an ignorance which might be enlightened, that it can in no way be diverted, brought back, reduced, and incorporated into idealistic humanism, like the shade of which Leibniz has written that it is necessary for the glare of daylight. (1965: 211)

In Chapter 8 I shall examine the occurrence in Shelley of the "same" image that Leibniz uses—the darkness that allows the apprehension of Intellectual Beauty—in examining the difference between the rhetoric of prayer and the rhetoric of mourning. But here I want to note that such an irreducibly nonsimple conception of the modern world and of the discourse of modernism suggests the unavoidable power it invests and realizes in its rhetoric. Literary criticism since World War II makes this modernist vision (and, more important, its rhetorical power) its own measure. New Criticism privileges "paradox"; phenomenology and reader-response criticism foreground the unresolvable difference between texts and writing and reading subjects; structuralism emphasizes the play between synchronic and diachronic understanding, between the grammar of literature and the manifestations of particular texts; and poststructuralism, like modernism, makes *irony* its central trope (see Schleifer 1981).

It has not always been so. English Romanticism depends on *synecdochical symbols* to articulate what Christopher Norris has called its "aesthetic ideology" "which equates the nature of language and meaning with the nature of empirical experience" (1988: 37) so that meaning seems to inhabit experience. Earlier, at the beginnings of the first industrial revolution, neoclassical imitations depended on *similes,* and those similes articulate the privatization of public life in the eighteenth century (Schleifer 1988: 38–39). Both of these modes of figuration can be subsumed under the Renaissance figure of *analogy,* which rhetorically marks the "centering" of European civilization, the establishment of Europe as the measure of humanity, and is very different from the *allegories* that engaged medieval literature.

In the face of the "end" of Europe, modernism favors irony and its paradoxes—that is, the undecidable play between synecdochic and metonymic orderings, between the random and the same, between competing conceptions of rhetoric—embodiments of what Nietzsche calls the "eternal contradiction," "the contrariety at the center of the universe" (1956: 33, 64). As is so often the case, Kafka articulates the global situation of modern irony. In *The Castle*

> it seemed to K. as if at last those people had broken off all relations with him, and as if now in reality he were freer than he had even been, and at liberty to wait here in this place, usually forbidden to him, as long as he desired, and had won a freedom such as hardly anybody else had ever succeeded in winning, and as if nobody could dare to touch him or drive him away, or even speak to him; but—this conviction was at least equally strong—as if at the same time there was nothing more senseless, nothing more hopeless, than this freedom, this waiting, this inviolability. (1974: 139)

In this passage Kafka combines an understanding of the time and place of K.'s situation as simultaneously meaningful and meaningless. This is itself a function of his perceived sense of the human situation as being what Geoffrey Hartman calls "an indeterminate middle between overspecified poles" (1970: 348)—a situation bred from the unresolvable contradiction between the senses of being "in between" in time and "in between" in space that inhabits discourse. Time seems to offer K. the freedom of an undetermined future, while the inviolability of space—his separateness, rather than his centeredness—cuts him off from any meaningful value in that freedom. Like the contradiction between death conceived as a synecdochical part of life and as life's metonymic other, and like the incompatibility of the signification and communication of rhetoric, here time and space seem irreducibly incongruent.

At the turn of the century, the complementarity of time and space broke down. Space came to be seen, in the sciences as well as the arts, as not simply a void but as "a constituent function" so that there was "no clear distinction between the plenum of matter and the void of space" (Kern 1983: 177, 183). In this conception of what Stephen Kern calls "positive negative space," space itself is a *material constituent* and "had one feature in common with the progress of political democracy, the breakdown of aristocratic privilege, and the secularization of life at this time: they all leveled hierarchies" (1983: 153, 177). One effect of this new conception of space, Kern argues,

> was a leveling of former distinctions between what was thought
> to be primary and secondary in the experience of space. It can
> be seen as a breakdown of absolute distinctions between the
> plenum of matter and the void of space in physics, between
> subject and background in painting, between figure and ground
> in perception, between the sacred and the profane space of
> religion. Although the nature of these changes differed in each
> case, this striking thematic similarity among them suggests that
> they add up to a transformation of the metaphysical founda-
> tions of life and thought. (1983: 153)

In this can be seen, as I argued in the preceding chapter, a reorientation toward the surface of things.

The same reorientation can be seen in the concept of time, even though time (as opposed to space) came to be understood as less and less material. Time came to be seen as a function of its measurement so that the "pastness" of the past, that great source of nostalgia and power in the Romantics, came to be seen as a function of present consciousness, floating, as it were, on the surface of things (Kern 1983: Ch. 1). Still, unlike "materialized" space, time came to be seen as a function as well as a determination of the rhetoric of language. As a *function* of rhetoric, as an effect of language, temporality exists or arises

in discourse and in the *possibility* of discourse as simply, in de Man's
terms, "the metaphor of temporality" (1979: 162). Of *The Social Contract* de Man writes, "the noncoincidence of the theoretical statement
with its phenomenal manifestation implies that the mode of existence
of the contract is temporal, or that time is the phenomenal category
produced by the discrepancy" (1979: 273). De Man is arguing that the
very "feel" of time—what Husserl calls the "phenomenology of time
consciousness" (1964)—becomes a distinctive, articulated "sense" by
means of linguistic operations. In this, time itself is a phenomenal
category—an experience—produced by linguistic activity; like all linguistic effects, it is subject to rhetorical analysis.

   In this opposition between space and time—as well as in de Man's
narration of the absolute "randomness" and contingency of temporal
occurrences—we can see why I am claiming that the rhetorical figure
that best describes the modernist movements in literature and criticism
is irony. Irony, like rhetoric itself, exists by virtue of the irreducible
opposition between time and space, between what Søren Kierkegaard
calls the "temporal ego" and the "eternal ego," between phenomenon
and essence (see Schleifer 1984). It arises out of the irreducible opposition between communication and meaning. "The act of irony, as
we now understand it," de Man says,

> reveals the existence of a temporality that is definitely not
> organic, in that it relates to its source only in terms of distance
> and difference and allows for no end, for no totality. Irony
> divides the flow of temporal experience into a past that is pure
> mystification and a future that remains harassed forever by a
> relapse within the inauthentic. It can know this inauthenticity
> but can never overcome it. It can only restate and repeat it on
> an increasingly conscious level, but it remains endlessly caught
> in the impossibility of making this knowledge applicable to
> the empirical world. It dissolves in the narrowing spiral of a
> linguistic sign that becomes more and more remote from its
> meaning, and it can find no escape from this spiral. (1969: 203)

Here de Man is describing the problem of rhetoric in general. In the
context of the historical determinations I examined in Chapter 2, this
problem resonates as part of the modernist movement. "Schlegel's
rhetorical question," he concludes, " 'What gods will be able to rescue
us from all these ironies' can also be taken quite literally. For the later
Friedrich Schlegel, as for Kierkegaard, the solution could only be a
leap out of language into faith" (1969: 204). Irony, then, like the "end"
of Europe, is a failure of consciousness, what de Man calls "the con-

sciousness of non-consciousness," "the end of all consciousness" (1969: 198) in the apprehension of meaning as noise, what the thunder said.

In the incompatibility of conceptions of time and space can be seen a version of the transformation from explanation conceived in terms of cause and effect to explanation conceived as a retrospective "accounting" of phenomena. In rhetorical terms, such incompatibility dissociates representation as communicating preexisting ideas and representation as conditioning those ideas. In this are the two conceptions of rhetoric that I have already discussed. One conceives of the aspect of language it studies as temporally situated and thus studies modes of persuasion and rhetoric; another conceives language in spatial terms and studies meaning as effected by configured structures and tropes. The incompatibility of time and space renders the relationship between the communicative and signifying aspects of language problematic: Are space and time material grounds for these competing conceptions of rhetoric, out of which meaning emerges (just as space comes to be seen a material condition of objects in space)? Or are the categories of space and time—the conceptual frameworks they create—themselves rhetorical effects created by the spatial configurations of language (just as time comes to be seen as a function and effect of a discursive or signifying system)? In either case—in both contradictory cases—modernist discourse is a function of a certain way of reading (perhaps its cause, perhaps its effect), an emphasis on rhetoric that uses contradiction to create power and knowledge. The contradiction between the constative and the performative aspects of discourse, between its more or less transcendental meanings and its specifically located interpersonal exchanges, between what the French call *énoncé* and *énonciation,* generates its affective power and its significatory meanings. Even my brief survey of English literature in terms of rhetorical tropes participates in the essentially rhetorical understanding of both literature and its history. Whether or not such a conception of language and phenomenal experience necessitates de Man's reduction of meaning and the experience of meaning to "random" events situated between a mystified past and an inauthentic future—whether it shows, as he claims of Shelley, that nothing ever happens in relation to anything else—is a matter to which I will return.

Such a conception of language and phenomenal experience allows us to find *Madame Bovary,* published in 1857 and often with justice called the first "realist" novel, a modernist text. In *Modern Poetry and the Idea of Language* Gerald Bruns claims that there is "a competition between language and reality, or between life and art" in Flaubert—a competition that can lead one to figure ink as life's poison or to conceive of rhetorical effects as the death of intentional significance. Just as there is this competition, Bruns continues,

> so there are two *Madame Bovarys,* one a representation of life, a tour de force in the realistic mode, the other an adumbration of an impossible book—a book which, given the nature of language as a semiotic system, cannot exist in a pure state but only in a relationship of competition with the reality which language seeks conventionally to articulate. One is reminded here of Valéry's observation that "the essence of prose is to perish—that is, to be 'understood'—that is, to be dissolved, destroyed without return, entirely replaced by the image or impulse that conveys according to the conventional language." (1974: 146, 148)

Whether or not these "two *Madame Bovarys*" are the "same" and the ways in which a thoroughgoing material understanding of rhetoric makes the category of the "same" a problem are issues closely related to de Man's austere understanding of meaning and experience. I take them up later in this chapter. But here I want to note that the "idea" of distinguishing between a conception of rhetoric as complementing reality and a conception of rhetoric as semiologically competing with reality participates in Saussure's founding assumption of the arbitrary nature of the sign and of signification. Linguistic meanings, Saussure argues, are not "motivated"; rather, they are arbitrary "articulations" of "vague, uncharted" phenomenal experiences that are delimited through that arbitrary articulation (1959: 112). Discourse will take up *any* material signifier in order to articulate and communicate its meanings: there is no reason why one sound rather than another is taken up to signify a particular concept. Given the arbitrary nature of the sign—and Saussure argues that not only the signifier, but even the signified itself is produced by the (un-"necessary") arbitrary articulations of discourse—even the absence of a material signifier can come to signify in the differential functioning of discourse.

If we return to *A Passage to India* in relation to de Man's reading of Shelley, the *materialist* implications of the arbitrary nature of the sign (as opposed to the *formalist* implications that Saussure himself stressed) will become clearer. When Mrs. Moore reads the semantic void of material sound "Boum" as a semantic discourse that "managed to murmur, 'Pathos, piety, courage—they exist, but are identical, and so is filth. Everything exists, nothing has value' " (1952: 149), the text is making the same assertion that de Man makes when he says that

The Triumph of Life warns us that "nothing . . . ever happens in relation, positive or negative, to anything" else (1984: 122). What is
striking here—in Forster, in de Man, in the functioning of language in
general—is the way discourse creates a relationship between materiality
and meaning (even when it asserts none exists). For Forster that relationship *ends* in meaning (or at least the "effect" or, in more charged
terms, the "illusion" of meaning); it realizes itself when the text can
narrate the way "despair" creeps over Mrs. Moore (1952: 150). In de
Man, however, the materiality of meaning is no way incorporated or
transcended in the realization of meaning: the very arbitrariness of the
signifier ensures that it cannot be incorporated into idealistic humanism. "The bottom line," de Man writes, "in Kant as well as Hegel, is
the prosaic materiality of the letter and no degree of obfuscation or
ideology can transform this materiality into the phenomenal cognition
of aesthetic judgment" (1984: 144). In other words, the transformation
of the arbitrary fragmentation of material things into the "wholeness"
of immaterial meaning is only an "aesthetic" effect or illusion of discourse, much like the illusions that Mrs. Moore and Forster create by
giving voice to material objects.

Derrida underlines the radical sense of the materiality of discourse
in de Man in a discussion that is less certain, less assertive than the
warning de Man offers in his reading of *The Triumph of Life*. "There
is," Derrida writes in his elegy for his dead friend,

> a theme of "materiality," indeed an original materialism in de
> Man. It concerns a "matter" which does not fit the classical
> philosophical definitions of metaphysical materialisms any
> more than the sensible representations or the images of matter
> defined by the opposition between the sensible and the intel-
> ligible. Matter, a matter without presence and without sub-
> stance, is what resists these oppositions. We have just placed
> this resistance on the side of thought, in its strange connivance
> with materiality. We might have associated it yesterday with
> death and with the allusion to "true 'mourning' " which makes
> a distinction between pseudo-historicity and "the materiality
> of actual history." (1986: 52)

The distinctions Derrida lists here between sense and intelligence,
pseudo-historicity and actual history, between metaphysical "materialism" and "matter" itself, are *rhetorical* distinctions. They are distinctions in which the opposition between the same and the other,
between thought and matter, are always threatening to reduce themselves to one or the other. In Forster they become a synecdochical

"speech" of things, parts speaking for the whole, materiality becoming meaning. In Eliot's *Waste Land* and in de Man they become the end of speech in the metonymic babble of random power.

Such threatened reductions are not simply accidental. They take place within the economy of the power of discourse and rhetoric to posit or delimit or assume meaning—the *restricted economy* of discourse in which the effects of meaning are possible in a world of seeming meaningless materiality. Such rhetorical economies offer the recuperated voices of the world that Forster (and Eliot in his "mythical method") suggest, but they also offer the free-floating, affective meaning of random power to which de Man continually returns, the simultaneous meaning and nonmeaning he figures as the power of death. What resists such reductive recuperations is the rhetoricity of rhetoric itself. Such rhetoricity, like the "matter of this sort, 'older' than the metaphysical oppositions in which the concepts of matter and materialist theories are generally inscribed" which Derrida imagines he discerns in de Man (1986: 53), resonates in contemporary criticism and the modernist discourses in relation to which contemporary criticism articulates itself. It resonates in the recovered signification of "meaninglessness" and "chaos" in Eliot and de Man, as well as in the recovered "understanding" of Mrs. Moore's experience which Forster "brings back" to idealistic humanism.

How is it that discourse encompasses the material and the significatory, "matter" and "materialism," random events and stable identities? In "Literature and Discontinuity," Roland Barthes asserts that "discontinuity is the fundamental status of all communication: signs never exist unless they are discrete. The esthetic problem is simply how to mobilize this inevitable discontinuity, how to give it a rhythm, a tempo, a history" (1972: 181). In *Structural Semantics,* following Saussure, Jakobson, and Hjelmslev, Greimas attempts to describe the nature of relations between the "discontinuous" elements of signification; he attempts to describe the mobilization of meaning and to inscribe that description in a "science" of signification. "We perceive differences," he writes, "and, thanks to that perception, the world 'takes form' in front of us and for us" (1983: 19). Yet the perception of differences requires that those different elements "must have something in common" as well as being "somehow different" (1983: 20). Randomness cannot be inscribed in language. Signification, he says, cannot be structured simply in terms of the discontinuities of presence and absence; semantic differences are not the presence and absence of an element of signification, the way a phonological difference can be understood in terms of the presence or absence of a distinctive feature—that of voicing, for instance—in the pronunciation of a phoneme. While the phonological difference is the presence or absence of voicing, marking the fundamental discontinuity of signs—what Greimas calls their "negative meaning, only a possibility of meaning" (1983: 33)—semantic differences are marked by the *presence* of different, opposing elements on what he calls a *semantic axis* (see Schleifer 1987: 21–25).

Such an axis creates a semantic "reserve," what Derrida, following Georges Bataille, calls a "restricted economy" of meaning, "a discourse, by means of which philosophy, in completing itself, could both include within itself and anticipate all the figures of its beyond, all the forms and resources of its exterior; and could do so in order to keep these forms and resources close to itself by simply taking hold of their enunciation" (1978: 252). Such a "reserve" describes Europe before its "end," the hegemonic centeredness of a particular culture. Within such a reserve, within the restricted economy of rhetoric and discourse, Derrida argues, philosophy—and cultural signification in general, I might add—completes itself and can articulate and express its "other" in its *own* rhetoric: as Derrida says, "in discourse (the unity of process and meaning), negativity is always the underside and accomplice of positivity" (1978: 259). In other words, the positive unity of discourse is always accompanied, metonymically, by its negative other.

In the unity of the hegemonic sphere of reserve comparison and continuity are possible, and in such terms the crossing of disciplinary rhetorics within contemporary "postmodern" criticism can be understood. Samuel Johnson, for instance, could write an "imitation" of Juvenal in "The Vanity of Human Wishes" because he believed that "Nature and Passion," as he says in *Rasselas,* ". . . are always the same" and that knowledge need only discern "general properties and large appearances," "those characteristicks which are alike obvious to vigilance and carelessness" (1958: 526–28). In this understanding of the world we can see the cause and effect of Johnson's horror of madness and death: madness inscribes discontinuity into a full world where everything is named and ordered, oppositions are positive and comparable, distinctions homogeneous; it inscribes death (or the "other") within the "same."

Johnson's conception of "the same" is based on a remarkable abstraction—Mikhail Bakhtin calls it "abstract objectivism" in another context—that takes place within the reserve of rhetoric and cultural hegemony. Such abstraction avoids both Kierkegaard's dialectic of repetition and Nietzsche's thought of the eternal return of the same. For Kierkegaard, the dialectic of repetition is "easy" in the combination of the repeated and the novel (1964: 52) governed by the strenuous "ease" of faith which creates the relationship between the same and the other (see Bové 1984: 36). For Kierkegaard, faith in God provides the "absolute purpose" of seemingly random events in the world, so that accidents can be governed, after all, by transcendental meanings—meanings (including the personal identity of a soul) that remain the same across time and space. For Nietzsche, the concept of "the same" does not function within either the "unconscious" restricted economy of Johnson's self-evident truths nor the more self-conscious "faithfully" determined economy of Kierkegaard's "leap out of language." Rather, "the same" (*Das Gleiche*), as Joan Stambaugh argues,

> does *not* express simple identity, and therefore does not, strictly speaking, mean the Same. It lies somewhere between the Same and the Similar, but means neither exactly. For example: If two women have the same hat on, they have, strictly speaking, one hat on at different times. . . . If two women have the "same" (in the sense of *gleich*) hat on at the same time, they have two hats which resemble each other so exactly that one could think that one woman had borrowed the other's hat, if one saw these women at different times. This is more than similarity, but it is not identity. (1972: 31)

This description repeats the dissociation of time and space I have already discussed. Moreover, it is very close to Saussure's examples of the "same" in the *Course in General Linguistics,* two "8:25 pm Geneva-to-Paris" trains or a street that is demolished then rebuilt. "We feel," Saussure notes, "that it is the same train each day, yet everything—the locomotive, coaches, personnel—is probably different." Of the street he asks, "Why can a street be completely rebuilt and still be the same?" It is "the same," he answers, "because it does not constitute a purely material entity; it is based on certain conditions that are distinct from the materials that fit the conditions, e.g., its location with respect to other streets" (1959: 108–9).

Saussure uses these examples to delimit linguistic entities and units. In this way different speakers in different situations can use the "same" entities of speech. But when Gerald Bruns speaks of "two *Madame Bovarys*" is he talking about the "same" text? When I use the "same" word, "cure," that de Man uses to describe the possibility of anatomy "curing" mortality (see Chapter 7) in ways that may or may not be ratified by his "intention," are these two occurrences of "cure" the same? Or have I transgressed the restricted economy of de Man's rhetoric—a "tactical" rhetoric (in Barthes's terms) restricted precisely by his intention? To answer I should say that the "conditions" that govern the "same," the relationships of the parts or "entities" to one another, might best be conceived in the double sense of rhetoric I am presenting as simultaneously a part of language and the whole of language. Rather than the absence of relationship de Man asserts, the "same" is a synecdochic *part* and essence of phenomena—the "kernel" of meaning and theme that Marlow doesn't quite narrate in *Heart of Darkness*. At the same time, it is, metonymically, *wholly* other to sensible phenomena, outside the reserve of rhetoric that conditions sensible phenomena. In this way the "same" is not quite simple: it describes both elemental entities (the physical materials of such and such a street, or the figure "cure" abstracted and abstractable from one context to another) and the very condition of the existence of such entities (the street itself or, more generally, signification itself). In the same way (or is it different?), *death* functions as a signified of discourse, a particular meaning inscribed and circumscribed by language, and it also functions to signify, more generally, resonatingly, material absence itself, materiality governed by the always present accidental and arbitrary possibility of its absence or presence.

If this is true, it is because the existence of linguistic entities—of repeated (the same?) significatory entities, of enunciated entities, best represented by the sign *death*—is different from the existence of other kinds of entities. "It seems to us," Emile Benveniste writes,

> that one should draw a fundamental distinction between two orders of phenomena: on the one side the physiological and biological data, which present a "simple" nature (no matter what their complexity may be) . . . ; on the other side, the phenomena belonging to the interhuman milieu, which have the characteristic that they can never be taken as simple data or defined in the order of their own nature but must always be understood as double from the fact that they are connected to something else, whatever their "referent" may be. (1971: 38–39)

Such a connection makes interhuman linguistic entities always complex, always directed toward their effects rather than their causes, at once equal to and more than the material comprising them; it makes them always rhetorical. Most of all, it makes meaning—including the interhuman meaning inscribed in the concept of "event"—different from the simple randomness of material phenomena (whether they be physical or biological).

In this sense, then, the "same" is rhetorical, an "effect of identity." It is also rhetorical to call attention to the difference of the "same," the difference between my use of "cure" and "event" and de Man's uses of these linguistic entities, for instance, or the difference between the intention of Roman Jakobson's figural language and its effects beyond intention discussed in the next chapter, or the difference between Kierkegaard's transcendental repetitions and Nietzsche's immanent repetitions. By inscribing the "same" within the "eternal return," Nietzsche accomplishes what Kierkegaard's (faithful) definition of repetition doesn't quite accomplish and what de Man's (faithless) randomness also fails to accomplish: it figures or describes an ambiguous "same" within time. It is precisely the temporalization—or better, the historicization—of identity that creates the ambiguity of the "same," the novelty of repetition, the marking of rhetoric.

If the "same," unlike physiological data, is not measured against an origin (or a cause), but is measured by its *effect,* then there is always a radical historicization of identity—a "scattering" of identity—in which the phenomenal "immediacy" of meaning and feeling to which language (and rhetoric) give rise is always connected to something else. That is, if the "same" is a species of Kierkegaard's repetition—future oriented, rather than the "recollection" of the Greeks that Kierkegaard describes—it produces in its very assumption of a (future) promise a mark of meaning beyond the local reserve of its discourse. (Such reserved discourse seems simply, as in Johnson, to be describing the world in transparent, "unmarked" language.) Yet the very fact that language requires a category of the "same" to allow repeatability at all—to allow language to be a means of communication—makes the effect of unmarked transcendental meaning beyond the randomness of material phenomenality, the effect of transparency, always a part of its functioning. (This, I think, is what Greimas means by the "substantifying" force of language discussed in Chapter 1.)

That is, if rhetoric marks its own rhetoricity, it always also functions precisely by not marking itself, by being transparent, as in Jakobson's "scientific" structuralism and, at least as a moment, in de Man's hypostatization of discontinuity and randomness. Such unmarked language creates the reserve of discourse that Derrida describes, and its marking—always in terror at the power of the randomness of the mark, and sometimes with pity as well—presents, momentarily, a sense of rhetoric without reserve that can lead, as de Man says of Kierkegaard, to an aporia requiring a "leap out of language into faith" (1969: 204). It can also lead, as in Johnson, to the constant anxiety to establish and reestablish the reserve of language and meaning. Unlike Johnson's discourse, which aims at order and keeping down its "other," rhetoric without reserve is finally *sacred,* a rhetoric of prayer, of mourning. Like Hegel in Derrida's description and like Jakobson as I will describe him, Johnson in his very spatialization of his vision blinds himself "to the experience of the sacred, to the heedless sacrifice of presence and meaning" (Derrida 1978: 257) that takes place alongside the meaningful orderings of language.

Johnson's reserved rhetoric incorporates (and thus desacralizes) the other by creating what de Man calls a "naively referential language" through the imposition of proper meaning—the limitations of a reserve—on the open structure of free-floating affect. "Like 'man,' " de Man writes,

> "love" is a figure that disfigures, a metaphor that confers the illusion of proper meaning to a suspended open semantic structure. In the naively referential language of the affections, this makes love into a forever-repeated chimera, the monster of its own aberration, always oriented toward the future of its repetition, since the undoing of the illusion only sharpens the uncertainty that created the illusion in the first place. (1979: 198. See also Derrida 1987: 399 for the "diverse, polymorphous, ungraspable, phenomenon" of "what is called" *pleasure.*)

In this, "love" conceals the arbitrary nature of signification by disfiguring the accidental historical determinations of its occasion. Unlike physiological data, signifying "data" are oriented toward the future of their repetition. Yet such repetitions are repetitions of things not quite identical, the "same" only in their effects (such as "love" or what is called "pleasure"). Such effects, however, possess their own "meaning-effects," the *power* of their meaning: they confer certainty on a "suspended open semantic structure." "Metaphor is blind," de Man says, "not because it distorts objective data, but because it presents as certain what is, in fact, a mere possibility" (1979: 151). In possibility—in its orientation to a future repetition—rhetoric creates its ambiguous sameness, the tactile immediacy of its communication and the future-oriented tactics of its significations which never quite coincide.

In the same way, however, that the correspondence of the concept "love" and its occasion, the "suspended open semantic structure" it closes off, remains problematic and "undecidable" yet creates the illusion of certainty, so de Man's own discourse conceals the historically situated nature of its signification in its propositional or constative assertion of the "blind" nature of metaphor. Christopher Norris argues that de Man, like Nietzsche, has "earned" the right to this "inconsistency"—the propositional assertion that all propositional assertions are illusions of proper meaning—in the "saving readiness" of his texts "to problematize their own most crucial working assumptions, and not take refuge in a premature appeal to method and system" (1988: 44). But the very *textual* nature of Norris's argument creates its own rhetoric of reserve. The "uncertainty" that occasions and conditions the assertion of the disfiguring nature of figurative language in de Man is the historical occasion of modernism and postmodernism I have described: the "end" of Europe. This "end"—in politics, economics, social structures, in the very phenomenal experience of life—even if considered, as de Man would very well consider it, in "textual" terms, presents suspended open semantic structures indeed.

By universalizing uncertainty de Man, like Eliot and like Johnson in another time, reduces the particular situation of his culture—the particular workings (effects) of textuality within his culture—to "all" human situations. Andrew Ross argues that *The Waste Land* figures the "bankruptcy" of Europe and the "problems of history" in historically specific terms of "failures": the death of Eliot's father and a personal sense of sexual failure (1986: Ch. 2). Norris likewise notes, in his thoughtful and sympathetic account of de Man's wartime associations with the pro-Nazi newspaper, *Le Soir,* that the universalizing assertions of de Man's later work must be modified in the context of de Man's early associations and the fact that he concealed them. (See also Jonathan Culler's short description of this matter [1988: 108] and Derrida's long rhetorical analysis of those early writings [1988a]. For a range of negative assessments of de Man's wartime associations, as well as discussions of these associations in relation to his mature work, see Hamacher et al. 1989.) With the revelations of those early writings, Norris argues, the assertions and pronouncements of de Man's later work demand to be understood as "something more than . . . purely diagnostic [textual] commentary." That later work could be the "constant, often agonized attempt to explain the sources of that powerful 'aesthetic ideology' which had played a prominent seductive role in his own youthful thinking" (1988: 179–80), or it could as easily be simply the wish to conceal the truth.

In any case, even in a rhetorician as subtle and thoughtful as de Man, the metonymies of rhetoric—the tactile immediacy that discourse creates, and its future-oriented tactics—constantly seem to come to rest in synecdochical order. Yet the very fact that discourse has a future, and that it calls for its own future in a way that is different from the *random* "futures" of "physiological and biological data," means that its "intentional" future will be beset by the accidents of its "natural" future. The *accidents* of its future are especially important. Thus Roland Barthes argues (as we shall see in Chapter 6) that the "origin of a spoken discourse does not exhaust that discourse; once set off, it is beset by a thousand adventures, its origin becomes blurred, and its effects are not in its cause" (1977: 206). Barthes is describing the blurring of its "intentional" occasion through the "history" of a discourse cut off from its author, but that "history" can also modify the intentional nature of discourse—its future orientation—by marking its occasion in historical-material terms. In these terms Derrida asserts, in his discussion of de Man's wartime journalism, that "the absolutely unforeseeable . . . is always the condition of any event. Even when it seems to go back to a buried past, what comes about always comes from the future" (1988a: 593). More elaborately, de Man argues in discussing *The Triumph of Life,* that future random occurrences—in this case, Shelley's drowning—are precisely what undermine the "monumentalization" of discourse, the imposition "on the senseless power of positional language the authority of sense and of meaning" (1984: 117). Just as Shelley's drowning leaves "entirely on the reader" the task of understanding his text in relation to his death—and the very "textuality of this event" of his death, the defaced body "present in the margin of the last manuscript page . . . an inseparable part of the poem" (1984: 121, 120)—so the "accidental" revelation of de Man's own past has created an unintentional future—a metonymic, *material* future—for his discourse. Living that future, we see what it was vouchsafed de Man never to see: namely, the "reserve" of his position, the personal reserve of his silence about his past and the discursive reserve of a simple conception of prosaic materiality in the constitution of events.

The very non-coincidence of the future-oriented intention of discourse and the accidents that constitute its immediate present create the always possible (even in Johnson) power and import of the sacred in discourse, the "meaning-effect" of the sacred. This is a far cry from the certainty of Johnson's "same," which, rather than seeking ambiguity and novelty, seeks an abstract objective identity transcending time ("always the same") in order to create the possibility of cognition, the possibility of "knowledge"—the possibility, finally, not of the sacred, but of the ordinary, the assimilable, rhetoric restricted within a "strategic" economy. "Knowledge," writes Nietzsche, is the making possible of *experience* by tremendous simplification of real events both on the part of the acting forces and on the part of our shaping forces: *so that there appears to be something like similar and identical things. Knowledge is falsification of the manifold and uncountable into the identical, the similar, the countable.* Thus *life* is possible only through such an *apparatus of falsification.* Thinking is a falsifying re-shaping; willing is a falsifying re-shaping. In all of this there lies the power of assimilation, which presupposes a will to make something like ourselves. (cited in Stambaugh 1972: 71)

Here Nietzsche is presenting a sense of rhetorical power, the reshaping power of signification. Even Johnson—even Jakobson—is "rhetorical" in this way. Johnson pursues knowledge, and his "same" is constituted by the falsifying reshaping of the abstract identity of nouns, the "equivalence" of nouns: it presupposes a will to create likenesses and creates the axis of comparison.

Such identity reduces the complex materiality of rhetoric—rhetoric at once arbitrary and necessary, tactical and tactile, a particularly *modernist* rhetoric inhabited by the materiality of death—simply to saying something that could be said otherwise. Such a reduction aims at preventing what Henry Staten calls "the admission of the not-itself into the citadel of the as-such," which is, in the terms I am developing, the admission of the arbitrary materiality of rhetoric into the constitution of meaning. It is the admission, finally, of the negative materiality of death into the relational economy of meaning. Such an admission, Staten goes on to argue, "appears to open the way to the flux Aristotle and Kant feared. This flux is the flux of particulars. The transcendental function of language is the heightening of the abstracting and generalizing power of words; transcendentality in the strict sense is only the highest flight of this power of generalization. To know is always to categorize" (1984: 23–24). The flux Staten mentions (like the random events de Man describes) creates the possibility of the *sacrifice* of presence and meaning in discourse—a *future* possibility that de Man doesn't allow himself or Shelley in his assertion of the "senseless power" of performative language. The flux of particulars transforms the transcendental abstraction of language to immanent rhetoric without recuperation. Two descriptions might conceivably describe the "same" event (the verbs "survey" and "remark," for instance), but two bets, to use an example from J. L. Austin (or two marriage vows), have a very different "sameness." While such "sameness" is not quite the same, neither is it the absolute unconnectedness de Man describes in prosaic materiality.

Later in this chapter I will follow Derrida and Bakhtin in the possibility of recuperating the "same" within a material understanding of discourse. Here, though, we can see the logic of Johnson's privileging of nouns (as opposed to Austin's privileging of first-person verbs), for nouns, such as "Passion," offer transcendental categories and the possibility of both knowledge and imitation. Thus there is an appropriateness to the beginning of "The Vanity of Human Wishes" with its remarkable number of words inscribed on the axis of "seeing," written by a man who was, like Greimas, a maker of dictionaries:

> Let observation, with extensive view,
> Survey mankind, from China to Peru,
> Remark each anxious toil, each eager strife,
> And watch the busy scenes of crowded life;
> Then say how hope and fear, desire and hate,
> O'er spread with snares the clouded maze of fate. . . . (1958: 47)

The tour de force of observation surveying, remarking, and watching the world ratifies study of a world in which things do not change and in which it is imaginable, as Swift thought, for language to be replaced by a satchel of things carried around by our servants.

This is all the more remarkable because Johnson, like Swift's Laputans, closes his ear to open his eye: Juvenal begins in the Humphries translation not with the clarity of eye, but with the mistake of ear: "In all the lands that reach from Gibraltar to the Euphrates / Few indeed are the men who can tell a curse from a blessing" (1958: 121). In the context of Juvenal's Latin text this is even more suggestive:

> Omnibus in terris, quae sunt a Gadibus usque
> Auroram et Gangen, pauci dinoscere possunt
> uera bona atque illis multum diuersa. (1938: 89)
> [In all the world, from Gibraltar to dawn and the Ganges,
> few can distinguish true good from everything else.]

The verb "dinoscere," which Johnson renders "survey" and "say" and which Humphries translates as "tell," more precisely means "to recognize as different, to distinguish." Thus neither the knowledge of the eye nor the telling of the ear—the spatialization of tropological rhetoric or the temporalization of persuasive rhetoric—quite accurately renders the difficulty of recognizing the difference that Juvenal writes about. Perhaps the great vanity, after all, is the sense that "knowledge" can distinguish the good (or, in de Man's negative discourse, the true).

Still, Geoffrey Hartman tells us that the blessing and curse of Humphries "are among the oldest types of formalized speech" (1981: 129);

moreover, they "undermine statement" (1981: 132). Because they are speech-acts rather than statements, enunciations rather than *énoncés,* in the vocative rather than the accusative case, they undermine the transcendental function of language (and Nietzsche's shaping power of language) without reducing themselves simply to unconnected random events. They are addressed to the ear—and like the Gospel, like psychoanalysis, even like mourning, they are addressed to a particular ear—rather than to sight. As such, they mark an encounter with another and mark the great cultural encounter with *its* other that has faced high European culture all through our century. "What, then," asks Derrida,

> is this encounter with the absolutely-other? Neither representation, nor limitation, nor conceptual relation to the same. . . . And first of all because the concept (material of language), which is always *given to the other,* cannot encompass the other, cannot include the other. The dative or vocative dimension which opens the original direction of language, cannot lend itself to inclusion in and modification by the accusative or attributive dimension of the object without violence. Language, therefore, cannot make its own possibility a totality and *include* within itself its own origin or its own end. (1978: 95)

Vocative and accusative, Derrida goes on to argue, are not comparable. The vocative, he says, "is not a category, a *case* of speech, but rather the bursting forth, the very raising of speech" (1978: 103). The vocative does not articulate the transcendental function of language, because it aims not at knowledge or entity but at power and articulation itself: rhetoric. It breaks up noisiness not for the sake of encompassing entity, not for the sake of synonymous survey, but for the sake of articulating difference (*dinoscere*). The vocative and accusative are not comparable, yet they occur in the same breath. This is a scandal to transcendentality, knowledge, identity, comparison. This is the scene of rhetoric, the moment of enunciation, always a part of language, but made clear in the glare of modernism's encounter with the other in general and with death in particular. Eliot and de Man present such encounters in their discourse, modern and postmodern; for both the transcendental function of language and its loss are matters of grave importance. For others, however, the very crisis of the seeming loss of transcendental truths is a kind of freedom. It is as if they, unlike Eliot and de Man and even Samuel Johnson, have less, both transcendentally and personally, to hide.

Moments of enunciation are very different from random events—just as rhetoric is different from a "primal cry," even though rhetoric can arbitrarily take up a primal cry as a signifier or a signified. In fact, rhetoric "enunciates" its signifiers and its meanings—it iterates and reiterates the elements of language and discourse—to effect its meanings and its powers. In this way, then, the concept of enunciation is crucial to understanding the materialist rhetoric of modernism and of contemporary criticism beyond de Man's aleatoric vision. Enunciation is a complex and difficult concept because it attempts to account for two seemingly incompatible but undeniable facts. On the one hand, language manifests itself as unique events which seem random and *essentially* unconnected to other events; and, on the other hand, language is, in its very nature, *intentional* and thus future oriented in its meanings.

In this way the concept of "enunciation" attempts to describe without figuring what Saussure described as language "taken as a whole." The whole of language, Saussure noted, "is many-sided and heterogeneous; straddling several areas simultaneously—physical, physiological, psychological—it belongs both to the individual and to society; we cannot put it into any category of human facts, for we cannot discover its unity" (1959: 9). Saussure goes on to argue that, as a consequence of the many-sided phenomena of language, the linguist must abstract the system of language, which he calls "*la langue*," from the heterogeneity of language in order to discover the "self-contained whole and principle of classification" (1959: 9) that is immanent, synecdochically, within language. In other words, language manifests itself in unique articulations of discourse ("*la parole*," which Saussure opposed to "*la langue*"), but it is recognizable as language—as discourse—only because these unique language-events are not random. They somehow articulate and repeat the encoded pattern of *la langue*.

Enunciation is clearly an aspect of language—as our parents say, we should strive to "enunciate" our words—yet it is neither a synonym for the whole of language nor reducible to any particular part. Enunciation cannot be understood as a synecdoche for language in the way Saussure suggests that *la langue* is a self-contained part by which the heterogeneous whole of language can be classified and understood. But neither is it *la parole* in the way that Saussure understands *parole* as idiosyncratic and random, "individual" (as opposed to social) and "more or less accidental" (as opposed to essential) (1959: 14). Perhaps it is closer to *parole*, but even here it is not a manifestation in relation to what is immanent (as opposed to manifest)—another synecdochical representation (not as the essence, but as an example). Enunciations are *occurrences* of language that are "self-contained" and "whole," but not "complete" or "finalized." In this way the concept of enunciation, like rhetoric itself, is not quite "pure"; rather, it inhabits a gray area between linguistic immanence and manifestation, neither essence nor example.

In this way, too, in Chapter 2, I examined European hegemony as a horizon of "all" understanding—the *whole* of understanding—which, nevertheless, can "end." Such hegemony is a mode of understanding that is "whole" in that it is coherent, exhaustive, and simple—the criteria both Hjelmslev and Greimas use to describe science in general (Schleifer 1987: 66)—but that, at the same time, is not *necessary* even though its "wholeness" produces the "effects" of self-evident, transcendental "necessary" truths. In this, temporality is not (or not solely) determined by discursive discrepancies between "theoretical statement" and its "phenomenal manifestation," as de Man asserts (1979: 273). "The metaphor of temporality" is not "generated" by "the indeterminacy of reference" (which also, according to de Man, generates "the illusion of a subject, a narrator, and a reader" [1979: 162]). Rather, time itself is a material base upon which discourse (including the "textual" sense of temporality de Man describes) is built. For this reason, the systematic structure or "building" of discourse is "whole," but it is not "complete" or "final": it is transformed by historical accident, what Eliot calls "the introduction of the new (the really new)" (1975: 38). In the same way, the systematic structures of *la langue* and, more specifically, of phonemes and their "distinctive features" are built upon the "base" of the actual materiality of human speech organs (vocal chords, teeth, nose, etc.) which, nevertheless, are accidental—determined in time—in their materiality. In this conception, temporal determinations are not the simple occurrence and existence of "random" events, even if events are unforeseeable and always incomplete. Rather, time and space are always also social and historical; as Benveniste says, they always belong to the "interhuman milieu" and thus are always "connected to something else" (1971: 39).

In *Mikhail Bakhtin: The Dialogical Principle,* Tzvetan Todorov offers a concise description of the problem of enunciation that will help to define the functioning of the materialism of rhetoric. Mikhail Bakhtin allows us to situate discursive phenomena—including the rhythm, tempo, and history of literary phenomena—beyond essentialist (or, as Bakhtin says, "philological") reading without falling into Forster's silence or de Man's despair.

Between the generality of the meaning of words, such as we
find them in the dictionary, and that of the rules of grammar,
and, on the other hand, the uniqueness of the acoustic event
that occurs when an utterance is proffered, there takes place a
process that permits the linkage of the two, which we call
enunciation. This process does not suppose the simple existence of two physical bodies, those of the sender and the receiver, but the presence of two (or more) social entities, that
translate the *voice* of the sender and the *horizon* of the receiver.
The time and space in which enunciation occurs also aren't
purely physical categories, but a historical time and a social
space. Human intersubjectivity is actualized through particular utterances. (Todorov 1984: 39–40)

"Enunciation" is of utmost importance in Bakhtin's "dialogic" poetics,
his rhetoric. Enunciation calls attention to the starting point of linguistics, the fact that the many-sided heterogeneity of language creates
the rhetorical effects of wholeness. In these effects, meaning seems to
be more than the sum of its parts—more than a random event—and
for this reason seems to transcend its historical time and social space.
But while linguistics attempts to understand this paradox of language
by dividing language into what is essential and what is accidental—
langue and *parole* on the social level of Saussure's analysis; "competence" and "performance" on the individual psychological level of
Noam Chomsky's analysis; "semiology" and "rhetoric" in de Man's
rhetorical analysis—Bakhtin attempts to understand the whole of language without recourse to the opposition between essence and accident
and the synecdochic representations that such an opposition implies.

Instead of seeing the "parts" of language as parts of an abstract
"whole" of meaning, in *Marxism and the Philosophy of Language,*
Bakhtin/Voloshinov argues that the relationship between "meaning"
and "theme" in discourse—terms Bakhtin later more clearly distinguishes as "meaning" in general and the "specific sense" of a discourse
(1986: 86)—is a relationship between different entities: "the *wholeness*
of utterance," he writes, "is subject neither to grammatical nor to
abstract semantic definition" (1986a: 101). Thus the distinction between the dictionary "meaning" (or signification) of words and the
"theme" (or global "meaning") of the text formed by the words is
absolute. "Theme," Bakhtin notes, "is the *upper, actual limit of linguistic significance*; in essence, only theme means something definite.
Meaning is the *lower limit* of linguistic significance. Meaning, in essence, means nothing; it only possesses potentiality—the possibility of

having a meaning within a concrete theme" (1986a: 101). In this distinction, the central problem of structuralist linguistic studies such as Saussure's *Course* or Greimas's *Structural Semantics*—the "semiology" that de Man undermines in relation to "rhetoric" (1979: 6–7)—is made clear. The "abstract objectivism" of such linguistics leaves out the essence of the phenomenon of language, the historically situated "definite" meanings of discourse (which Bakhtin here calls "theme"). It assumes that the meaningful whole of discourse is simply another hierarchical *level* of language formed by and parallel to (or "isomorphic" with) other linguistic levels. In this way structural linguistics and semiology proceed on the assumption that linguistic phenomena are *synecdochically* analyzable and that a part can stand for the whole of language. This conception, I think, governs abstracting the "same" from various phenomena through the isolation of synecdochical "invariables"; it is what de Man is opposing in the warning he takes from *The Triumph of Life.* That is, de Man opposes the hierarchical structures of linguistics and semiotics not by turning (as Bakhtin does) to particular historically situated meanings of discourse, but by asserting that these meanings are themselves the repetition of "a historical and aesthetic system" of denying the very fact that "nothing, whether deed, word, thought, or text, ever happens in relation to anything" else (1984: 122), and that this system "repeats itself regardless of the exposure of its fallacy" (1984: 122). If abstract objectivism creates abstract and objective "wholes" in language and experience—which is to say wholes "complete" in their abstraction—then de Man opposes this systematization by destroying the possibility of any "definite" meaning—even when it is "unfinalized"—beyond illusion. (In this, I think, de Man parts from his master, Nietzsche, whose "eternal return of the same" aims, impossibly, at "essentializing" rather than dismissing accident, at holding both synecdoche and metonymy within a single thought.)

The synecdochical understanding of "meaning" in abstract objectivism mystifies and *dematerializes* language. It makes meaning some kind of "spirit" hovering behind and within discourse, at its "kernel" or "heart" in Conrad's terms. It trivializes its rhetorical expression as simply one manifestation of that spirit among many (inconsequential) possibilities. In Coleridge's phrase, describing the essentially *synecdochical* conception of Romantic symbolism, "the symbol is characterized by the translucence of the special in the individual, or of the general in the special, or of the universal in the general; above all by the translucence of the eternal through and in the temporal" (cited in de Man 1969: 177). In this, as de Man argues, not only is the symbol "always a part of the totality that it represents"; more remarkably, in synecdoche "the material substantiality [of a symbol] dissolves and becomes a mere reflection of a more original unity that does not exist in the material world" (1969: 176, 177). Through synecdoche, language creates the effect of an essential "whole" that transcends its particular instances of enunciation, a whole that transcends materiality and death.

The metaphor I have opposed to this conception of transcendental meaning is the "resonation" of the material "overtones" of meaning, the ringing of meaning's materiality in the same way that material sounds produce sympathetic vibrations at different frequencies. I have followed this metaphor to inscribe the "spirit" within a material understanding—Derrida's "materialism of the idea"—without spiritualizing or "dematerializing" it (as Coleridge does) or reducing meaning to being *simply* illusory (as de Man does). If, as de Man suggests, Coleridge's apprehension of the eternal through the temporal is an illusion, a question still remains: How, in material and historical terms, are the illusions of transcendental meanings created?

In this I am following Bakhtin, for whom such mystification does not suggest that signification is always "aberrant." For Bakhtin, understanding can take place only in the particular historical time and social space of an enunciatory situation: time is always time, and place is always and only place. In opposition to de Man's position that events occur outside of relationships, Bakhtin argues that signification *realizes* relationships; only *in* discourse do deeds, words, thought, or texts happen in relation, positive and negative, to things that precede, follow, or exist elsewhere. He doesn't want to argue for or against "randomness": for him, language realizes and manifests an effect of intentionality that responds to and counters the random power of death. Thus Bakhtin argues that "*any true understanding is dialogic in nature.* Understanding is to utterance as one line of a dialogue is to the next. Understanding strives to match the speaker's word with a *counter word.* Only in understanding a word in a foreign tongue is the attempt made to match it with the 'same' word in one's own language" (1986a: 102). Such a "counter word" is not a part for the whole, but a kind of radical metonymy in which word answers word, not with its "essence," but with a materialism that fully situates discourse as many-sided and heterogeneous—situates it in relation to the "other" rather than the "same," but still *in relation to* the other. "Counter" itself is such a word, resonating with "encounter" and signifying "coin," and de Man himself, in his resistance to the synecdochical "aesthetic ideology," situates his thought in relation to its other. For this reason Bakhtin objects to the oppositions between a words's "usual" and "occasional" meanings, "between its central and lateral meanings, between its denotation and connotation, etc." (1986a: 102). For Bakhtin, *all* meanings are "occasional" in a material-historical sense, but occasions themselves are not simply or wholly "random." Occasions themselves, read retrospectively—that is, rhetorically—substantiate relationship. Rhetoric, for Bakhtin, is the *site* of relationship, the *site* of the "same," the foundation of the interhuman milieu.

Throughout *Marxism and the Philosophy of Language,* Bakhtin/Voloshinov distinguishes the abstract objectivism of synchronic linguistics, which attempted to articulate the synecdochical invariants of language—what he calls here the "same"—from the study of "living speech as actually and continuously generated." Traditional linguistics, he argues, is "guided by philological needs" and so "has always taken as its point of departure the finished monologic utterance—the ancient written monument, considering it the ultimate realium" (1986a: 72). The "basis of linguistic thought" has always been attention "*on the study of defunct, alien languages preserved in written monuments,*" in an attempt to "revive" "the cadavers of written languages" (1986a: 72, 71). Such a resurrection in language, like the anxious need so often articulated in modernist rhetoric for a "past" and a "tradition" to which to belong, marks the dematerializing force of synecdoche. It offers an immaterial "essence" of meaning that transcends its occasion, just as the theological figure Bakhtin employs ("reviving" the dead) answers the problem of what precisely is resurrected, what part of the individual life becomes the whole of everlasting life, with its concept of the immaterial soul.

Such a concept, like the synecdochical definitions in a dictionary, in some ways betrays what we must mean by "life" when we talk of the everlasting life of resurrection. My grandmother delimited this problem when she told me that she would be resurrected as a thirty-five-year-old woman, strong in body as well as in soul. I have a picture of her at that age carrying a pail of milk and possessing the healthy look of a kind of peasant angel—which is to say a *situated* angel. Her religious discourse is a form of synecdoche; it abstracts a "representative" part from the placeable situations that, taken together, constituted her life, and it asserts that one part, one moment, was "essentially" what she was. In this way her discourse creates the effect of the "same" soul—of a monological meaning—governing her varied life. But even the monological, as Bakhtin says, is "an inseverable element of verbal communication," an element of the larger metonymies of language. "Any utterance," he goes on, "—the finished, written utterance not excepted—makes response to something and is calculated to be responded to in turn. . . . Each monument carries on the work of its predecessors, polemicizing with them, expecting active, responsive understanding, and anticipating such understanding in return" (1986a: 72).

This can be better seen in opposing Eliot's authoritative tradition to Joyce's scaffolding of tradition in *Ulysses. The Waste Land,* Franco Moretti argues, "is a code that allows for the *assimilation* of elements taken from different codes: the 'all-inclusiveness' that appears on the poem's surface is the consequence of this deep formal procedure: and this, in turn, functions substantially as a *mythic system*" (1983: 219). In the terms I have been developing, Eliot's mythic system is a recuperation of a "deep" synecdochical hierarchy in the face of the metonymic cultural explosion of Europe at the end of the nineteenth century. It is, as Bakhtin would say, a work of philology. ("Philology," with a strong positive valence, is a term governing George Steiner's lament in *Real Presences.) Ulysses,* on the other hand, dramatizes what Patrick McGee calls "the repressed truth behind every work of art in lacking not only a final meaning but a final value supported by a historically transcendent code" (1988: 7). More than this, I suspect, *Ulysses* dramatizes the repressed truth behind the hegemony of Western cultural assumptions, namely that its values are not historically transcendent. For this reason, McGee concludes, "the mythical structure which the early criticism of Joyce focused on can now be seen as less a principle of order giving shape to the chaos of modern life, as Eliot insisted, than as a layer of ideological coding associated with those hierarchical kinship societies from which the modern world inherited paternal values and male dominance" (1988: 193).

In this *Ulysses* is not philological but dialogical; it resonates on its "surface" with the voices of Homer and Shakespeare and Mozart, so that, in Moretti's negative reading, it "uses myth only to desecrate it, to parody Bloom with Ulysses, and Ulysses with Bloom; to create an order which gives greater relief to the absence of order." In Joyce, unlike Eliot, myth and history neutralize one another, "and it is impossible to establish [as Eliot does] a formal or ideological hierarchy between the two" (1983: 192). Both Joyce and Eliot, then, record and enact the failure of synecdoche in the modern world, but for Eliot, as for de Man, such breakdown is the occasion of grave concern, anxious recuperation, the despair of free-floating anxiety. For Joyce, on the other hand, it is the occasion for metonymic laughter, the material word and counter-word enunciated at a particular time and place. (This is why Moretti and McGee can so strongly place Joyce in the "immigrant culture" of British modernism [Moretti 1983: 190; see also McGee 1988: 141–42].)

Bakhtin's material-historical understanding of discourse is directly relevant to an understanding of the appropriation and transmission of texts beyond the despair of unconnected events that de Man and Eliot articulate in their different ways. That is, it offers a way, as Joyce does, of recuperating the "same" in discourse without mystification, and thus a way of understanding and recuperating the modernist rhetoric that responds to a world very much like the one de Man conceives of. There is a difference between metonymy—even Bakhtin's and Joyce's *radical metonymy*—and the randomness that de Man describes and Eliot enacts. Metonymy exists within the historical and social institution of language; even when the "deep" and transcendental truth is lost, the interhuman "play"—the transmission—of discourse goes on. Walter Benjamin notes that Kafka presents "a sickness of tradition" in which the "consistency of truth" has been lost. He "was far from being the first to face this situation," Benjamin says; "many had accommodated themselves to it, clinging to truth or whatever they happened to regard as truth and, with a more or less heavy heart, forgoing its transmissibility. Kafka's real genius was that he tried something entirely new: he sacrificed truth for the sake of clinging to its transmissibility, its haggadic element" (1969: 143–44). In the same way Joyce, unlike Eliot, clings to the *transmissibility* of truths without the authority of a "past."

In "Discourse in the Novel" Bakhtin explicitly addresses this question of the historical transmission of discourse through historically determined genres. "When verbal disciplines are taught in school," he writes,

> two basic modes are recognized for the appropriation and transmission—simultaneously—of another's words (a text, a rule, a model): "reciting by heart" and "retelling in one's own words." The latter mode poses on a small scale the task implicit in all prose stylistics: retelling a text in one's own words is to a certain extent a double-voiced narration of another's words, for indeed "one's own words" must not completely dilute the quality that makes another's words unique; a retelling in one's own words should have a mixed character, able when necessary to reproduce the style and expressions of the transmitted text. (1981: 341)

In this passage Bakhtin is articulating not only the stylistic opposition between Eliot's citations and Joyce's retellings. He is also articulating the "dialogics" of discourse, his sense that discursive significance is always and only to be understood as historically and socially situated *enunciated* discourse (whether or not that enunciation recites or retells). For him, language always materially embodies in the speaker's own words the social forms and genres of discourse; such a sense of language, as he says here, always has a double-voiced, mixed character that allows the other's words to resonate in discourse. In other words, it is precisely because of language and rhetoric that the random power of death de Man describes can be put in the service of meaning and relationship. It is precisely because of language that we will never be able to conceive of human existence as random events. "We can never get back to man separate from language," Benveniste writes, "and we shall never see him inventing it. We shall never get back to man reduced to himself and exercising his wits to conceive of the existence of another." Rather, it is through language—through the metonymic "instances of discourse" which always take place, contiguously, with others—"that man constitutes himself as a *subject*" (1971: 224, 217, 224).

The dialogic double voicing of Bakhtin is significantly different from the doubling of *langue* versus *parole* in Saussure's understanding of language and the "semiology" and "rhetoric" in de Man's understanding. The double voices contend in the "condition of fierce social struggle outlined by Bakhtin in 'Discourse in the Novel,' in which the dialogical forces of language actively contest the social and political centralization of the culture" (Hirschkop 1986: 74), but they do so without the possibility of reducing (synecdochically) one to the other. It is easy to see how de Man transforms social and political strife to monadic and metaphysical strife in his reading of Shelley, just as Eliot transforms it to the melodramatic "ruin" of Europe in his writing. But in Bakhtin it is also easy to see (and hear) the wide range of senses of "enunciation" (including de Man's) contending endlessly with one another: to enunciate means to say it again, more clearly, to make it clear in this particular unique (and unconnected) instance of discourse, to situate "meaning" within a "concrete theme," to create a particular occasion for a "counter word," a dialogue. Each instance of enunciation, like the stylistic play in the late chapters of *Ulysses,* seems without relation to anything that precedes and follows from it; yet together, in their radical metonymy, they constitute the rhetoric of meaning responding to a world in which the "same" is a problem, a world of time and death.

While rhetoric offers such polyphonious strife, then, it also presents the possibility of "the appropriation and transmission—simultaneously—of another's words" (Bakhtin 1981: 341). In this we can discover a *material* sense of genre in which the "habitual" modes of speech—its "habits" being governed by recurrence of more or less "accidental" (that is, historically determined) social situations—help to determine the "unfinalized whole" of an utterance. Such a whole is a function of genre, but because it is not finalized, such "wholeness" is not synecdochically analyzable. It cannot be represented by a part—especially a "nonmaterial" part, such as traditional conceptions of genre—even though it is made up of parts whose relations to one another (like the relations of facial features in family resemblances) are not wholly arbitrary and random. Rather, the wholeness of genre is the unity of a *position* of discourse that is defined as responsive to other generic positions in a kind of metonymic strife, in the same way that the subject of discourse, in Benveniste's description, is always *positioned* in relation to other subjects. As Bakhtin/Medvedev says in *The Formal Method in Literary Scholarship* (echoing *Marxism and the Philosophy of Language*), while the theme of discourse "always transcends" the abstract meanings of language, "the thematic unity of the work and its real place in life organically grow together in genre" (1985: 133). They do so because genre, in its accidentally and historically determined "forms"—forms which function, Bakhtin says, as a kind of collective memory responding to basic material human needs—allows discursive utterances *to function* as wholes, as "finalized structuredness," in particular situations (1985: 129, 184). That is, a genre is an "enunciation," a dialogic moment within the historically determined development of genres. It manifests the effect of discursive relationship by being a function of memory and relationship, which are themselves conditioned by discourse.

With a similar *rhetorical* understanding of genre and discourse—a *nonsynecdochical* understanding—Derrida asserts that "every text participates in one or several genres, there is no genreless text; there is always a genre and genres, yet such participation never amounts to belonging" (1980: 65). Derrida is implicitly answering de Man's vision of randomness with an irreducibly nonsimple response. In this, genre is a subcategory of the more general iterations of language Derrida discusses in "Limited Inc.": generic iteration, like general linguistic iteration, is never "pure"; it is always marked by "disruptions" (1977: 190). "One might even say," Derrida goes on to say in "The Law of Genre," that the disruptions of genre are engendered "by citation or re-citation *(re-cit)*. . . . A citation in the strict sense implies all sorts of contextual conventions, precautions, and protocols in the mode of reiteration, of coded signs, such as quotation marks or other typographical devices used for writing a citation" (1980: 58).

Genre for Derrida, like the classroom recitation Bakhtin describes, is a moment of "enunciation" in the various mixed senses of that concept. (Certainly here a teacher, like a parent, might tell a student to enunciate his or her words.) It is a simultaneously global and metonymic category that participates in the same "impurity" of all discourse, the radical metonymy of its "internal division . . . , impurity, corruption, contamination, decomposition, perversion, deformation, even cancerization, generous proliferation, of degenerescence" (1980: 57). As such, it is determined by material rhetoric, both rhetoric's diacritical tropology and the power of its interpersonal enunciations. That is, it is determined by the irreducibly complex conception of rhetoric I have described in this chapter: the linguistic articulation of the "same"—and of "knowledge" itself—in tropological patterns, and the simultaneous enunciated power of its articulations to create interhuman relationships of persuasion and effect, neither of which can be fully (or purely) isolated in the rhetoric of discourse.

For de Man, the impurity of discourse is the perverse deformation of unconnected random events, the perversity of rhetoric that can never coincide with semiology while never being able to mark that noncoincidence. For Bakhtin, however, this impurity of discourse and signification—like the "impurity" of contingent material historical accident—is, in fact, a "generous proliferation" of meaning and meaningful historical relationships. Bakhtin creates, in his material-historical understanding of discourse, the possibility of future transformation, even radical transformation, on all levels of human social life. For him— and for Derrida, I believe—language, like history, offers the possibility of change and development—the *future* itself—precisely because it is many-sided and heterogeneous. It offers what de Man despairs of in his understanding of meaning and relationship. For Bakhtin—and Derrida—discourse raises up its meanings in the face of death, not to (synecdochically) deny death, but neither to succumb too quickly to its random power. As Bakhtin notes in *Problems of Dostoevsky's Poetics,* generic tradition exists but "is reborn and renewed in each [particular author] in its own way, that is, in a unique and unrepeatable way" (1984: 159). Such "rebirth" is not resurrection but transmission, another instant of enunciation, unique but not without positive and negative relationships to things that precede, follow, or exist elsewhere.

The fact is, relationships themselves are *effects* of discourse, *rhetorical effects.* To discount them (as de Man does) simply because they participate in the double-voiced ambiguity of all discourse—of phenomena belonging to the interhuman milieu—is to fail to recognize (as Derrida claims Heidegger also fails to do) the "rhetoricity of rhetoric," the exhilaration and generosity as well as the aporetic problematics of discourse. In this way Bakhtin's historicization of genre—which is, after all, the historicization of rhetoric—allows for the very kind of cluttered materialist understanding of discourse and rhetoric that modernism itself calls for. Such a "heteroglossia" of discourse irreducibly confuses the heterogeneity of voices in the discourse that modern literature and modern criticism present.

Modernist Postmodern Rhetoric

The critics examined in this book—including Paul de Man and Mikhail Bakhtin in this chapter and even George Steiner in the Introduction—are all responding to and participating in the world I have been describing. The rhetoric inhabiting this world can be most clearly seen in modernist literature as responses to the metonymic materiality that discourse and life seem to present—the self-conscious configured "textual" response I examined in Chapter 3, and the response of "imperial" modernism in Eliot, Steiner, and Jakobson that I examine in the next chapter. These critics raise their voices, as modernism does, against the clamor and noise of polyphonic strife and the resonating overtones of nothingness, non-sense, and death. They are responding to the "end" of Europe, just as the modernist writers earlier in the century responded to the breakdown of the self-evident "truths"—the consistency of truth—in their time. I believe this is the best sense in which the critics who came into their own after the final breakup of European hegemony in World War II can be called "postmodern." In Part II, I shall explore these responses as the postmodernist rhetoric of criticism in the work of Barthes, Lacan, and Derrida in studies tutored by the writings and readings of Anglo-American modernism. I begin, however, with an examination of the "modernist" rhetoric in Jakobson's work, in an attempt to describe the simultaneous assertion and failure of synecdoche in his "scientific" criticism. In each chapter a critic is paired with a major modernist literary figure—Yeats, Lawrence, Conrad, and Stevens—but the focus is not so much on the literary figure as on the articulation and situation of rhetoric shared—or at least paralleled—by the contemporary thinker and the modernist writer. Such an examination will help us to understand the language of contemporary criticism and of modernism; it will help us to discover a larger sense of the responsiveness—the rhetorical nature—of twentieth-century discourse.

The chief feature of this responsive language is the "enunciatory" aspect of discourse. Perhaps "aspect" is a misleading term, because the difference between "enunciation" and "statement" is not the difference between different "parts" or "aspects" of discursive phenomena: discourse is all enunciation, and at the same time it is all statement. When I said in chapter one that the relationship between the modern and the postmodern is the "translation" of metaphysical elegy into "simple" rhetoric, I was hardly marking a difference: discourse is "metaphysical" insofar as it participates in the tendency Greimas notes of "substantifying" the relationships it articulates by means of synecdoche; it is "rhetorical" insofar as its communicative function is (metonymically) asymmetrical with its significatory function. In this way, Derrida's definition of "translation" is and is not different from Jakobson's. Derrida describes "translation . . . from one language into itself (with the 'same' words suddenly changing their sense, overflowing with sense or exceeding it altogether, and nevertheless impassive, imperturbable, identical to themselves, allowing you still to read in the new code of this anasemic translation what belonged to the other word, the same one, before psychoanalysis, that other language, makes use of the same words but imposes on them a 'radical semantic change')" (1979a: 5). This description falls within *and* outside—it is a "part" and an "other"—of Jakobson's definition of meaning as "the translation of a sign into another system of signs" (Jakobson 1977: 1029).

Enunciation imposes this kind of "translation" onto statement, and the difference between modernism and postmodernism is a difference both global and hardly there at all. That is, the "translation" of modernism into postmodernism is the "translation," examined in Chapter 1, of synecdoche (and synecdochic metonymy) into the radical metonymy of de Man, Bakhtin, and Derrida. In fact, the "difference" between de Man and Bakhtin, as I have suggested in this chapter, is a translation of modernist rhetoric of crisis into a postmodern rhetoric of play—again, a difference both global and hardly there at all. In a parallel way, the next chapter argues that Jakobson's translation of Yeats's sense of the crisis of modernism—the crisis of synecdoche—into universal, imperial truths is global and imperceptible. In subsequent chapters the practitioners of postmodern discourse theory engage in similar "translations," with the "same" words changing and overflowing their sense and still identical to themselves and their earlier functioning within modernism. Roland Barthes enunciates Jakobson's linguistic analyses of literature as "textual" analyses; he translates linguistic synecdoche into textual metonymy. Jacques Lacan situates and enunciates Freudian psychoanalysis as a discursive practice—the talking "cure"—in the subtle transition from physician to teacher. And Jacques Derrida enunciates the metaphysics of prayer (most indebted, in his project, to Nietzschean metaphysics) as the rhetoric of mourning. In this way the "postmodern" writers I explore resituate modernist linguistics, psychology, and metaphysics—language, the subject, and being itself—within a world and a historical moment where the negative materiality of death and the radical metonymy of discourse are there and not there all the time, just on the edge of vision, a small unfocused blur. In this, the postmodern answers and fulfils the modern and offers, at the same time, its other. The "modernist postmodern" rhetoric of Part II enacts a similar relationship, with "modernist" both a synecdochical adverb, modifying "postmodern," and a simple apposition. In this, the relationship between modernist and postmodernist is like the relationship between missionary and African that Jakobson narrates to describe the global power of language: they are complexly, metonymically linked, with the "face" of meaning and the "nakedness" of materiality everywhere.

Part Two

Modernist Postmodern Rhetoric

5

The Rhetoric of Passivity

Roman Jakobson, Imperial Modernism, and the Science of Criticism

> and after these
> To gradual Time's last gift, a written speech
> Wrought of high laughter, loveliness and ease.
> —W. B. Yeats, "Upon a House Shaken
> by the Land Agitation"

The preceding chapters examined two conceptions of rhetoric—what I've called the doubled-voiced ambiguity of discourse—both of which account for meaning and signification in material terms, allowing for the existence of meaning without "dematerializing" its force and understanding or its historical occasion. In one conception, rhetoric is conceived as the *structural* and *diacritical* condition for the phenomena of meaning—the phenomena of what Nietzsche calls "similar and identical things" that make "experience" possible. Such a conception, at least in its manifestation in Saussure, is *formal,* but it allows for (although it does not always manifest itself in) an understanding of "form" as a function of a material base. The second conception of rhetoric is a more thoroughgoing materialism: in it, rhetoric is conceived as the discursive manifestation of social and interpersonal relationships, what Bakhtin calls the "dialogic" nature of understanding. Unlike the "structural"—or Paul de Man's "semiological"—model, however, it does not fully interrogate the nature of the "same" in its perception of repetition and reiteration. The first of these two conceptions of rhetoric—as more or less formal "tropology," rather than "persuasion" (again to use de Man's terms)—has governed contemporary literary study, and, indeed, the study of literature since the advent of modernism.

In fact, it is reasonable to argue that early formalisms—Russian Formalism in the 1920s, the New Criticism in the 1930s, even Prague structuralism—are themselves species of modernism. They respond to a world in which the future seems impossible, in which, as Nietzsche says in *The Use and Abuse of History,* existence is "an imperfect tense that never becomes a present" so that "when death brings at last the desired forgetfulness, it abolishes life and being together, and sets the seal on the knowledge that 'being' is merely a continual 'has been,' a thing that lives by denying and destroying and contradicting itself" (1957: 6). The response of formalism, like Eliot's suggestion of a "mythical method" in modernism, is to attempt to recuperate meaning and significance in the face of the explosion of metonymy—in the face of the "end" of European world hegemony—the "extreme case" Nietzsche describes of "the man without any power to forget who is condemned to see 'becoming' everywhere" (1957: 6). Such recuperation takes the form of the assertion of synecdoche in what Christopher Norris aptly calls the "aesthetic ideology" everywhere present in Anglo-American modernism. Against such aestheticism one should recall de Man's striking readings of Nietzsche: " 'Only as an *aesthetic phenomenon* is existence and world forever *justified*': the famous quotation, twice repeated in *The Birth of Tragedy,* should not be taken too serenely, for it is an indictment of existence rather than a panegyric of art" (1979: 93).

There are, of course, historical reasons for the ascendant power of formal (and "aesthetic") rather than persuasive conceptions of rhetoric governing literary, linguistic, and philosophical modernism. Such formalism, after all, responds to conceptions of life and being such as Nietzsche's and the vision of the absolute material dissolution of death that are also articulated in modernism. Bakhtin, from his vantage as a historical-materialist, describes the "alarming instability and uncertainty of the ideological word" in the modern world, what he calls the "*transformation of the word into a thing,* the stage of *depression in the thematic value of the word*" (1986a: 159), and he suggests that the absence of an Absolute Knowledge—and the concomitant metonymic endlessness of material and discursive existence—governs such transformations and depressions. De Man emphasizes the futility and meaninglessness of such materialism. The historical "causes" and "effects" of this state of affairs are also related, as I argued in Chapter 2, to a growing awareness of the *semiotic* nature of value—including capital—and the reorientation of modes of conceiving of and apprehending value as effects of material relationships of one sort or another at the end of the nineteenth century. Formal and structural accounts, however, governed as they are by binary oppositions—unlike Bakhtin's accounts (he writes about "the extreme *heterogeneity* of speech genres" [1986: 60])—are not under pressure to offer material and historical accounts of such phenomena even when they conceive of them as *material*: they conceive "events," as de Man does, as more or less "random." Thus, Greimas and Courtés note in their encyclopedic dictionary, *Semiotics and Language,* that the ascendancy of formalist rhetoric is more or less accidental, that "a set of historical and pragmatic factors has given binary structures a privileged place in linguistic methodology" (1982: 25).

The privileged place of binary structures may indeed be "accidental," but it is so in a historically determined context. Binary structures—structures of one-to-one opposition—are a function of the perception of the breakdown of hegemonic self-evident truths: when truths are self-evident, then there is no need to self-consciously define the true against its opposite. In this way, as Jacques Derrida has attempted to show from the beginning of his career, binary oppositions are "never the face-to-face opposition of two terms, but a hierarchy and an order of subordination" (1982: 329). As de Man notes, "binaries, to the extent that they allow and invite synthesis, are therefore the most misleading of differential structures" (1986: 109). In this way, then, the historical and pragmatic factors that have given binary structures a privileged place in linguistic methodology are the factors of the breakdown of the hierarchic ordering of experience and perception at the end of the nineteenth century and the felt need, in the face of this "futility and anarchy," to reestablish synecdochical order. Binaries are most misleading because they present, in all their "oppositions," a sense of metonymic truth and counter-truth at play; at the same time, they *respond* to the radical metonymy of their historical situation by covertly reestablishing the hierarchical power of synecdoche, the sense that one of the elements of the binary opposition can always be seen to embody the general term that encompasses the *whole* of the opposition. (I describe this "neutralization" of binary oppositions in greater detail in "Deconstruction and Linguistic Analysis" [1987a].)

The greatest proponent of the functioning of binary structures in discourse and semiotics is Roman Jakobson. Unlike other twentieth-century linguists, he consistently argued for the isomorphic functioning of binarism across *all* levels of the functioning of language, from the "distinctive features" which, in "bundles" of binary oppositions, comprise the phonemes of language, to the binary oppositions that govern the semantics of poetry and discourse in general. For this reason, Lévi-Strauss was able to develop the narratology of structuralism based upon

Jakobson's binarism. In his understanding of narrative, each character, "far from constituting a single entity—forms a bundle of distinctive features like the phoneme in Roman Jakobson's theory" (1984: 182). For this reason also, Jakobson, with Saussure, is the object of Derrida's early deconstructive critique of linguistic science in *Of Grammatology.* The "scientificity" of linguistics, Derrida argues, "serves as the epistemological model for all the sciences of man" (1976: 29).

Derrida also focuses his critique on the continental phenomenology of Husserl in *Speech and Phenomena,* published in the same year as *Of Grammatology,* and a few years later he focuses his critique on the Anglo-American speech-act philosophy of J. L. Austin and John Searle in "Signature Event Context" and "Limited Inc." The work of Austin—and, behind him, the late Wittgenstein—is basically "enunciatory" in its understanding of discourse, and as such it is a major source of American "reader-response" criticism (see especially Fish 1980; see also Felman 1983 and Staten 1984). In the next chapter I shall examine postmodernist enunciatory literary theory in Roland Barthes, but there are other reasons—not altogether innocent—to make Jakobson's structural reading of literary texts "representative" of modernist discourse theory. Most obviously, the historical and pragmatic factors in American criticism—the hegemony of New Critical formalism, situated in its beginnings in the Old South, where hierarchical social structures, like those of Europe, were succumbing to futility and anarchy—calls for such a strategy. The remarkable reception of continental linguistics-based discourse theory in America is, in fact, as Frank Lentricchia has argued, a function of the post-Kantian formalism that dominated the academic study of literature for most of this century (1980; see also Norris 1988 for a fine discussion of Paul de Man's response to the "aesthetic ideology" of post-Kantian formalism).

But more to the point, the hegemony of formalism is a function, in large part, of the rhetorical power of the spatial figures—the seeming naturalness of conceiving of phenomena as substantial—that Nietzsche attempts to show to be figural in *The Use and Abuse of History* and elsewhere. Greimas describes this as the tendency of discourse to "substantify" relationships so that "whenever one opens one's mouth to speak of relationships, they transform themselves, as if by magic, into substantives. . . . Any metalanguage that we can imagine to speak about meaning is not only a signifying language, it is also substantifying" (1970: 8; see also Schleifer 1987: 40–43). Greimas is describing the nature of language which, as he sees it, gives rise to phenomenally substantial referents for its designations: when language *says* something, even when it describes a relationship, the act of designating that relationship causes it to seem to be not simply conceptual connections between other things but a thing itself. For instance, Saussure's word *signifier* (the French *signifier,* literally the "signifying") transforms relationship into a spatially locatable substance.

The power of spatial figuration answers flux and becoming and death—in larger cultural terms, it responds to the "end" of Europe—with the rhetorical effect of "objective" scientific phenomena that can be manipulated and configured, just as the phenomena that science studies can be. This is why, as Bakhtin says, "the *declaratory* word remains alive only in scientific writing" (1986a: 159): in such writing the existence of things and their possible future remains "alive." This is also why Jakobson so insistently parallels grammar and geometry in his work (see esp. 1968: 132–35). In *Structural Semantics* Greimas makes explicit the function of geometric tropes by analyzing discourse in terms of its articulated or substantified *agents*—what he calls the "actants" of narrative—rather than its represented *activities*—what he calls (following Propp) the "functions" of narrative. By focusing on the aspects of language that call for a rhetoric of space, Greimas demonstrates greater possibility of analysis and, of course, of configuration (1983: xxxviii). Most extremely put, without some kind of "mediating structures," conceived more or less consciously in spatial metaphors, the "social system" of language, as Greimas and Courtés note under the heading "Enunciation," can only be "scattered into a infinite number of examples of speech (Saussure's *parole),* outside all scientific cognizance" (1982: 103). At this extreme, enunciation becomes events with no relation, positive or negative, to anything that precedes, follows, or exists elsewhere.

It is precisely to avoid such non-discursive "non-sense" that de Man situates Bakhtin's understanding of discourse within its own binary structure. Bakhtin is a formalist insofar as dialogism is "a still formal method by which to conquer or sublate formalism itself." In this, de Man argues, "dialogism is here still a descriptive and metalinguistic term that says something about language rather than about the world" (1986: 109). This is one moment in Bakhtin—one "pole" in the binary opposition that governs *his* discourse—of which the other is the *extropy* of dialogism, the "voices of radical alterity" that Bakhtin hears in Dostoevsky or, we might imagine, in Joyce, not because they are different from the voices of their ("authoritative") authors, "but because," de Man says, "their otherness *is* their reality" (1986: 109).

In the same way, Derek Attridge situates Jakobson's poetics within an opposition between conceiving of poetry as functioning "to heighten attention to the meanings of words and sentences . . . [by means of] the particular forcefulness with which it presents its semantic content" and conceiving of poetry as "a linguistic practice that specially emphasizes the material properties of language . . . [which] provide pleasure and significance independently of cognitive content" (1988: 130; see also Peter Steiner 1984: Ch. 3). This opposition, which Attridge suggests functions unconsciously in Jakobson, like the opposition de Man sees in Bakhtin, opposes a formal and structural understanding of meaning to a material and historical—that is, *enunciatory*—understanding. It suggests that even the seemingly material effects of language can be accounted for within the structures of binary opposition and that, in Derrida's paraphrase of Husserl, "meaning is everywhere" (1981a: 30). Doing so, it reiterates, in the face of its denegation, a chief tenet of the ideology of liberal bourgeois society, in which, as Franco Moretti describes it, the real is rational and the free market guarantees the "rational functioning" of society, "automatically regulating its conflictual, irrational, and private foundations" (1983: 183).

The opposition between the semantic and material moments in his poetics presents a further reason for making Jakobson's structuralist criticism representatively modernist. In terms of the two species of rhetoric I have been discussing, Jakobson's "structuralist," tropological understanding of rhetoric (*Darstellung*) does not preclude a "persuasive" understanding of rhetoric (*Vorstellung*). That is, the configured tropes of structuralism (as opposed to a social and interpersonal conception of rhetoric) do not ignore the persuasive power of discourse. Greimas's very "actantial" analysis, for example, does not preclude "functional" analysis; rather, it attempts to create a metalanguage—a rhetoric—in which it can be most fully examined, the language of "actants." The formalist-structuralist assumption of the *hierarchic* nature of "interhuman" phenomena grounds itself in the situation of interpersonal enunciation. As Greimas says in a key passage of *Structural Semantics,* "linguistic activity" appears first as "essentially . . . a series of messages," each of which is hierarchically structured ("hypotactic") but which, taken together, are unconnected enunciatory acts between a sender and a receiver. Then, "a systematic structure . . . is superimposed on this [series] and establishes the message as an objectivizing projection, the simulator of a world from which the sender and the receiver of a communication are excluded" (1983: 134). In this view, the aim of linguistic activity is to transcend the situation of the sender and receiver: it is to make all the materiality and contingency of that situation disappear in an objectivizing projection—in Baudrillard's term, a "simulation"—of meaning and being in the world.

This description of linguistic activity transcending its momentary occasion aptly captures one aim of modernist formalism from Eliot's attempt to recuperate a "deep" and "transcendental" meaning from the flux of Joyce's and his own experience to the hypostasizations of irony and paradox of the New Criticism, which also attempts the recuperation of transcendental value. (The implicit opposite of this aim, the foregrounding of negative materiality within discourse and other social institutions, governed Part I of this book.) Structuralism, however, as Claude Lévi-Strauss has argued, aims at *situating* such formalism. Unlike Russian or New Critical formalisms, whose forms are abstract paradigms completely separate from the actual, temporally situated phenomena they study, structuralism arrests and apprehends the "logical organization" of phenomena "conceived as a property of the real" (Lévi-Strauss 1984: 167; see Galan 1985: 35 for Mukarovsky's earlier criticism of formalism in similar terms). The structures of structuralism do not simply assert the existence of nonmaterial abstract entities, such as Frye's opposition between comedy and tragedy figured as the opposition between Spring and Fall; rather, they attempt to recuperate, spatially, the temporal and phenomenological process of apprehension and organization. The structures of structuralism, like the binary opposition of presence and absence in the distinctive features of phonemes, allow the phenomena studied to exist *as* phenomena: without the binary structure of distinctive features, no phonemes—themselves "real" objects whose existence is based upon the structural network, the logical organization, in which they occur—would exist. In the same way, the phenomena of narrative—the King and Shepherdess of folktale whom Lévi-Strauss mentions (1984: 187)—exist and function as narrative units *because* of logical organizations apprehended as real (in this case the logical binarism of sexual and social differences). In this way, then, the structures of structuralism—and the rhetoric of structuralism—arise within the particular enunciatory context of the crisis of European culture.

Such structuralist rhetorical configurations recuperate signification from time and space—from the *situation* of discourse and, by extension, from the material nothingness and pure non-sense of death. What they do—as Western metaphysics, in Derrida's and Staten's readings, have always done—is create a *reserve* for rhetoric within material chaos: a measure of language and meaning against the nature of things conceived phenomenally. Phenomenal—gestalt—apprehension is a function of hierarchy and hierarchical configurations (as opposed to random configurations). Steiner claims that Husserl's phenomenology, like the aspect of modernism I am calling "imperial," is "the heroic but doomed rearguard action in defence of this principle" (1989: 132), and, as I have already mentioned, Jakobson is the great proponent of linguistic and "scientific" hierarchy in twentieth-century discourse theory. For this reason Jakobson participates more directly and fully in modernism than the other writers I am examining here: he most fully follows the combinations of a materialist-formalist understanding of science that Saussure articulated in the *Course of General Linguistics* and in his studies of anagrams. (See the fine discussion by Todorov [1982: 255–70] examining the practical effects of the contradiction between Saussure's material and formal conceptions of the sign; see also Starobinski 1979.)

In his scientific study of discourse Jakobson has focused on grammar as a *level* of linguistic phenomena that can only be understood in the larger context of a conception of the world in which the real is "rational." The poet, he says, must reckon with the "obligatory character of grammatical processes and concepts": "either he strives for symmetry and sticks to these simple, repeatable, diaphanous patterns, based on a binary principle, or he may cope with them, while longing for an 'organic chaos.' I have stated repeatedly that the rhyme technique is 'either grammatical or antigrammatical' but never agrammatical" (1968: 132). Grammatical or antigrammatical, the materiality of rhyme remains within the reserve of rhetoric, the reserve of material serving the *hierarchically* superior end of meaning. Without such reserve, discourse, for Jakobson, is reduced to enunciatory chaos.

Such a reserve is effected by the "scientific" transformation of the radical metonymy of enunciation into a synecdochical hierarchy of reserve. Throughout his work Jakobson more or less equates metonymy and synecdoche under the larger category of "contiguous relationships" (1956: 111). In "Two Aspects of Language," for instance, he distinguishes the Freudian structure of dream imagery on the basis of "contiguity (Freud's metonymic 'displacement' and synecdochic 'condensation') or on similarity (Freud's 'identification and symbolism')" (1956: 113) without noting that the equation of displacement and condensation replaces the possibility of the radical contingency and accident of displacement with the *motivations* of condensation. In other words, this equation answers the *arbitrary* nature of contiguity—and the consequent conception of discourse, in Nietzsche's terms, as "shaping forces," as "falsifying re-shaping" (cited in Stambaugh 1972: 71)— with a conception of contiguity that is not arbitrary but determined by the nature of things, the *relations* among their parts. The equation of metonymy and synecdoche replaces what Jakobson calls the "codified contiguity [of signification], which is often confusingly labeled 'arbitrariness of the verbal sign' " (1960: 87), with what he calls "the synecdochic nature of language" (1932: 459), which functions by means of the hierarchical relationship between part and whole.

Such a "replacement" redeems time by making chance meaningful, by finding a reserve of meaning wherever it looks. As Jakobson notes, "during the Middle Ages, *ignorance* was responsible for the dismemberment of classical statues; today the sculptor does his *own* dismembering, but the result (visual synecdoche) is the same" (1934: 369). In the same way, as Hugh Kenner argues in *The Pound Era,* modernism creates its effects by "imitating" the ways in which the passage of time "dismembers" and fragments intentional meaning so that "happenings in the world . . . [are converted] into something that happens in language" (1971: 123). Equating synecdoche and metonymy (condensation and displacement) Jakobson, like the postsymbolist modernists Kenner is describing, renders the real rational by analogizing the self-evident hierarchical and intelligible structures of language to the far from self-evident intelligibility of historical events (see Schleifer 1987: 16–18 for a similar discussion of Lévi-Strauss). In this way the synecdoches of language create the "effect" of what Eliot prays for in *Ash Wednesday,* to "Redeem / The time. Redeem / The unread vision in the higher dream / While jeweled unicorns draw by the gilded hearse" (1963: 90).

The equation of metonymy with synecdoche can be seen from another vantage on Jakobson's work. From early in his career Jakobson attempted to reintegrate "diachronic" linguistics within "synchronic" linguistics, but not to reintegrate the historical time and social space within the field of human signification that Todorov describes in relation to Bakhtin (1984: 40). Rather, Jakobson attempted to demonstrate the hierarchical nature of these categories, their *synecdochical* nature; he attempted to show how the structural, spatial model of language that Saussure's work implies and calls for could help us understand the "unread" but *readable* function of time as well as space in linguistic phenomena. Like the great modernists—at least in one moment of their work—he attempted to account rationally for the experience of otherness. As he wrote late in life,

> Saussure's ideology ruled out any compatibility between the two aspects of time, simultaneity and succession. As a result, dynamism was excluded from the study of the system and the *signans* was reduced to pure linearity, thus precluding any possibility of viewing the phoneme as a bundle of concurrent distinctive characteristics. Each of these mutually contradic-

tory theses sacrificed one of the two dimensions of time, one
by renouncing succession in time and the other by renouncing
coexisting temporal elements. (1983: 59)

Such a concept of time is fully reserved: it transforms "pure linearity"—
"pure" metonymy—into the motivated hierarchy of synecdoche.

Jakobson attempts to bring the two dimensions of time together
not only in the "distinctive features" of phonology, as he says here,
but also in his linguistic analyses of poetry. The most elaborate of these
analyses is one of his latest, *Yeats' "Sorrow of Love" through the Years,*
a study that attempts to bring both dimensions together as it examines
the poem in terms of its synchronic structure and its diachronic history
of Yeats's repeated revisions. There Jakobson attempts to deal with
the imperial rhetoric of modernism in its most pronounced form.

Behind this attempt is a more profound conjunction of structuralism and phenomenology in Jakobson—and, more than implicitly, in
the rhetorical tropology of modernism as well. Saussurean linguistics—
and Jakobson is a faithful follower in this—*begins* with the "givenness"
of meaning, the fact that, *phenomenally,* meaning is apprehended in
discourse. What Derrida says of Husserl is true of Jakobson as well:
in Husserl's phenomenology, Derrida writes, "all experience is the
experience of meaning (*Sinn*). Everything that appears to consciousness, everything that is for consciousness in general, is *meaning.* Meaning is the phenomenality of phenomenon" (1981a: 30). In the same
way, Jakobson tells an anecdote to demonstrate that "poeticalness is
not a supplementation of discourse with rhetorical adornment but a
total reevaluation of the discourse and of all its components whatsoever": "A missionary blamed his African flock for walking around with
no clothes on. 'And what about yourself?' they pointed to his visage,
'are not you, too, somewhere naked?' 'Well, but this is my face.' 'Yet
in us,' retorted the natives, 'everywhere it is face.' So in poetry any
verbal element is converted into a figure of poetic speech" (1960: 93).
Implicit in this passage is a definition of poetry as an encounter with
otherness—just as such otherness, as I argued in Chapter 3, is implicit
in modernism's rearguard response to the breakdown of European hegemony. In this, Jakobson is defining poetry, as the Russian Formalists
did, as the renewal of language and perception through "defamiliarization." This passage makes clear the relationship of such a modernist
understanding of poetry to European imperialism; it also indicates how
that imperialism participates in the binary opposition of center and
periphery. The concept of defamiliarization recuperates the other for
the same; it allows for the equation not only of face and breast, but of
black face and white face, of black face and face-in-general.

In poetry for Jakobson, then, as in discourse more generally, everything (including otherness) signifies; meaning is effected everywhere. Unlike American structuralism, which methodologically avoids considering meaning and meaning-effects (see Schleifer 1987: 56–61), continental structuralism *begins* with the apprehension of meaning—what Greimas calls, using a spatial metaphor, "the vague, yet necessary concept of the *meaningful whole* set forth by a message" (1983: 59). Such a beginning incorporates phenomenology into structuralism, creating what Elmar Holenstein calls the "phenomenological structuralism" of Jakobson's life work (1976; see also Peter Steiner 1984: Ch. 3). "It was in poetics," Jakobson noted late in life, "that the vital relation of the parts and the whole were most clearly apparent, and this stimulated us to think through and verify the teachings of Edmund Husserl (1859–1938) and of the Gestalt psychologists by applying their principles to the fundamental cycle of questions" (1983: 11). In his poetic studies Jakobson wants to account for the phenomenal "effects" of poetry—its meaning-effects, its subliminal effects, its affectiveness in general; whatever is "noticeable."

In his criticism, as in his linguistics, Jakobson begins with the phenomenon of meaning and the assumption that this phenomenon, because it is a function of a *synecdochical* hierarchy—a hierarchy that finally effects the "same" and makes "objective" meaning possible— is susceptible to analyses that are objective, repeatable, and verifiable. Thus Jakobson attempts to articulate a critical practice that will account for literary meanings in analyses whose rhetoric itself creates the effect of scientific objectivity, substantified structures, and intelligibility. The rest of this chapter will examine the rhetoric of his criticism as one side of the modernist enterprise, the "imperial" side that recuperates everything—the phenomenality of phenomena—for intelligibility. The next chapter will examine Barthes's "enunciatory" rhetoric in its attempt to capture the ways in which language *uses* the unintelligibility of discourse to effect its strategies and tactics and create the illusion of a future, a practice Stanley Fish describes as extremely "different . . . from the positivist-formalist project. Everything," Fish continues, "depends on the temporal dimension, and as a consequence the notion of a mistake, at least as something to be avoided, disappears" (1980: 159). Jakobson is not a positivist; his emphasis on the phenomenal givenness of meaning precludes that, even though his work presents elements that Attridge can characterize as "crusading positivism" (1988: 135). Yet for him mistakes are real simply because the effects of language are real, verifiable, and subject to intellectual accounting. Meaning is everywhere, a kind of "imperialism," because discourse reserves for itself, as Derrida says, the ability to achieve "completion": to "include within itself and anticipate all the figures of its beyond, all the forms and resources of its exterior ... by simply taking hold of their enunciation" (1978: 252). For Jakobson, then, criticism can legitimately aspire to a scientific discourse in which the material fact and radical otherness of death is forgotten, even if, as the cost of such forgetting, a future is lost as well.

"Meaning," Jakobson has repeated throughout his career, "is the translation of a sign into another system of signs" (1977: 1029; Jakobson is quoting C. S. Peirce). Every part of his distinguished career, which literally transformed the nature of linguistics and "modernized" discourse theory in general, has been governed by the assumption that the laws of language are a simple set of postulates and procedures subject to the kinds of translations he speaks about. That is, the motor behind Jakobson's career has been the simple proposition that all the effects that language gives rise to—from the minutest discriminations of the relationship between sound and meaning to the vaguest global effects of poetry and prose—are governed by homogeneous linguistic laws of binary logic and hierarchical relationships within and among the materials of language, laws that are humanly apprehensible and, for that reason, capable of being rigorously and objectively formulated. Besides bringing his remarkable sensitivity and learning to bear on strictly linguistic problems—with Trubetzkoy, as part of the Prague School, he produced the most scientifically verifiable models of linguistic sciences in his work on systematic phonology (including, as he mentioned, the verifiable bundles of "distinctive features" of phonemes)—he has also produced studies of morphology, syntax, and semantics.

 As part of his groundbreaking work in linguistics and semiotics he has turned his attention to the practical criticism of literary studies that aims to account for the effects of poetry—its meaning-effects, but also its ability to provoke particular feelings in its auditors. As I mentioned already, a culmination of Jakobson's life-long study of poetry is his relatively late analysis (1977) with his collaborator, Stephen Rudy, of a high modernist text, Yeats's early and late versions of "The Sorrow of Love." In Yeats' "Sorrow of Love" through the Years he and Rudy continue the translations of poetry into grammatical analyses he described in "Linguistics and Poetics" in 1960. His late Yeats study in many ways follows the procedures of his earliest and still best-known linguistic analysis of a poem, written in 1962 in collaboration with Lévi-Strauss, "Baudelaire's 'Les Chats.'" It geometrically dissects, as

Victor Erlich has noted, "along criss-crossing—vertical or horizontal—lines, the poem [which] emerges as a system of systems, an intricate web of binary oppositions" (1973: 7).

Jakobson himself has claimed that "the binary grammatical parallelism becomes the pivot of the plot and carries the whole dramatic development" of poems under analysis (1968: 126). Such parallelism becomes the "intense dramatization" (1968: 122) of Jakobson's literary criticism as well, as he describes the morphological, syntactical, and semantic distributions between stanzas of a poem, its center and periphery, its global divisions. "Any noticeable reiteration of the same grammatical concept," Jakobson has written, "becomes an effective poetic device." That is, "any unbiased, attentive, exhaustive, total description of the selection, distribution and interrelation of the diverse morphological classes and syntactic constructions in a given poem surprises the examiner himself by unexpected, striking symmetries and antisymmetries, balanced structures, efficient accumulations of equivalent forms and salient contrasts . . . [which] permit us to follow the masterly interplay of the actualized constituents" (1968: 127). In the simultaneous synchronic and diachronic analysis of Yeats's "Sorrow of Love" Jakobson displays his masterly skill, his wealth of discriminating attention. In reading a poem to surprise and inform his reader, Jakobson helps one return to Yeats with a greater sense of his art and with increased attention and admiration for the functioning of his language.

While such a "return"—informed by a fuller awareness of the complexity of Yeats's lyric and, indeed, the complexity of his poetic development—is, in some ways, the best that practical criticism can achieve, nevertheless my description of the critical achievement of Jakobson and Rudy demands some qualification. In its "objective" and scientific study, *Yeats' "Sorrow of Love" through the Years* fails to account for the material rhetoric of modernism—the non-imperial rhetoric—that I described in Part I; it fails to situate Yeats's poem—and his poetry in general—as Yeats himself does, as a cry to let something remain in a world where things fall apart. In *A Vision* Yeats describes Paul Valéry's *Cimetière Marin* as "chilling" in its most moving part: "in a passage of great eloquence [it] rejoices that human life must pass. I was about to put his poem among my sacred books," Yeats continues, "but I cannot now, for I do not believe him. My imagination goes some years backward, and I remember a beautiful young girl singing at the edge of the sea in Normandy words and music of her own composition. She thought herself alone, stood barefooted between sea and sand; sang with lifted head of the civilisations that there had come and gone,

ending every verse with the cry: 'O Lord, let something remain' "
(1966: 219–20). Throughout his career Yeats, like Jakobson, attempted
to make some sense out of the "unpurged" images of experience, the
complexity, fury, and "mire of human veins" (1956: 243). Yet, unlike
Jakobson, he never does so without remembering that against the imperial "justice" of meaning and significance, everywhere apprehensible,
resonates the "reality" that occasions the need for justice, the "reality"
of death and non-sense. This is precisely what makes Yeats's modernism complex—what makes it "modernist" in the first place.

In other words, Jakobson's description of the functioning of Yeats's
poetry does not address the occasion for the particular rhetoric—the
complex *modernist* rhetoric—of this poem. In this way, the structural
linguistic analysis Jakobson offers presents a prolegomenon to a study
of Yeats through the years, rather than a full account of his significance.
In *Structuralist Poetics* Jonathan Culler has most thoroughly described
the limitations of linguistic analysis in criticism, limitations that arise
out of the kind of order it produces. The "process of progressive differentiation," Culler writes, "can produce an almost unlimited number
of distributional classes, and thus if one wishes to discover a pattern
of symmetry in a text, one can always produce a class whose members
will be appropriately arranged" (1974: 57).

This is the recurrent criticism of Jakobson's poetic analyses:
namely, that they disclaim the discrimination of the critic and claim
objectivity and verifiability in a rhetoric of passivity; that they make
the claim, impossible for criticism, of being unbiased and exhaustive,
of basing their procedure, and their resulting order, as Jakobson says
in "Linguistics and Poetics," solely on an "empirical linguistic criterion" (1960: 71). Jakobson has attempted to develop a system of analysis that eschews the discriminating judgment of its practitioners: it is
to this ostensibly objective procedure of analysis that René Wellek
responded when he said "Baudelaire's 'Les Chats' " tells us nothing
about "the aesthetic value of the poem" (Erlich 1973: 22); this is the
object of the qualification Nicolas Ruwet makes for linguistic analysis
when he says linguistics cannot determine the *poetic* pertinence of the
materials it uncovers (1970: 297); this is, finally, what Michael Riffaterre questions when he asks how structural linguistics can determine
what structures are "literarily active" in a text (1970: 191). Such "activity," I think, is a function of the persuasive power of the poem,
conditioned, as persuasion always is, by the resonations of its enunciatory situation.

Jakobson's very language, in his reading of Yeats and elsewhere,
emphasizes his objective, scientific posture. Recurrent constructions

in his prose imply the factuality of data over the judgment of the critic. Thus the Yeats study repeatedly offers passive constructions—"It is significant . . . ," "It is worth noting . . . ," "the contrasting images . . . were apparently related to the author's gradually maturing mystical doctrine later systematized in *A Vision*"—which emphasize "fact" over perception, binary opposition over the mind that apprehends the relationship, the passive revelation over the active assertion. To use Jakobson's terms, these constructions emphasize the "referential" aspect of the critical language he develops. "The readiness with which he accepts his interpretation," Culler writes, "suggests that he thinks it correct *because* it has been reached by linguistic analysis" (1974: 73)— because, that is, it has been reached by a definite, repeatable procedure of analysis (one not affected by its particular practitioner, as long as he or she is unbiased, attentive, exhaustive), a procedure he and Rudy call in the Yeats study "a detailed and objective comparison" (1977: 221).

Throughout his work Jakobson obscures the judgment of the critic—and often it has been a fine and discriminating judgment—amid the passive constructions of his analyses. Thus he speaks, in "The Grammar of Poetry," of "noticeable" similarities of elements of the poem (1968: 127) without suggesting that noticed similarities are often discovered, as the "same" is discovered, by passing over other possible relations between the linguistic elements; thus the very "noticing" of similarities involves a discriminating act. In the passage from *"Sorrow of Love" through the Years* which asserts that Yeats's "gradually maturing mystical doctrine" is "later systematized in *A Vision*," the text passively relates Yeats's images to *A Vision* while silently passing over the problems suggested by the (teleological) notion "gradually maturing" and by the phrase "*later* systematized in *A Vision*." Jakobson assiduously avoids first-person pronouns so that judgments are often borne by adverbs and adjectives—"dramatically," "strikingly," "patently," "astounding," "apparently"—and remain passive, seemingly descriptive, attached to linguistic "entities" (Jakobson also calls them "intrinsic constituents of the verbal code . . . and not at all 'grammarians' conveniences' " [1968: 123]) and arising, apparently unbiased, from the text itself. That is—and I shall return to this—Jakobson offers metaphors as description, and his passive observations often suggest, in their rhetoric of passivity, that their "subject" is the reader.

These remarks are true for what Erlich calls "the standard Jakobson analysis" (1973: 20), but what is most "striking"—a recurrent Jakobsonian adjective—about the study of Yeats's modernist texts is its attempt to add an apparent diachronic opposition to its intricate web

of binary oppositions, offering, as Jakobson and Rudy say, "the com-
prehensive investigation of the basic oppositions which determine the
relation, on the one hand, between the different parts of the poem in
each version and, on the other, between" the two versions themselves,
the 1892 version of "The Sorrow of Love" *(SL)* and its "altogether
new" version, as Yeats called it, of 1925. Such an addition raises the
issue of Yeats's extensive revisions of his poems, which he himself
notes in the epigraph to his 1906 *Collected Works.* Jakobson and Rudy
cite it, "When ever I remake a song, / It is myself that I remake" (1977:
217). Such "remaking"—"making it new"—is closely related to the
modernist project in general, to the problematic sense that the old is
dying without any new European order coming to birth. It is closely
related to the great discoveries in discourse theory that Todorov describes in relation to Jakobson: "just as people had to recognize finally
that Europe was not the center of the earth, nor the earth the center
of the universe, so, in the same movement of differentiation between
the self and others, the same struggle with infantile egocentrism, we
have to stop identifying language with the part of it we know the best"
(1982: 282–83). Yeats's struggle to remake himself in his poetry takes
its place in the great cultural struggles of the twentieth century—the
revolution in spirit Steiner describes—yet throughout Jakobson's study
of Yeats, in the analyses of the different parts of the poem as well as
in the analysis of the relations between the different versions themselves, only an "infantile," egocentric conception of *transformation*
remains, one in which the problematics of difference, identity, and
repetition are all seen as configurations of the "same."

The simple conception of transformation in Jakobson's study is all the
more striking because the problematics of transformation are central
to "The Sorrow of Love," just as they are central to Yeats's emerging
modernism. The poem depicts an enormous change in the world from
the first to the third stanza, paralleling the enormous change in Yeats's
poetic practice through the years. The most important ("striking")
difference between Yeats in the 1890s and Yeats after World War I—a
difference Forster articulates at the end of *A Passage to India*—can be
seen in the very opposition between passive and active voices in his
poetry itself. Yeats wrote to Florence Farr in 1906 that he had learned
he could move people by active personal power rather than "charm"
or "speaking beautifully": "even things seemingly beyond control," he
wrote, "answer strangely to what is within—I once cared only for images
about whose necks I could cast various 'chains of office' as it were. . . .

Now I do not want images at all, or chains of office, being content with the unruly soul" (1954: 469).

In this opposition of passive to active Yeats conceives of poetry in terms of the two conceptions of rhetoric I am presenting, the rhetoric of tropes and the rhetoric of persuasion. Moreover, he enacts in his poetry the opposition that Baudrillard elaborates between the scheme of the "productive" repetition of the same in the nineteenth century and the scheme of "simulation"—the complex transformation in which what I described as the "negative materialism" of the play of structures and values replaces the "positive materialism" of resistant *things* in the world. Yeats recurrently conceives this opposition in terms of the opposition of seeing (positive "things") to speaking (a differential code): the joy of creation, he wrote in 1907, "remains in the hands and in the tongue of the artist, but with his eyes he enters upon a submissive, sorrowful contemplation of the great irremediable things" (1968: 254–55). (I shall return to this opposition between eye and ear in Chapter 8.) In his *Autobiography* Yeats describes his work of the 1890s in terms reminiscent of both Jakobson's visual (i.e., geometrical) metaphor for linguistic analysis and Baudrillard's description of repetitive production: "image called up image in an endless procession, and I could not choose among them with any confidence" (Yeats 1965: 181).

The failure of choice, the lack of confidence, is the failure to achieve what Yeats called in 1909 "active virtue as distinguished from the passive acceptance of a current code" (1965: 317), the failure of passivity. Such passivity is the hallmark of Yeats's verse of the '90s, which, as Northrop Frye has written, "depends not on things, but the qualification of things, not on a pattern of images, but a background of attributes" (1947: 4). Frye's description of Yeats describes Jakobson's analysis as well (especially its use of "the qualification of things," of adjectives and adverbs to make its judgments, and its phenomenological configuration of background and foreground). Even what Leo Bersani says of Jakobson—that his close reading makes the poem entirely invisible—can also be applied to Yeats's early verse: like Jakobson's criticism, it makes the speaking voice all but disappear so that the poem (the analysis) seems to speak itself in a "dislocated" enunciation (Schleifer 1985).

In his early poems Yeats is articulating the situation of modernism—to which Jakobson as well as Eliot responds—the "body of death" that Mallarmé apprehends in the endless metonymic progression of the world. The only answer Yeats devised in the '90s is the apocalyptic vision with which these "endless" poems end, the recurring "fading" and disappearance of the world, "a departure from the world," Derrida says in "Force and Signification," "toward a place which is neither a *non-place* nor an *other* world, neither a utopia nor an alibi, the creation of 'a universe to be added to the universe' " (1978: 8). In Jakobson's terms, the early poems offer the "metaphoric substitution" of a visionary world that quite literally *substitutes* itself with apocalyptic vehemence for the world we live in. In terms of this study, this is a response to the decentering of Europe. Later, Yeats replaces this apocalyptic end to metonymy—his "rage / To end all things, to end / What my laborious life imagined, even / The half-imagined, the half-written page" (1956: 431), to end, that is, the very *metonymic* fact of endless preparation for what doesn't happen—with its subordination within the aesthetic order of his later poetry and the "structural" order of *A Vision*.

Like Jakobson, Yeats comes to respond to the crisis of Europe by conceiving of "universal" experience in terms of a synecdochical hierarchy. He does so by turning to Nietzsche's early theory of tragedy as the heroic achievement of self-realization within an image. For the early Nietzsche of *The Birth of Tragedy* as well as for the later Yeats, the fulfillment of tragedy is such an achievement, which takes place by means of synecdoche: the hero "discovers" himself in a *part* of his life that stands for the whole. "The arts are at their greatest," Yeats wrote in 1904, "when they seek for a life growing always more scornful of everything that is not itself and passing into its own fullness, as it were, ever more completely as all that is created out of the passing mode of society slips from it; and attaining that fullness, perfectly it may be—and from this is tragic joy and the perfectness of tragedy— when the world itself has slipped away in death" (1962: 169–70). Tragedy—at least within the aesthetic ideology of *The Birth of Tragedy*— achieves its strength by scorning contiguity in favor of synecdochical hierarchy. It sees everything as "part" of completeness, the very completeness of the phenomenal givenness of meaning that does not occur, as Bakhtin's "finalized structuredness" does, as a moment in an ongoing endless series. (Later Nietzsche developed his conception of the eternal recurrence of the same precisely in response to this early aestheticism, precisely to situate his meanings as *enunciated.*) In this way, tragedy, as Yeats and Nietzsche both suggest, is an active virtue that wrests from life "the best that art—perhaps that life—can give" (Yeats 1968: 239). In this, the very activity of art and life, like linguistic activity itself, is synecdochical.

But it is a strange synecdoche, a *modernist* synecdoche that is, at the same time, entirely *coded* and thus entirely metonymic, entirely inscribed by metonymy so that it is very different from the hierarchic structures that govern nineteenth-century Europe, positivism, and even Jakobson's linguistic readings. Within this conception of tragedy resonates the otherness of negative materiality that can in no way be diverted, brought back, reduced, and incorporated into idealistic aestheticism. Within the tragic image, in Heidegger's description, is "the terrible in the sense of the overpowering power which compels panic fear, true fear" (1959: 149). Such power—the negative materiality of otherness itself (Heidegger describes it as "the uncanny [*das Unheimliche*], as that which casts us out of the 'homely,' i.e., the customary, familiar, secure" [1959: 150–51])—can be actively resisted by the tragic hero, but that activity itself participates in the overpowering violence of otherness and always results in the otherness of death, which "is an end beyond all consummation, a limit beyond all limits." In other words, the tragic "activity" Yeats describes is neither infantile nor egocentric: it decenters the actor precisely by making him or her uncanny, Daimonic, not altogether a "self," inscribed by otherness and death. "This strange and alien [un-heimlich] thing," Heidegger continues, "that banishes us once and for all from everything in which we are at home is no particular event that must be named among others. . . . It is not only when he comes to die, but always and essentially that man is without issue in the face of death" (1959: 158). In this tragic "activity" (as in much of his writing) Heidegger participates in the modernist response to the "end" of Europe. So do Nietzsche and Yeats. (For a fuller discussion of Yeats's Nietzschean conception of tragedy, see Schleifer 1979; and for a brilliant discussion of Heidegger's participation in the complex modernism I am describing, see Derrida 1989.)

Such "activity" is and is not very different from the passivity of Jakobson's "scientific" modernism and the passivity of Yeats's early verse. It is a conscious (as opposed to unconscious) version of it, understood in a context in which, to paraphrase Jakobson, consciousness is always slightly unconscious and the unconscious always has a hint of consciousness. The burden of passivity in Yeats's early verse is borne by the ubiquitous *and.* In relation to this *and,* Jakobson's opposition between metaphor and metonymy in "Two Aspects of Language and Two Types of Aphasic Disturbances" is quite illuminating. In this study Jakobson describes two global forms of language impairment which correspond to the two global "axes" of language that Saussure described—the "paradigmatic" axis of "metaphoric" substitution (or "selection") of one element of language for another, and the "syntagmatic" axis of "metonymic" definition of linguistic elements based upon the combinations of contiguity. With these rhetorical terms Jakobson describes the great Saussurean principle of the *structures* of language based upon processes of contrast and combination (see Schleifer 1987: 1–7). In "Two Aspects of Language," Jakobson describes aphasics who suffer from "Similarity Disorder," those who cannot perform metaphoric substitutions yet are unimpaired in constructing and recognizing metonymic relations between contiguous elements of a sentence. Such people exhibit speech that is "merely reactive" (1956: 100): they tend to omit the subjects of sentences, cannot follow monologues, and replace specific nouns by general nouns, often preserving pronouns, pronominal adverbs, and connectives. Their speech, then, is governed by contiguity so that *knife,* as Jakobson notes, might be spoken *knife-and-fork* (1956: 102). However, such contiguity, as Jakobson says, "maintains the hierarchy of linguistic units" (1956: 109). That is, linguistic contiguity is more synecdochic than metonymic: for Jakobson, contiguity functions, as it does for Greimas, hypotactically rather than paratactically, as a hierarchy rather than a series.

In this analysis of the accidental impairments of language, however, Jakobson leaves out the occasion for the parataxis of Yeats's early modernist poetry, its attempt to escape the referentiality of language. That is, Yeats's early poetry aims at asserting the power of language over nature in a paratactic discourse of *ands*; to this end it presents, in Derrida's terms, "the materialism of the idea" in its "manifold play of a scene that, illustrating nothing—neither word nor deed—beyond itself, illustrates nothing" (1981: 208; Schleifer 1985: 392–93). Jakobson's omission can be seen in his comparison of the central stanza of "The Sorrow of Love" in its two versions.

1892

And then you came with those red mournful lips,
   And with you came the whole of the world's tears,
And all the sorrows of her labouring ships,
   And all the burden of her myriad years.

1925

A girl arose that had red mournful lips
And seemed the greatness of the world in tears,
Doomed like Odysseus and the labouring ships
And proud as Priam murdered with his peers;

Of this central stanza Jakobson and Rudy have much to say. As I. A. Richards said of Jakobson's and Jones's study of Shakespeare's Sonnet

129, there is "an immense concentration and convergence on giving clarity and salience to the central theme of the poem embodied in its central distich" (1970: 589). In this study, Jakobson and Rudy concentrate on the central stanza of the two versions of the poem, and everything they say attempts to conceive this stanza—and the paratactic lines of the early poem—as part of a whole.

Structural analysis is governed by such synecdochic conceptions, governed precisely by what Derrida describes as the ability of the *reserve* of discourse to "include within itself and anticipate all the figures of its beyond" (1978: 252). This is the means by which intelligence—including Jakobson's remarkable intelligence—resists nothingness and pure non-sense (including the resonation of nothingness in Yeats's early verse): by means of the structurality of structure, by means of synecdoche. Jakobson and Rudy describe the theme of "The Sorrow of Love" as related to "the irreconcilable divergences between the two levels" of the poem, "the upper sphere, which may be labeled the 'overground' level, . . . treated in the first three lines of each outer quatrain," and "the lower level . . . focused upon the four lines of the inner quatrain and in the fourth line of each outer quatrain" (1977: 220, 219). Jakobson and Rudy call the lower level "terrestrial" for the 1892 version and "human" for the 1925 version. To these structures Jakobson and Rudy apply "Yeats' creed as poet and creative visionary . . . namely his view of development as 'a temporal image of that which remains in itself,' to quote Hegel as cited by the poet [in *Vision*]" (1977: 220). Thus the poem exhibits the "continual conflict" between being and its opposite, encompassing "coexistence" and "succession" (1977: 220). In these terms "coexistence" and "succession" describe the metaphoric and metonymic axes of language, but they do so precisely because "succession," as in Hegel, is never quite accidental, never fully metonymic.

This description comes the closest of any in *Yeats' "Sorrow of Love" through the Years* to describing the theme of the poem, and it is both accurate and limited. It is accurate in that it does describe the conflict—celestial/terrestrial (1892); celestial/ human (1925)—of Yeats's poetic. After all, as late as 1930 Yeats wrote "Passion is conflict; consciousness is conflict" (1962: 331). Moreover, it even finds, as Jakobson claimed in "Linguistics and Poetics," the semantic value of rhymes—"sky," for instance, part of the "overground" rhyming with its opposite (earth's or man's) "cry" (underground) (1977: 223). In fact, one of the most useful aspects of Jakobson's poetic analyses is their marshaling of thematically and poetically significant structures, even "down" to the phonological level of poetry. In the Yeats study Jakobson and Rudy demonstrate the relation of "tenor" to "vehicle" in ways that substantiate Jakobson's larger claim about the nature of poetry: "the poetic function projects the principle of equivalence from the axis of selection into the axis of combination" (1960: 71). Thus they show that the poem in both versions reveals unexpected, striking symmetries, structures, and salient contrasts: 1925: $_1$*girl* is tied to $_2$*greatness* /gr/ *of the world* /rl/; 1892: II $_2$*world* is tied to I $_2$*full round* /lr/ and is "echoed by /rl/ in II $_3$*her lab(ou)ring*" (1977: 236).

Moreover, in showing how the grammatical categories of the early version of the poem present but do not emphasize the opposition of the stanzas—I and III (overground) against II (underground)—the authors indicate the complex metonymic play of identity and difference to which the poem and Yeats's own modernism respond. Charles Rosen has asserted that Jakobson's readings "rarely . . . substantially affect or alter" more traditional readings of verse (Erlich 1973: 26), yet the informed attention he brings to linguistic details of the poem forces his reader to recognize the poetic function of much that he or she was unaware of. In the case of Yeats, it forces the reader to see in Yeats's own mature description of his poetic—that of conflict, between man and his Daimon, emotion and its expression, the hero and his world—a description of the "unconscious" (Jakobson calls it "subliminal") workings of his early verse. As Yeats himself said, his early poetry was governed by its "unconscious drama" (1965: 69). Discourse itself is the locus of the play of identity and difference, of metaphor and metonymy, of the synchronic and the diachronic. Jakobson and Rudy, by thematizing the structures of "The Sorrow of Love" and at the same time reading it "through the years," direct attention to this profound poetic and critical fact. In the wealth of their linguistic observations they offer a new context—a "translation"—that simultaneously alters and reinforces traditional readings of Yeats, playing the same identity and difference the analysis discovers within Yeats's text(s) against critical readings.

Still, Jakobson's and Rudy's description of the poem also reveals the limits of "scientific" structuralism and Yeats's own late synecdochical aestheticism: what they call the "irreconcilable divergences" within and between the two poems are, in fact, "reconciled" in their hierarchical reading, just as what Yeats calls the "unconscious drama" of his poetry apparently achieves conscious articulation in Yeats's own autobiographical reading of his poetry. Neither Jakobson nor apparently Yeats recognizes the possibility of the radical *otherness* of the unconscious, the possibility that the "meaningful whole" of discourse will not be achieved or "finalized," that, in Roland Barthes' terms, "the origin of a spoken discourse does not exhaust that discourse; once set off, it is beset by a thousand adventures, its origin becomes blurred, all its effects are not in its cause" (1977: 209). Specifically in relation to Jakobson's analysis of Yeats, as the acknowledged and unacknowledged references to Yeats's prose suggest, the study bases it reading on the "mature" poem, the *later* systematization of *A Vision*. That is, offering a naive sense of diachronic development, the study reduces the "equivalence" of the two versions to subordination and reads the poem's history as unproblematic development, as "maturing" and "disclosure," a movement from part to whole.

Doing this, the analysis fails to explore the most striking binary opposition it presents, that between the "terrestrial" center of the 1892 version and the "human" center of the later version, the heroine of the inner 1925 quatrain who "is identified—through a chain of similes (II $_2$*seemed,* $_3$*like,* $_4$*as*)—with the tragic and heroic human world" (1977: 220). Here is the opposition of an almost Heideggerian chthonic power to human power, "you" to "A girl," a passive structure of *ands* (a structure of coordination) to that of equational connectives (a structure of subordination) (1977: 232). Thomas Parkinson says the later version gives "the impression of an active man speaking" (1951: 176), and George Russell noted that "the later selfconscious artist could not let the earlier halfconscious artist be" (cited in Parkinson 1951: 131). As we have seen, Yeats himself in the *Autobiography* distinguishes his early from his later work in terms of an opposition of unconscious to conscious drama—an opposition that confronts passivity and activity.

Jakobson and Rudy never explore this opposition, because despite their claim of describing "the basic oppositions which determine the relation" between the two versions of the poem, they never take the 1892 version as *opposite*—that is, as fully *other* than—the later poem. In a 1939 phonological study Jakobson described two global types of opposition: one, "oppositions of *contradictory* terms, is a relationship between the presence and absence of an identical element"; a second, "oppositions of *contrary* terms, is a relationship between two elements 'which are a part of the same genus and which differ the most from one another . . .'" (1939: 273; see Schleifer 1987: 23–30). This topology leaves out the possibility of a *nonreductive, nonsynecdochical* opposition, the opposition of otherness. It leaves out the *material,* nonsensical aspect of discourse: the fact that its elements are opposed not only to their contrary elements or to their own specific absence, but also to absence in general, to nothingness itself, to the always present possibility of non-existence: death. That is, it leaves out the laughter

Derrida describes breaching the "reserve" of meaning or the "tendency" dictated by mourning—itself an effect of a wholly "other" sense of temporality—"to accept incomprehension, to leave a place for it, and to enumerate coldly, almost like death itself, those modes of language which, in short, deny the whole rhetoricity of the true" (1986: 31).

Greimas describes such a material opposition in his (negative) description of narrative as "neither pure contiguity nor a logical implication" (1983: 244), and Barthes—at least after passing through the structural modernism of Lévi-Strauss, Jakobson, and Greimas—conceives of reading as the "pure contiguity" of pure diachrony. But Jakobson, at the extreme of structuralism, conceives of narrative temporality as the "purity" of "logical implication." To do this, he conceives of temporal oppositions as "contrary," which is to say he apprehends the logical organization of diachronic data in terms of their "spatial form," a kind of axis on which events can be placed. Yet instead of such a "logical" conception, the study of Yeats unwittingly offers a "contradictory" relationship between the versions of the poem in which the later version presents elements—"consciousness," "disclosures," "mature" ideas—absent in the early version. In this way the study, seemingly "unconsciously," complicates (without abandoning) its binary logic and subordinates the early version to the later. Doing so, it avoids the very *terror* of modernism, the terror Yeats felt, perhaps unconsciously, in the plenitude, the meaningless material fullness of images following one another in an endless procession of his early verse. It domesticates metonymy to synecdoche.

The very rhetorical structure of Jakobson's analysis betrays the occasion of Yeats's modernist rhetoric by "unconsciously" subordinating the part to the whole, the periphery to the center, the beginning to the end. Each section of the Yeats study—sections are devoted to linguistic categories such as "Finite Verbs," "Nouns," "Connective," "Prenominal Attributes," and so forth—examines *first* the 1925 version, then the earlier one, *first* the outer stanzas, then the inner one. And for all the authors' claims of not preferring one version to the other, their choice of Yeats's later writing—*A Vision* (1925; 1938), *Dramatis Personae* (1935), "The Phases of the Moon" (1919)—as a final context for the poem indicates their preference. Jakobson's very procedure suggests that discourse, in fact, contains an immaterial essence which, as Kenneth Burke says, is revealed in the *ends* of discourse. Thus Jakobson and Rudy write that the 1925 version, "displays an astounding symmetry in the distribution of the major grammatical categories among the three quatrains, a symmetry which is either lacking or muted in the early version. It may indeed be considered a persuasive example of the 'geometrical symbolism' which was so vital a force both in the poet's subliminal imagery and in his abstract thought" (1977: 239). The spatial metaphor of geometry—one that Jakobson uses recurrently to examine the relationship between the functions of grammar in poetry and of relational geometry in painting (1968: 132)—reveals the underlying assumption that balance, equivalence, and ultimately knowledge (as opposed to "power" in Yeats's own opposition) are preferred poetic values.

The metaphor taken from *A Vision* is revealing in other ways as well, for it underlines Jakobson's recurrent recourse to spatial metaphors in describing Yeats's poem. The use of these metaphors suggests a radical criticism of Jakobson's definition of the poetic function as a projection of the principle of equivalence from the axis of selection to that of combination. Of the 1892 poem the authors write, "Although the inner quatrain is composed like the outer quatrains, of coordinated subjects with a joint predicate, . . . in the outer quatrains the predicate is placed after the subject, whereas in the inner it appears before them. . . . In terms of *A Vision,* 'these pairs of opposites [subject and predicate] whirl in contrary directions.' The same may be said of the distinctive criterion for the opposition of inner versus outer quatrains in *SL* 1925" (1977: 233; brackets in original). In another instance, describing the adverbs of the 1892 poem, "obliterated in *SL* 1925," the authors notice the later version is "in agreement with *A Vision,* 'every image is separate from every other, for if image were linked to image, the soul would awake from its immovable trance' " (1977: 243). In these figures the study uses and gives priority to *spatial* tropes, tropes that utilize the elements of contiguity—*linked* images, the complementary *movement* of whirling pairs. Yet situated in the center of these metonymic tropes is the "immovable soul," the center around which subject and object whirl; in the center is *metaphor,* both the "soul" and the unspoken metaphor of "center" itself. Thus Jakobson's attempt to give clarity and salience to the central distich of the poem, to "the border between the two halves of the poem" (1977: 241–42), is one of the least persuasive aspects of his analyses here and elsewhere: categories of symmetry and balance break down before the need to find a synecdochic "center."

This is why Jakobson can assert that "in poetry, where similarity is superinduced upon contiguity, any metonymy is slightly metaphoric and any metaphor has a metonymic tint" (1960: 85). In poetry, as in discourse, where meaning is everywhere, both metonymy and metaphor are preserved within the reserve of synecdoche: both are "parts" of the "whole" of meaning. For this reason the figures of the study are not centered and grounded in metaphor; rather, like Yeats's own later modernist practice, they are grounded in the synecdochic play between metaphor and metonymy: the play between the metonymic "name" of linguistic analysis, "geometrical symbolism," which passively allows itself geometrical representations of the verse pattern and, more generally, of language itself; and its metaphoric "name," which actively substitutes an *equivalence* for poetry by attributing animate qualities to language: "*words obey [the poet's] call*" (1977: 249). In the first instance, the poet (and critic) passively respond to the geometry of language, to its "geometric symbolism," which can be taken as a metaphorical substitution for language or its metonymic attribute (in Jakobson's synecdochical understanding of metonymy, a part for the whole). In the second instance, the poet (and critic) actively produce the response of language, now conceived alternatively in terms of its "animate" attributes (part for the whole) or as a speaking (responding) subject. In this study, then, metonymy and metaphor, passive succession and active selection, are brought together by means of synecdoche.

They are brought together by synecdoche, but the complex division of rhetoric as trope and rhetoric as persuasion that they embody remain metonymically juxtaposed. Which is projected onto which? Which, to follow Hillis Miller, is figure, which is ground? Miller suggests that, given the radically figural nature of language—its *rhetorical* nature— there is no ground for choosing (1976: 17; see Miller 1985), yet Jakobson and Rudy give priority to metaphor (conceived figuratively as kinds of "centers"), the *disclosed* metaphors of *A Vision*, the *projected* metaphors of poetry. They do so silently, in passive assertions that obscure the choice and judgment involved: the recurrent "in terms of *A Vision*" gives priority to and seemingly literalizes the terms—the rhetoric—of *A Vision*, the spatial geometrical tropes of *its* structural analysis.

Toward the end of their study, Jakobson and Rudy finally read "The Sorrow of Love" against the phases of the moon, "translating" the poem into the "system of signs" of *A Vision*. For the first time *A Vision* becomes primary, read "in terms of *SL* 1925" (1977: 246). They suggest that in the revision of the first stanza "The brilliant moon . . . Had blotted out man's image and his cry" reveals phase 14 of Yeats's lunar cycle, and that in the last stanza "A climbing moon . . . Could but compose man's image and his cry" reveals lunar phase 16. The middle stanza, they claim, has the privileged position of phase 15, "a phase of complete beauty" (1977: 245–47). "The reference to Troy" in the central stanza, the authors write, "later openly disclosed in *SL*

1925, remains rather obscure in the early version" (1977: 247). This "open disclosure" discloses the authors' use of Yeats's own late definition of development, "a temporal image of that which remains in itself." Such a definition seems hardly developmental, only illusorily "temporal," and inadequate to a discussion of Yeats's complex modernist rhetoric, what he calls his self-transformation through the years. In other words, what the authors call the "antithetical struggle and harmonious complementarity" of the two versions (1977: 220) becomes a synecdochical binary structure completing one version by the other.

Jakobson and Rudy fail to oppose the metonymy of the 1892 stanza II to the metaphoric equivalence of the 1925 stanza because they fail to *situate* Yeats's poem as an enunciation that is a function of power as much as of knowledge, and to take into account its nature as a response to something, a rhetorical counter-word. They fail to do so because they overlook Yeats's modernism altogether, his historically situated counter-word to death. For Jakobson, Yeats becomes simply one poet in a series—Shakespeare, Marvell, Poe, Baudelaire, Pushkin, etc.—whose poetry can be analyzed simply as a (synecdochic) example of discourse in general. Moreover, Jakobson and Rudy fail to situate Yeats's modern sense of death in the same way that Heidegger fails to situate modern death in describing the tragic and "essential" homelessness of humanity. In this, Yeats's case is particularly instructive. His modernist poetry never fully articulates *its* homelessness: namely, the destruction of Protestant Ireland at the end of the nineteenth century, a microcosm of the subsequent "end" of European hegemonic power. Yeats's career, as Malcolm Brown has persuasively argued, is a reaction to a felt sense of the loss of the privileged tradition of Protestant rule in Ireland, a tradition that was not one of "high laughter, loveliness and ease" which Yeats describes in an early poem lamenting the loss of Lady Gregory's estate (and which describes as well the "written speech" that is the object of Jakobson's poetic analyses), nor one of "tragic gaiety" (in Nietzsche's term, which Yeats borrowed). Rather, as Brown describes it, the Irish gentry that infatuated Yeats "will be remembered instead for its cheerful non-Yeatsian Benthamite good sense, since it provides history with its solitary example of a social class that took solid money in exchange for its privileges and went away quietly" (1972: 300). In this way Yeats's modernism, like Jakobson's structuralism, attempts to erase the specific enunciatory situation of discourse from its utterances (Schleifer 1985, 1990; see also Kenner 1973a).

Without situating Yeats's poetry as a modernist *enunciation,* Jakobson and Rudy cannot adequately (*metonymically*) oppose the chthonic power that Yeats articulates to human knowledge. Such power is the "furious" power of death, earthly, material power, historical power that is always plural, always a material plurality, always overwhelming. Such furious power enunciates itself as the "noisiness" of the first stanza of both versions of Yeats's "Sorrow of Love," *material* noise that "hides" *(SL* 1892) and "blots out" *(SL* 1925) meaning. Such noisiness *occasions* Yeats's discourse, the wheels and gyres of *his* "structuralist" account of existence in *A Vision,* and the subtler discourse of his constant attempt to "remake" himself and achieve that future which, he says in his *Autobiography,* "never happens" (1965: 71). In Yeats the division between chthonic power and human meaning—between the power of persuasive rhetoric and the "knowledge" (of the "same") that tropological rhetoric creates—situates and enunciates modernism itself.

More specifically, Yeats's development through the years is his attempts to refashion the chthonic power of the "immortal Moods" of his early poetry, before which the poet passively stands, into the "masks" of the later poetry, the spoken similes of the 1925 poem. By the time of the 1925 version of "The Sorrow of Love," Yeats had abandoned the term "moods"—Jakobson and Rudy quote Yeats's description of their passive nature as "disembodied powers, whose footsteps over our hearts we call emotions" (1977: 234)—and adopted (again from Nietzsche) an almost completely different term, "masks." Yeats's masks, like the "impersonality" of Eliot and Pound, aestheticize experience in the face of the breakdown of cultural power. Like Nietzsche's, they are ambiguously metonymical: each mask is also "face" because, as the African answered the missionary, in a world of meaning, in an economy of "reserve," "face is everywhere." As such they are slightly, resonatingly synecdochic. Such resonations, however, like those in the early verse, "illustrate" nothing. Instead, they attempt to remake disembodied powers into active human *powers*—not *knowledge*—to offer a situated response to a world which, in its endless noise, hides and blots out meaning and presents, instead, *incomprehensible* metonymic plenitude, endless rhetoric. With his masks Yeats attempted to fashion what he later calls the Daimon with *its* human/inhuman face, what Jean-François Lyotard calls the "faceless figure" of art (1977: 397; see Schleifer 1979).

To "translate" this description into the linguistic context Jakobson and Rudy offer, Yeats's development through the years is marked by the translation of the pronoun "you" of the early poem "with [its] inherent reference to context" into a proper noun ("Helen" who stands behind "A girl"), "the main subordinating agent of the sentence" (1956: 101). It is the simple transformation of "the whimsical metathetic confrontation of the two sociative prepositions *with* ... and ... the series of summarizing totalizers ... in the early version" into "the system of metaphors underlying the inner quatrain of *SL* 1925" (1977: 221). This is the self-conscious project of structuralism, embodied in its substantifying "geometrical" rhetoric, just as it is the unconscious project of formalism: namely, to replace linguistic activity with linguistic agents, metonymy with metaphor (and the "unconscious" metaphor, synecdoche), the other with the same.

The translation of deathly chthonic power into human power, of a faceless face (like the one the African presents to the missionary) to mask, is more than such "replacement," however, even if Yeats—and especially his own species of structuralism in *A Vision*—is closest of all the modernists to Jakobson's comic vision. Synecdoche is the figure of comedy, just as metonymy, as I have argued elsewhere, is the figure for tragedy (see Schleifer and Velie 1987). Synecdoche erases the *other* from experience; it conditions wholeness and the same. In this way the Jakobsonian priority of metaphor—his teleological argument that the later poem *discloses* the metaphor—indicates yet refuses to acknowledge the strength of Yeats's tragic vision of otherness, nothingness, and non-sense, the radical opposition of word and counter-word. Paul de Man describes this opposition in describing the way "Among School Children" "makes synecdoche into the most seductive of all metaphors," but then he also presents the opposite possibility, that sign and meaning are in an accidental metonymic relationship in which "dancer and the dance are not the same" (1979: 11–12). In this, the opposition between synecdoche and metonymy, like the opposition between the two version of "The Sorrow of Love," is not reducible, even when the binary form it takes, like the relationship between European and aborigine, invites the synthesis of one to the other.

The aesthetic synthesis and stasis that so many of Yeats's later poems present in a world that seems to offer neither is answered by the very fact of his revisions, the word and counter-word of versions of "The Sorrow of Love." In 1892 the human ("you") reveals itself, passively, to be chthonic power, her tears, sorrows, years, of the dark underground itself. In the later version history "arises" with the human, not only with the girl, but also with the voice that can create an aesthetic order and subordination in the world of things. Both versions together present, through the years, the irreducible complicity of co-existence and succession, being and becoming, activity and passivity.

They present what Yeats called late in life the "truth" and "counter-truth" of all that he did (1962: 307). This complicity emphasizes, to the point of making problematic, the notion of "transformation" in Yeats's work—the "translation" that Jakobson sees as the essence of meaning itself.

To define meaning as translation, as Jakobson does, is as radically metonymic as Derrida's "definition" of linguistic dissemination: it displaces essence, putting it outside, before or after. Taken far enough, to the lengths that dialogic play itself takes "translation," it deconstructs essence, identity, and presence itself, just as death destroys these things. Yeats recognized this when he understood that vision arises in terror. We gaze at poets like Villon and Dante "in awe," he wrote in his *Autobiography,* "because we gaze not at a work of art, but at the re-creation of the man through that art, the birth of a new species of man, and, it may even seem that the hairs of our heads stand up, because that birth, that re-creation, is from terror" (1965: 183). Such a recognition motivated Yeats's complaint of the "unconscious drama" of his early verse, what he finally understood, I think, as the "easiness" and distortion of the apocalyptic substitution of another world for our seemingly endless world, for the seemingly endless play of rhetoric.

Recognized or not, rhetoric creates the drama of our lives; it creates, as Jakobson has shown, the drama of addresser and addressee, of what Yeats calls truth and counter-truth. The counter-truth of Jakobson's and Rudy's study of Yeats through the years and, more generally, of Jakobson's "scientific" criticism is the fact that it reads temporally *different* enunciations of the "same" poem as structural *opposites,* at times giving priority to one over the other through acts of the very discriminating judgment his science overtly denies. The counter-truth to their comedy of universal meaning—to the "justice" by which Yeats described the "miracle" of meaning which necessarily overwhelms whoever is "in the midst of it" (1966: 25), in the same way, finally, that Jakobson's discriminating intelligence overwhelms us in his readings of poetry—is the faceless "tragedy" of meaningless materiality, the furious terror in the "reality" that Yeats opposes to "justice" and that Jakobson does not take into account.

The study of Yeats, like all of Jakobson's "scientific" linguistic criticism, is not unbiased. Neither is it total—the play of truth and counter-truth, the drama of rhetoric, goes endlessly on—but this work resonates with the very modernism it studies, and it opens and suggests fruitful ways of understanding Yeats and modernist literature. In these terms, the failure of this "scientific" criticism is the failure of consciousness in Yeats's sense of the term; it is the failure to answer the "justice" of a system—the spatial geometry of Jakobson's reading—with the modern "reality" of the play of translations, the surface play of voices, the terror of material plenitude. Jakobson's linguistic criticism discriminates among translations and voices, but it does so unconsciously, in a rhetoric of passivity that fails to acknowledge its own material situation. Rhetoric is the act of persuasion and the language of value; while all language carries value—all language is rhetorical—it does so in the face of terror and futurelessness that Yeats acknowledges in ways that Jakobson does not.

Of all the writers I treat in this book, Jakobson is the most committed to "knowledge" in its common sense, yet he does not *acknowledge* the power embedded in knowledge as Yeats, for all his evasions, does—the Nietzschean sense of knowledge that the other, "postmodern" figures I examine in the following chapters do acknowledge to one extent or another. For this reason, I think, he is also the least interested in the play between contemporary criticism and modernism, least interested in the *enunciation* of modernism and the relationship between mortality and meaning. Modernism itself is not a concern of his criticism. For Jakobson, meaning, like the Africans' faces, is everywhere, so there is no need to situate it as a response to the homelessness, the terror, and the standing chill of death that Yeats and modernism and postmodernism more generally enunciate.

6

The Rhetoric of Textuality

Roland Barthes and the Discomfort of Writing

To Gudrun this day was full of a promise like spring. She felt an approaching release, a new fountain of life rising up in her. It gave her pleasure to dawdle through her packing, it gave her pleasure to dip into books, to try on her different garments, to look at herself in the glass. She felt a new lease of life was come upon her, and she was happy like a child, very attractive and beautiful to everybody, with her soft, luxuriant figure, and her happiness. Yet underneath was death itself.

—D. H. Lawrence, *Women in Love*

This chapter will examine the conception of textuality in the work of Roland Barthes as it relates to literary studies. Very different from the scientific criticism of Roman Jakobson, this conception is a function of the radically *metonymic* sense of the functioning of language in Barthes. It is a sense, as he says in a late essay on Proust, of the power of metonymic *disorder* in discourse. "Although Proust speaks on one occasion," Barthes notes, "of the 'depths of our unconscious,' this sleep has nothing Freudian about it; . . . it is constituted by the depths of consciousness *as disorder*." Thus, he goes on, the Proustian episode is "held suspended in a sort of grammatical scandal: to say 'I'm asleep' is in effect, literally, as impossible as to say 'I'm dead'; writing is precisely that activity which tampers with language—the impossibilities of language—to the advantage of discourse" (1986: 280). This "tampering" with language is the rhetoric of "textuality" that Barthes examines and produces, and it is linked in a powerful way with the possibilities that language and discourse afford of articulating and conceiving of death as well as sleep—and of articulating the material "pleasures" of the text that Barthes, like D. H. Lawrence, attempts to circumscribe in his language. As Barthes says elsewhere, the enunciation "I'm dead," in its transformation of the metaphorical into the literal, "is impossible": "the enunciation 'I am dead' is literally foreclosed (whereas 'I sleep' remained literally possible in the field of hypnotic sleep). It is, then," Barthes concludes, "if you like, a scandal of language which is in question" (1981b: 153). For Barthes, it is a scandal precisely because he is committed, above all, to intelligibility, to sense (as opposed to non-sense), to understanding.

Unlike Lawrence, Barthes has an important commitment to the *articulation* of material pleasure, to what he calls in the late Proust essay "the uniformly intellectual nature of my previous writing (even if a number of fictive elements taint their rigor)" (1986: 289). Like Jakobson, then, Barthes is a kind of intellectual hero, one with (for most of his life) an overriding faith in explanation and clarity (see Tavor Bannet 1989: 66–67), even when, unlike Jakobson, he focuses on the metonymic special case, rather than the synecdochical representative case. In this late essay Barthes approvingly cites Nietzsche's assertion that "we must reduce the universe to crumbs, lose respect for the whole" (1986: 282), and throughout his work he pursues the metonymic enunciations of discourse. Yet in this *enunciatory* task—in what he calls its "radical materialism" (1975: 64)—Barthes, like Jakobson, rarely addresses the nothingness and non-sense of death in the ways modernism does, as in the constant resonation of material mortality in Lawrence's metonymic discourse.

Rather than such resonation, Barthes describes the "unexpected flash which sometimes crosses" the field of perception (1981: 94–95). This "flash" is, as he calls it here in *Camera Lucida,* the unique detail or *punctum* of a photograph (as opposed to the coded meaning of its *studium*) which "rises from the scene, shoots out of it like an arrow, and pierces me." This "accident which pricks me (but also bruises me, is poignant to me)" (1981: 26–27) does not reveal or present nothingness and terror; rather, in its momentary "flash" it is a kind of aesthetic intelligibility, revelation itself, which arouses, above all, sympathy, connection, "pity." "In the love stirred by Photography (by certain photographs)," he concludes, "another music is heard, its name oddly old-fashioned: Pity" (1981: 116).

Still, if Jakobson's discourse attempts to discover the invariants among the variations of enunciation, that which remains the same amid the incessant random scatterings of discursive events, then Barthes' is the opposite task: he attempts to discover the meanings of scatterings, to recuperate significance and pleasure in the material multiplicity of language, to rejoin what Jakobson never feels to be sundered, metonymy and synecdoche. In this he, more than Jakobson, is sensitively *aware* (in the sense of the physical, material "awareness" that Lawrence circumscribes in his discourse) of the sheer power of modernist rhetoric. He describes and defines the physical awareness of what Proust calls the "pinnacle of the particular" of enunciation in the figure of *"writing aloud"* with which he ends *The Pleasure of the Text*. "*Writing aloud*," Barthes says, "is not phonological but phonetic; its aim is not the clarity of messages, the theatre of emotions; what it searches for (in a perspective of bliss) are the pulsional incidents, the language lined with flesh, a text where we can hear the grain of the throat, the patina of consonants, the voluptuousness of vowels, a whole carnal stereophony: the articulation of the body, of the tongue, not that of meaning, of language" (1975: 66–67). What he seeks, then, is a kind of *materialism* of the sign, yet one in which the significatory force of the sign is not lost in its materiality. He seeks, as Jacques Derrida says of his work, to allow the unique detail or event of the *punctum* to lend itself to metonymy conceived of as "a system of substitutions"—to let the "absolutely other" compose "with the same"—so that "if the photograph bespeaks the unique death, the death of the unique, this death repeats itself immediately, as such, and is itself elsewhere" (1988: 285).

In other words, if Jakobson—who was, after all, in an important way Barthes' teacher—attempts to recover a text's "meaning" and its meaning-effects and to account for the existence of the phenomenal "effects" of meaning we experience, Barthes' task is different. Rather than recovering intelligible meaning, he attempts to recover meaningfulness as an active force in human affairs. "A literary work," he writes,

> is a very special semantic system, whose goal is to put "meaning" in the world, but not "a meaning"; the work, at least the work which ordinarily accedes to critical scrutiny—and this is perhaps a definition of "good" literature—the work is never entirely nonsignifying (mysterious or "inspired"), and never entirely clear; it is, one may say, a *suspended* meaning. . . . This disappointment of meaning explains . . . why the literary work has so much power to ask the world questions (undermining the assured meanings which ideologies, beliefs, and common sense seem to possess), yet without ever answering them. . . . (1972: 259)

Questions without answers constitute the form of Barthes' discourse, what he calls, describing Flaubert, "an irony impregnated with uncertainty [that] achieves a salutary discomfort of writing" which is "the very being of writing (the meaning of the labor which constitutes it)," namely, "to keep the question *Who is speaking?* from ever being answered" (1974: 140). What Barthes does in his literary studies is to marshal the *power* of enunciation, its essential *interpersonal* power embodied in questions without answers, rather than to account for the "givenness" of texts themselves. In his terms, he explores "texts-as-reading" rather than "authorial" texts. This is a closely *enunciatory* task: Barthes does not attempt to reconstitute either reader or writer; rather, he attempts to reconstitute reading as an activity (1986: 30, 31).

Such a reconstitution is what he calls the "third meaning" of discursive activity, an obtuse meaning beyond the communicative and symbolic meanings Jakobson is concerned with. "By contrast with the first two levels, communication and signification," Barthes writes, "this third level—even if the reading of it is still hazardous—is that of *signifiance,* a word which has the advantage of referring to the field of the signifier (and not of signification) and of linking up with, via the path opened by Julia Kristeva who proposed the term, a semiotics of the text" (1977: 54). Elsewhere Barthes writes that

> when the text is read (or written) as a mobile play of signifiers
> [*signifiants*], with no possible reference to one or several fixed
> signifieds, it becomes necessary to distinguish carefully be-
> tween signification, which belongs to the level of the product,
> of the statement [*énoncé*], of communication, and the signi-
> fying work, which belongs to the level of production, enunci-
> ation, symbolisation: it is this work that we call 'signifi-
> ance.' . . . 'Signifiance,' unlike signification, cannot be reduced
> to communication, to representation, to expression: it puts the
> (writing or reading) subject into the text, not as a projection
> . . . but as a 'loss'; . . . whence its identification with 'jouiss-
> ance': it is through the concept of 'signifiance' that the text
> becomes erotic. . . . (1981a: 37–38)

In this definition, however, *signifiance*—the activity of signification, of rhetorical "play," the elemental *production* of meaning—remains within the reserve of meaning, of signification; it remains, as Barthes says here, an effective concept. Here Barthes inscribes the materiality of language within discourse, but that material enunciation still maintains itself within the reserved economy of signification: this metonymy, like that of Jakobson, includes (or in included within) the synecdochical economy of meaning-effects.

Still, in this there is a certain obscurity (obtuseness), as Greimas as well as Barthes notes, a "discomfort" of meaning; in this there is the material non-sense of pleasure that inhabits discourse, what Barthes calls variously the "grain of the voice" and the "rustle" of language. But there is also—though it seems Barthes fails to notice or focus upon this until near the end of his life—the materiality of mortality that governs, after all, the scatterings of enunciation, the *events* of pleasure. "The 'middle of life,' " he wrote in 1978, "is perhaps never anything but the moment when you discover that death is real, and no longer merely dreadful. Journeying thus, there occurs all of a sudden this obvious situation: on the one hand, I no longer have time to try several lives: I must choose my last life, my new life, *Vita Nuova . . .* ; on the other hand, I must emerge from that shadowy state (medieval theory called it *acedie)* to which the attrition of repeated tasks and mourning dispose me" (1986: 286). In the middle of life—a middle that, sadly, was closer to the end of his life two years later—Barthes discovered that however random the remarkable changes of his intellectual life were, they were banal since changing "doctrine, theory, philosophy, method, belief" was simply the nature of intelligence, "the very pulsion of the intelligence, once it is attentive to the world's surprises" (1986: 286). Moreover, he learned that however random the punctuation of events was, in order to produce significance it was necessary to set some sort of limit to the scattering such punctuation effects.

Barthes' own career, beginning with the high structuralism of *Elements of Semiology,* down to the deconstructive multiple "structurations" of *S/Z,* to the fragmentary and seemingly arbitrary musings of *The Pleasure of the Text* and *A Lover's Discourse,* seems, indeed, to be "several lives." But what is striking in these "lives" (until the "middle" of his life, marked by the death of his mother described in *Camera Lucida)* is that, like Jakobson, they are rarely informed by a sense of death or mortality, rarely focused on the nothingness and pure non-sense of a materiality beyond meaning-effects (including the subliminal meaning-effects of pleasure). Even in his study of the Marquis de Sade in *Sade/Fourier/Loyola,* death is rarely discussed, rarely circumscribed as a "third meaning"; when it is discussed, it is as an element of semiology. Barthes and Jakobson, then, both share a kind of faithfulness in intelligibility, an attempt to recuperate experience to the human and the comprehensible. For Jakobson, that experience is intelligible itself—susceptible to the accountings that the discovery of the "same" of invariants allows. For Barthes, that experience can be obscure and obscurely powerful, but, as in Jakobson's view, it remains always within an economy of textuality, a reserve of the humanly meaningful (just as "pity" remains within the reserve of the humanly meaningful).

This chapter will focus on the economy of textuality that Barthes delimits—the economy of his enunciation. Such an economy complements the economy of scientific intelligibility that governs Jakobson's criticism, in the same way that the enunciatory rhetoric of power complements the tropological rhetoric of the same. I need to say here, however, that Barthes' textual economy is self-consciously rhetorical; it subscribes to the surface—the *aesthetic* surface—of the experience of intelligibility that in its very "superficiality" obscures the clarity and vision of Jakobson's scientific "intelligence." Such obscurity is an important part of Barthes' textual aesthetic. There is obscurity that grows out of imprecision of thought or language, a lack of an "ear" for language or an "eye" for pertinence; but these imprecisions are, for Barthes at least, accidental and trivial. (They are so even if, as I shall argue in the next chapter, in the work of Jacques Lacan such enunciatory "slips" carry with them a power beyond intelligence that is not as easily recuperated as meaning—even as a "third meaning"—as Barthes' work suggests.) Another kind of obscurantism, one close to Jakobson's rhetoric of passivity, is more serious because it stems from a blind adherence to unquestioned assumptions about the nature of clarity, reason, and precision itself. Derrida addresses this kind of obscurity when he argues that "the principle of reason may have obscurantist and nihilistic effects. They can be seen more or less everywhere," he writes, "in Europe and America among those who believe they are defending philosophy, literature and the humanities against these new modes of *affirmation,* and new ways of taking responsibility" (1983: 15). Such obscurity is part of the passive and seeming unconscious affirmations—the *nonresponsible* affirmations—inhabiting Jakobson's "scientific" criticism which Barthes passed through in his varied career.

In examining Barthes' rhetoric of textuality, I want to address neither the first of these obscurities nor, except peripherally, the second. Rather, I shall examine the obscurity of textuality itself. Barthes, more than any other critic, has made this the object of his writing and, finally, the shaping power of his intelligence. This brand of obscurity seems to me closely linked with literature and its simultaneously tactical and tactile rhetorical strategies—its textual strategies—*intending* to invigorate the inertias of our common life. "Language," George Steiner notes in *After Babel,* "articulates sense; it is intended to externalize and communicate meaning. In what ways can it fail to do so, and which of these ways can, possibly, be construed as intentional?" (1975:

178). The articulation and exploration of such "intentional obscurities" of rhetoric have been the object and motor of Barthes' literary criticism.

Barthes' criticism more than anything else has focused on the *situation* of the author and reader of literature—"the (writing or reading) subject" (1981a: 38)—which is represented in language by those elements of the verbal code that Jakobson defined as "shifters" (1957). "Though coded," Barthes writes,

> ... the shifter thus appears as a complex means—furnished by language itself—of breaking communication: I speak (consider my mastery of the code) but I wrap myself in the mist of an enunciatory situation which is unknown to you; I insert into my discourse certain *leaks of interlocution* (is this not, in fact, what always happens when we utilize the shifter *par excellence*, the pronoun *I*?). Which leads him to imagine shifters . . . as so many social subversions, conceded by language but opposed by society, which fears such leaks of subjectivity and always stops them by insisting on reducing the operator's duplicity. . . . (1977a: 166)

Literature foregrounds the "operator's duplicity" that Barthes describes as embedded in the enunciation of language. Literature—prose and poetry, drama and oratory—imitates voices. It presents and represents what has been called the "voice shaken by feeling," "a man speaking to men," "overheard" speech.

The great illusion of literature from Homer to the present is the illusion of voice—the imitation of *situated* discourse—even when, in Mallarmé or Joyce or Borges, literature sometimes calls attention to this illusion by parodying and imitating writing rather than speech. "Voice," Barthes says, "is what is really at stake in modernity, the voice as specific substance of language everywhere triumphantly pushed forward" (1977: 175). Even when the poet eschews voice, as Steiner argues in "On Difficulty" that Poe, Mallarmé, and Heidegger do, so that "it is not so much the poet who speaks, but language itself" (1980: 46), voice in its absence is still the touchstone of literature. "The act of stating," Barthes asserted in his Inaugural Lecture, Collège de France, "by exposing the subject's place and energy, even his deficiency (which is not his absence), focuses on the very reality of language, acknowledging that language is an immense halo of implications, of effects, of echoes, of turns, returns and degrees." But it also "assumes the burden of making understood a subject both insistent and ineffable, unknown and yet recognized by a disturbing familiarity" (1982: 464).

Such "familiarity" is the source of pity for Barthes; it "makes knowledge," as he says here, "festive."

The *imitation* of voice, however, always "leaks" interlocution. It always marks the noncoincidence of its "enunciatory situation" and its unintended linguistic meanings; it always shifts between the "intention to speak" and communicate which inhabits voice (Barthes 1967: 19) and what is communicated beyond that *situated* intention. In the passage from *Roland Barthes* describing how the shifter breaks communication—as in the book as a whole—Barthes enacts the noncoincidence of enunciation and unintended meanings in the shift from the first-person to the third-person pronoun in the same way that Lawrence shifts from the third person to the first person in *The Rainbow*.

Within this shifting are the two senses of rhetoric with which I began: rhetoric aiming at persuasion, a kind of intersubjective strategy; and rhetoric as the condition of meaning conceived of as an effect, including the "effect" of a scientific, and ultimately godly, rhetoric of passivity which seeks above all to achieve knowledge, to reduce the operator's duplicity and create a relationship between the human subject and his world. In these two contrasting ideas of rhetoric one can see the difference between what Barthes describes as language considered "as a pure instrument of transmission" and language considered as stylized, composed, arranged—the whole *written* discourse of "textual productivity," of *signifiance*. Barthes offers these descriptions in response to Julia Kristeva's articulation of "the entire problem of current semiotics . . . : do we continue to formalize semiotic systems from the point of view of communication . . . , or do we initiate within the problematics of communication . . . that other scene—the production of meaning anterior to meaning" (Barthes 1985: 139, 13), anterior even to signification. This contrast between communication and the production of meaning, as I have argued elsewhere (1987a), constitutes a major motive to poststructuralist discourse and rhetoric.

Within Barthes' understanding of language—and the enunciated voices of language—is this contrast between language considered as communicative and language considered as significative. It is most useful here, I think, to examine this opposition from the vantage of the rhetorical "voices" of these two conceptions. In "Writers, Intellectuals, Teachers," Barthes traces the opposition between writing and speech in terms of voices. Speech, says Barthes, "is irreversible: a word cannot be *retracted*, except precisely by saying one retracts it. To cross out is here to add: if I want to erase what I have just said, I cannot do it without showing the eraser itself (I must say '*or rather* . . .' 'I expressed myself badly . . .'); paradoxically, it is ephemeral speech which is indelible, not monumental writing. All that one can do in the case of spoken utterance is to tack on another utterance" (1977: 190–91). The "monument" of speech aligns itself on the side of the authority of the person who speaks, on the side of communication—the authoritative presence of the speaking subject.

In speech the burden of what Bakhtin calls the "specific sense" of discourse, the "*wholeness* of utterance," is shifted onto the enunciation of its speaker, the ostensible antecedent of its "person" pronouns. In this conception, speech, unlike literature, offers a single voice seemingly without the duplicity of rhetoric. In *Problems in General Linguistics* Emile Benveniste examines the persons or "shifters" of speech, the difference between the first and second persons ("I" and "you") and the third person. " 'Person,' " Benveniste says, "belongs only to *I/you* and is lacking in *he*" (1971: 217). Thus Arab grammarians note that "the first person is . . . 'the one who speaks'; the second, . . . 'the one who is addressed'; but the third is . . . 'the one who is absent' " (1971: 224). All person pronouns, however, "*do not refer to a concept or to an individual,*" but to an act of individual discourse in which they are *pronounced* (1971: 226). Thus speech, Benveniste implies—speech as contrasted with writing, insofar as writing always more or less "imitates" speech and thus more or less obscures the antecedents of its pronouns—constitutes the subject. It is Kurtz's *voice* that so fascinates Marlow, a voice on which he bases his monumental "my": "You should have heard him say, 'My ivory.' Oh yes, I heard him. 'My intended, my ivory, my station, my river, my-----' everything belonged to him. . . . The thing was to know what he belonged to, how many powers of darkness claimed him for their own" (Conrad 1971: 41). In performing, everything belongs to the subject. All is "present" in the self-evident clarity of a "person" standing before you, sharing Jakobson's intention, as Steiner says, "to externalize and communicate meaning."

This is why Benveniste argues that the purpose of speech is intersubjective communication:

> The importance of this function [of pronouns] will be measured by the nature of the problem they serve to solve, which is none other than that of intersubjective communication. Language has solved this problem by creating an ensemble of "empty" signs which are nonreferential with respect to "reality." These signs are always available and become "full" as soon as a speaker introduces them into each instance of his discourse. Since they lack material reference, they cannot be misused; since they do not assert anything, they are not subject to the condition of truth and escape all denial. (1971: 219–20)

Benveniste's "instances of discourse" are Barthes' "enunciatory situations," the ground of the purely relational discourse of communication. The spoken pronoun asserts (constitutes) identity by creating the basis (or the illusion of the basis) for grounding "empty" linguistic shifters. Such grounding creates the possibility of clarity as opposed to obscurity, relationships as opposed to random events, pity as opposed to terror.

The very conception of identity—self-same, single and coherent, precise—is necessary for communication. "Context," Barthes writes, "is a structural given not of language but of speech and it is the very status of context to be reductive of meaning. The spoken word is 'clear'; the banishment of polysemy (such banishment being the definition of 'clarity') serves the Law—*all speech is on the side of Law*" (1977: 191). The Law, above all, is the Law of non-contradiction, the Law of identity, what Derrida calls the principle of reason serving "information"—that is, "the most rapid and the clearest (univocal, *eindeutig)* stockpiling, recording and communication of news" (1983: 14). Communication aims at passing on self-identical information—the "significance," the "production," the "intention" of the speaker. "Communication," Derrida says elsewhere, "communicates a determined content, an identifiable meaning, a describable value" (1982: 309). It is in the context of its *communicative* function that Barthes asserts that speech "is nothing but a flow of empty signs, the movement of which alone is significant. The whole of speech is epitomized by the expendability of words . . ." (1967: 19). These "empty signs" are "filled," as Benveniste says, as soon as "a speaker introduces them into each instance of his discourse"—which is, for Benveniste, a particular context of discourse. They are filled, or predetermined, by his physical presence and the intention *behind* his words, both of which are defined in relation to the interlocutor, the second person of speech. In this way language performed (i.e., enunciated) constitutes subjectivity: in the service of communication.

In this the persons of discourse and the shifting between and among them imply two rhetorical strategies. One strategy is that of the "first person" of the subject of enunciation—Kierkegaard figures this as the ironist who was the first inhabitant of the position "individual," a "first" person indeed (Schleifer 1984: 188–89). The other is that of the "third person" who is the object of transcendental "knowledge." Yet for Barthes, the third person is neither Jakobson's knowledge nor de Man's sense of the absolute randomness of experience. Rather, it is closely linked to the "second person" of the reader, of interlocution, of dialogue, to the ghostly resonation of some other presence "who always walks beside you," as Eliot describes it in *The Waste Land*:

> When I count, there are only you and I together
> But when I look ahead up the white road
> There is always another one walking beside you
> Gliding wrapt in a brown mantle, hooded
> I do not know whether a man or a woman. . . . (1963: 67)

Barthes' third *meaning* (*sens*) haunts the second person; it is "ghostly" in the definition of ghost that Derrida articulates in relation to *Camera Lucida*, "the concept of the other in the same, the *punctum* in the *studium*, the dead other alive in me" (1988: 267).

That is, because the third meaning is "a signifier without a signified," not filled out, but in "a permanent state of *depletion*" (1977: 61, 62), it depends (like shifters) on the interlocutor and the situation of enunciation (interlocution). For Barthes, the third meaning remains within the economy of signification because, linking it so closely to enunciated interlocution—and consequently so closely to the second person—he fails to fully discern the *otherness* of this third "meaning," its terror as well as its pity. Unlike the uncanniness (*unheimlich*) that Heidegger describes in the face of death, for Barthes the photograph, though traversed by death, is punctuated by the desire to inhabit it; it is "*heimlich*, awakening in me the Mother (and never the disturbing Mother)" (1981: 40). The strange and uncanny otherness (as in the third figure whom Eliot suggests is Christ) is that of the sacred which escapes Barthes' aesthetic textuality. In Chapter 8 I shall argue that Derrida discerns such a sacred *act* in the arbitrary assertion (affirmation) of meaning within the arbitrary nature of the sign. The sacred, for Derrida, is the Other that cannot be fully encompassed by language, by textuality, but also cannot be bracketed and shunted aside from language and its meanings. It is what Derrida calls the rhetoricity of rhetoric itself, and it is sacred because it asserts meaning in a world inhabited by death and non-sense. As such, it is an act informed by terror as well as pity.

Lawrence understood the sacred in language as well as—perhaps better than—Eliot; in his rhetoric he achieves the uncanny effect of what Kristeva calls the production of meaning anterior to meaning. In *The Rainbow*, for instance, he offers this discourse when Tom Brangwen participates in his daughter's wedding:

> How did one grow old—how could one become confident? He wished he felt older. Why, what difference was there, as far as

he felt matured or completed, between him now and him at his own wedding? He might be getting married over again—he and his wife. He felt himself tiny, a little, upright figure on a plain circled round with the immense, roaring sky: he and his wife, two little, upright figures walking across this plain, whilst the heavens shimmered and roared about them. When did one come to an end? In which direction was it finished? There was not end, no finish, only this roaring vast space. Did one never get old, never die? That was the clue. He exulted strangely, with torture. He would go on with his wife, he and she like two children camping in the plains. What was sure but the endless sky? But that was so sure, so boundless.

Still the royal blue colour burned and blazed and sported itself in the web of darkness before him, unwearyingly rich and splendid. How rich and splendid his own life was, red and burning and blazing and sporting itself in the dark meshes of his body: and his wife, how she glowed and burned dark within her meshes! Always it was so unfinished and unformed! (1976: 135)

Lawrence offers here, as he does throughout his fiction, a kind of radical metonymy. Not only does this passage "detach" itself from its discursive context—Tom Brangwen, a peasant farmer sitting nervously and a little drunk in church, watching the stained glass as he awaits his daughter's marriage—so that it cannot come to stand, synecdochically, for that situation itself. In its very indirection—its "indirect discourse"—it also detaches itself from the discursive possibilities of the speech of its subject: the passage's metaphorical and discursive resources of language are so far beyond those available to Brangwen that we are left with Barthes' question, *Who is speaking?*

The answer for Lawrence is not simply the character, as it would be in Chekhov's realism; nor is it a narrator curiously attuned and *limited* to the discourse of his subject as in Joyce; nor, finally, is it even Barthes' "pleasure-effect" of discourse (though it is close to this). Rather, Lawrence articulates here (as throughout his most powerful work) the *impersonal* situation of earthly, material life—marriage, death, birth, courtship—a materiality that includes but exceeds the materiality of Barthes' textual "pleasure." Such materiality, above all, is *not* personal, not even in terms of discursive, textual "persons"; such "basic," material life-activities, as Barthes says in another context, "are not those of a user but those of a demiurge" (1972a: 54). That is, the force of such materialism is not limited to the subject or the subject-position of discourse; like the "burst of laughter" that Derrida describes exploding the reserve of significance (1978: 256), it pervades the whole of experience beyond the limits and oppositions of textuality. Such a "demiurge" is basic, "elemental," a species of the "original materialism" Derrida describes before the "classical" oppositions "between the sensible and the intelligible," "matter without presence and without substance, . . . what resists these oppositions" (1986: 52).

In Lawrence's "Odour of Chrysanthemums," Elizabeth Bates describes the smell of that flower—its "cold, deathly smell of chrysanthemums" (1961: 296), as the story says—as inhabiting, in a similar way, the most elemental events of human life: "It was chrysanthemums when I married him, and chrysanthemums when you were born, and the first time they ever brought him home drunk, he'd got brown chrysanthemums in his button-hole" (1961: 289). At the end of the story, Walter Bates's death is also marked by vases of chrysanthemums. In the same way, the discourse of *The Rainbow* is that of neither a subjective first person nor an objective third person: it wavers across or beneath all the persons of discourse on the boundlessness of material existence, articulated before "the immense, roaring sky," the sureness of the endless sky, the ongoingness of human life—courtship, marriage, children, death, on and on and on—and the terrifying unsurety of individual personal existence.

In *Camera Lucida* Barthes comes close to describing the terror of Lawrence's rhetoric that somehow rustles beneath the difference between the enunciatory rhetoric of the first person and the tropological rhetoric of the third person, that aims at circumscribing the *elemental* production of meaning anterior to meaning. In one of the few places where Barthes historicizes the bodily affect he attempts to circumscribe in his discourse, he describes the "flat" death that inhabits modernism. "Photography," he writes,

> must have some historical relation with what Edgar Morin calls the "crisis of death" beginning in the second half of the nineteenth century; for my part I should prefer that instead of constantly relocating the advent of Photography in its social and economic context, we should also inquire as to the anthropological place of Death and of the new image. For Death must be somewhere in a society; if it is no longer (or less intensely) in religion, it must be elsewhere. . . . Contemporary with the withdrawal of rites, Photography may correspond to the intrusion, in our modern society, of an asymbolic Death, outside of religion, outside of ritual, a kind of abrupt dive into literal Death. . . .

> With the Photography, we enter into *flat Death*. One day, leaving one of my classes, someone said to me with disdain: "You talk about Death very flatly." —As if the horror of Death were not precisely its platitude! The horror is this: nothing to say about the death of one whom I love most, nothing to say about her photograph. . . . The only "thought" I can have is that . . . I have no other resource than this *irony*: to speak of the "nothing to say." (1981: 92–93)

Barthes is situating death between his unanswerable rhetorical question of voice—"Who is speaking?"—and Jakobson's answerable, scientific question—"What is happening?" Moreover, he is situating it in the radical metonymy of "between" (see Derrida 1981: 219–22), of conceiving of death somehow, impossibly, *outside* the reserve of dialectic and meaning, what Barthes describes earlier in *Camera Lucida* as his own "total, undialectical death" (1981: 72). Here he is trying to interrogate experience not, as he says, "from the viewpoint of pleasure, but in relation to what we romantically call love and death" (1981: 73).

Usually, however, Barthes does interrogate experience from the viewpoint of pleasure, the vantage of aesthetics. He does so by creating a dialectic between the questions of communication and signification in a "third meaning" which he attempts to understand in terms of *jouissance* and what he calls Nietzsche's "*absolute flow of becoming*," "a true science of becoming" (1975: 60–61), a science of enunciation. This dialectic is created through the synthesizing force of the *figurative* meanings of its elements. *Jouissance,* as Eve Tavor Bannet notes, "is untranslatable in modern English, but has an equivalent in the Renaissance word 'to die,' which meant orgasm, death, and the moment of self-obliteration (of death) at the height of sexual pleasure" (1989: 64). By using this term figuratively—creating a "dialectic" between its literal and figurative meaning (just as Jakobson creates a dialectic between the literal and figurative meaning of metonymy)—as well as figuring Nietzsche's becoming in terms of an "absolute flow" and a "science," Barthes attempts to understand the "sensuousness" of discourse without acknowledging, as Nietzsche and Lawrence did, that *jouissance* and becoming have their torture as well as their exultation in radical metonymy, in the boundless and impersonal nothingness and non-sense of death that resonates, literally, alongside their significance.

Barthes' *literary* question remains: *Who is speaking* in *The Rainbow* at the Brangwen wedding? Without the "presence" of enunciation, in the *imitated* speech of literature—in its contextless rhetoric—communication can no longer be the sole aim of language. Literature imitates voices, but it also frees voice from context: it wraps the enunciatory situation in a mist. In literature the significance of "the movement alone" is no longer the sole significance of language: rather, rereading, marking, indexing, pausing, rearranging—all forms of detachment from the "enunciatory situation"—are possible (see Perloff 1985: 511; and Tavor Bannet's description of Barthes' practice of "the '*fiche*' or index method" of fragmentary composition, 1989: 72–83). The spoken voice intends a message and repeats itself—it enunciates its discourse—until that communication is received; the rhetorical voice—the voice of signification—detaches such repetitions from intention. Communication uses the movement of repetition as a pure instrument of transmission so that its redundancies are *always* "expendable" once that communicative goal is achieved. Literature, on the other hand, as Greimas has argued, takes up the redundancies and noise of language for significatory—not communicative—ends (see Schleifer 1987: 159–63). Citing Freud's observation that "*nothing is gratuitous except death, as everyone knows,*" Barthes says that "for the text nothing is gratuitous except its own destruction" (1975: 24).

Barthes offers a dialectical understanding of literature by synthesizing the opposition between the two conceptions of rhetoric and representation that I have presented. He accomplishes this synthesis by handing them over to the "second" person of the reader. In this understanding, the genius of literature is its ability to be understood in another way, as spoken in another context (and thus by another "person"), so that the univocal communication of speech is undermined to become "meaning" without "a meaning"—a kind of third meaning. It is, as Barthes says, to create "an 'intention' of reading" (1981: 78). To conceive of literature as rhetorical in this dialectical sense—as the imitation of speech without a *situated* speaker—destroys the line of speech that is imitated, the line of communication. With the destruction of the line, it destroys also the possibility of filling empty signs, discovering antecedents for pronouns and other parts of speech. "Once the Author is removed," writes Barthes,

> the claim to decipher a text becomes quite futile. To give a text an Author is to impose a limit on that text, to furnish it with a final signified, to close the writing. Such a conception suits criticism very well, the latter then allotting itself the important task of discovering the Author ... beneath the work.... In the multiplicity of writing everything is to be *dis-*

entangled, nothing *deciphered*; the structure can be followed, 'run' (like the thread of a stocking) at every point and at every level, but there is nothing beneath: the space of writing is to be ranged over, not pierced; writing ceaselessly posits meaning ceaselessly to evaporate it, carrying out a systematic exemption of meaning. In precisely this way literature (it would be better from now on to say *writing*) by refusing to assign a "secret," an ultimate meaning, to the text (and to the world as text), liberates what may be called an anti-theological activity, an activity that is truly revolutionary since to refuse to fix meaning is, in the end, to refuse God and his hypostases—reason, science, law. (1977: 147)

As we have seen, Jakobson installs the Author by giving priority to the "mature" Yeats over the young Yeats. Once the Author is removed, Barthes faces us with radical reader response, phenomenology without a subject. He doesn't replace the Author with the psychology of the reader (as, for instance, Norman Holland does); neither does he replace the reader with social conventions (as J. L. Austin and Stanley Fish do). He replaces the Author with subjectless writing, with textual activity, the production of meaning, *signifiance*; he replaces the *strategies* of (persuasive) rhetoric with aimless *tactics*. This sense of writing creates the central problem of literature: it imitates the gesture of a "person," but it does not "present" or "constitute" that person. In writing, Barthes says earlier in this essay, "it is language which speaks, not the author; to write is, through a prerequisite impersonality . . . , to reach that point where only language acts, 'performs,' and not 'me' " (1977: 143). Whatever the imitative "performance" of literature is, it is not the performative language of "communication"; it is not simply an absent address.

In addition to creating the central problem for literature, the removal of an authoritative author creates—or, rather, occasions—a sense of its mystifying power, its ability to create the "effect" of textual activity that somehow transcends its own occasion. In this, it creates the power that literature presents to erase—to forget about—death and nonsense and nothingness. For Barthes, as for Jakobson, "language is *everywhere,* and not simply *close by*" (Barthes 1986: 160); for Barthes, even the "pleasures" of textual activity are *readable* and *sayable* precisely because they exclude (or seem to exclude) the very death that inhabits language. Barthes' "pleasure," that is, finds its energy in what Julia Kristeva calls the "*abject,*" which "draws me toward the place where meaning collapses" (1982: 2). It is, she says, "something rejected from which one does not part, from which one does not protect oneself as from an object. Imaginary uncanniness and real threat, it beckons to us and ends up engulfing us" (1982: 4). Modernism understands such "abjection," as in the image of Brangwen, tiny and lost in the vast, "endless" materiality of sky, or in the image Marlow offers of "the great wall of vegetation, an exuberant and entangled mass of trunks, branches, leaves, boughs, festoons . . . like a rioting invasion of soundless life, a wave of plants, piled up, crested, ready . . . to sweep every little man of us out of his little existence" (Conrad 1971: 30). Here, as in the passage from *The Rainbow,* torture and exultation, darkness and rich and splendid life are brought together, but not quite joined in synecdoche so that, as Barthes says of the "third meaning," there occurs "a multi-layering of meanings which always lets the previous meaning continue, as in a geological formation, saying the opposite without giving up the contrary" (1977: 58). Here is how Kristeva describes it: "handling that repetition, staging it, cultivating it until it releases, beyond its eternal return, its sublime destiny of being a struggle with death—is it not that which characterizes writing? And yet dealing with death in that manner, making sport of it, is that not infamy itself?" (1982: 24).

Barthes' definition of "literature," however, even in its "third meaning," is related to but finally very different from *this* sense of the "sublime" affective power of discourse, the resonating effects it creates which reiterate (as in de Man) the power of death. For Barthes, literature seeks, as John Fowles says when his character meets the French Lieutenant's woman in conversation, "an intelligence beyond convention," to find a world different from our own, but possible (1969: 141). Herman Melville says the same thing: "It is with fiction as with religion: it should present another world, and yet one to which we feel a tie" (1967: 260). Thus Barthes writes that "there is no such thing as a timeless essence of literature, but under the rubric 'literature' (itself quite recent, moreover) a process of very different forms, functions, institutions, reasons, and projects whose relativity it is precisely the historian's responsibility to discern" (1972: 251; see also Lentricchia 1980: 129–45). That the world of literature is not our own—that it is a world of rhetoric without intention—is its obscurity and its difficulty. Yet, since it is one that allows at least the illusion of intercourse, it creates "a distinct sense in which we know and do not know."

What Barthes describes as "literature" (under the metaphors of "writing" and "textuality") is a process simultaneously active and passive, a process in which that distinction breaks down: the writer is both agent and vehicle. "Writing," says Barthes, unlike speech, "develops like a seed, not a line" (1967: 20), and like a seed it confuses beginning and end, the agent and the vehicle. Unlike Kurtz's voice, writing avoids possession, self-assertion, even love. In literature, in other words, the pronoun is lost: writing, the possibility of rereading, rearranging, etc., is a form of waiting that does away with the "instance of discourse," the "occasion of enunciation" of which Benveniste speaks. But it does not, for Barthes, do away with the future. Writing, with the possibility of rereading standing *before* it (and not *behind* it, as stand the persons of speech), does not present itself as the (self-identical) "work" of speech; rather, it creates the possibility of literature.

A clear example of rhetoric without intention is the indirect discourse of literature, such as Joyce's description of Maria on the tram, which I examined in Chapter 3. Indirect discourse presents the rhetoric of voice without locating it: who says "nice" in "Clay"? A more striking example is the shimmer of Lawrence's indirect discourse from *The Rainbow*. Lawrence's description is more instructive than Joyce's because it so clearly *situates an intention* in its indirect discourse, yet it does so in relation to a "person" who simply does not have the resources of language that the passage utilizes and that, being utilized, explode the limits of that situated discourse. In other words, what Frank Kermode calls the visionary "cruxes" of Lawrence's narratives, which seem only minimally linked together in the discursive diegesis (1968: 36), enact the *theatricalization* that Barthes describes as "not designing a setting for representation, but unlimiting the language." Sade, Fourier, and Loyola, Barthes continues, have substituted "volume of writing" for "platitude of style":

> The style supposes and practices the opposition of matter and form; it is the lamination of a substructure; the writing reaches a point at which it produces a row of signifiers, such that no language matter can still be recovered; because it is conceived as "form," style implies a "consistency"; the writing, to use Lacan's term, only recognizes "instances." . . .
>
> Thus, if Sade, Fourier, and Loyola are founders of a language, and only that, it is precisely in order to say nothing, to observe a vacancy (if they wanted to say *something*, linguistic language, the language of communication and philosophy would suffice: they could be *summarized*, which is not the case with any one of them). (1976: 5–6)

In this way, too, Lawrence offers "instances" of discourse—enunciations—in which language *stands for* itself in a third meaning that is the same and different at the same time, the "unlimiting" of language. It is the same and different precisely because underneath the experience represented is, as Lawrence says in *Women in Love,* "death itself" (1982: 568).

In other words, if style offers "language matter," writing can simply "present" it in the unique "instances" of material signifiers. It is in the rhetoric of presentation—always metonymic—that Barthes' *concepts* (his *representations)* of "textuality" and "pleasure" and the "radical materiality" of discourse can best be understood. For this reason Barthes opposes "texts" (as another figure for literature) to "work":

> The difference is this: the work is a fragment of substance, occupying a part of the space of books (in a library for example), the Text is a methodological field. . . . the text is a process of demonstration, speaks according to certain rules (or against certain rules); the work can be held in the hand, the text is held in language, only exists in the movement of discourse (or rather, it is text for the very reason that it knows itself as text); the Text is not the decomposition of the work, it is the work that is the imaginary tail of the Text; or again, *the Text is experienced only in an activity of production.* (1977: 157)

The difference is that the work is a work of "communication," self-identical, informational, intentional, while the text is an activity and a process. Texts are subject to dispute; they are constantly being rewritten because *no one*—except for the ghostly imitation of a person—stands behind them. If a work combines communication and signification in the figure of the author (with such "work" being precisely what Jakobson attempts to account for through structural linguistic analysis), then the text is neither communication nor significance, but a possibility of meaning determined by the "empty" positions, waiting to be filled, that discourse presents. In this, text, writing, *signifiance* destroys in its *rhetorical* activity the intentional meaning, the work, and ultimately the "person" of the author as well; above all, it destroys the clarity of communication. Such *possibility* of meaning, like Barthes' refusal to fix meaning, is "obtuse" indeed: it is a process that is more than communication, the process of what Barthes calls "literature" and "writing," a process that Barthes seeks to articulate, circumscribe, and utilize in his own critical discourse.

In this Barthes is describing the metonymy of modernism that can escape even the limits of textuality itself. That is, if Joyce "textually" situates intentions in the more or less realist moments of his indirect discourse, then Lawrence's indirect discourse presents another, more radically metonymic realism in its distance between the language of its situated character and its unlimited textual language. Take the remarkable description of the killing of the officer by his orderly in "The Prussian Officer":

> The orderly watched the lid of the mug, and the white hand that clenched the handle, as if he were fascinated. It was raised. The youth followed it with his eyes. And then he saw the thin, strong throat of the elder man moving up and down as he drank, the strong jaw working. And the instinct which had been jerking at the young man's wrists suddenly jerked free. He jumped, feeling as if it were rent in two by a strong flame.
>
> The spur of the officer caught in a tree-root, he went down backwards with a crash, the middle of his back thudding sickeningly against the sharp-edged tree-base, the pot flying away. And in a second the orderly, with serious, earnest young face, and underlip between his teeth, had got his knee in the officer's chest and was pressing the chin backward over the farther edge of the tree-stump, pressing, with all his heart behind in a passion of relief, the tension of his wrists exquisite with relief. And with the base of his palms he shoved at the chin, with all his might. And it was pleasant, too, to have that chin, that hard jaw already slightly rough with beard, in his hands. He did not relax one hair's breadth, but, all the force of all his blood exulting in his thrust, he shoved back the head of the other man, till there was a little "cluck" and a crunching sensation. . . . Heavy convulsions shook the body of the officer, frightening and horrifying the young soldier. Yet it pleased him, too, to repress them. It pleased him to keep his hands pressing back the chin, to feel the chest of the other man yield in expiration to the weight of his strong, young knees, to feel the hard twitchings of the prostrate body jerking his own whole frame, which was pressed down on it. (1961: 109–10)

Of this passage we could again ask Barthes' question *Who is speaking?*, and the answer here, I think, would be more difficult than that of Joyce. Here, instead of voice, Lawrence is offering a strong sense of the *materiality* of experience—a strong sense of its metonymic force. Everything narrated in this passage takes place in terms of things: it is as if there is *no* intention, even while the text plays with the intentions of author, character, and reader. What is striking here is how synecdoches become metonymies as body parts take on lives of their own, particpate in a kind of "demiurge," without reintegration into a "person."

To put this differently, Lawrence plays with the materiality of experience by unlimiting language to the point of *effacing* intention, even if he enunciates it in a powerfully intentional discourse. That is, in Lawrence the "persons" of discourse are enunciated in an altogether different way from that of Barthes' and Benveniste's intellectual schemas of linguistic persons. It is different, too, I think, from the "persons" inhabiting Joyce or Eliot or even Conrad. If Conrad, as I shall argue in the next chapter, is a kind of intellectual hero, a hero of cognition, who attempts, like Jakobson, to transform the first person to the third person (just as Barthes transforms the first to the second person), then Lawrence wants to unlimit the third person, to transform the "knowledge" to which the third person gives rise into the "presence" of materiality beyond knowledge, multiple demiurgic presences of the "radical materiality" that Barthes describes but rarely engages within his uniformly intellectual writing.

In this passage from "The Prussian Officer" the binary opposition between first and third person disappears in a textuality that includes within its metonymic particularities the starkly metaphoric description of flame and the metaphoric response of "sickeningly" (*whose* response is it?). In another mode, in Chapter 10 of *The Rainbow,* for instance, Lawrence ends his third-person narration of the Brangwen Christmas with a kind of rhapsodic exclamation about the resurrection and the life so that the very narration itself is crossed, as in a geological formation, by a cry bursting through in the first person: "Why, when Mary says: Rabboni, shall I not take her in my arms and kiss her and hold her to my breast. Why is the risen body deadly, and abhorrent with wounds?" (1976: 281). In this, the question *Who* is speaking? makes less sense than *What*—what force, what cry, what "powers of darkness"—is taking up and destroying discourse altogether?

Like Barthes, Lawrence has a fascination with what he calls in "The Prussian Officer" "dark, expressionless eyes, that seemed never to have thought, only to have received life direct through is senses, and acted straight from instinct" (1961: 97). Unlike Barthes, however, Lawrence doesn't want to "account for" this material life; rather, through language, he wants to make its power felt. He achieves this, I think—as Barthes does in particular passages of his work, and as he continually aims to do in his later work (tutored as he is by modernism)—by making the *unlimiting* power of death itself felt resonating through the meanings of his discourse, through the significations of literature. Barthes' "pleasure" may well find its energy, unconsciously, in Kris-

teva's *"abjection,"* located where meaning collapses not into nothingness, but into pure metonymic effect, material effect, in a strange combination of the persons of enunciation. It may well combine, as
Lawrence does, the synecdochical strategy of persuasiveness—the rhetoric of the power-effects of discourse—and the tactical play of knowledge—the rhetoric of meaning-effects.

Such a configuration of persons helps define Barthes' great contribution
to literary criticism, the "tactics" of reading that he developed. In
Roland Barthes he describes these tactics in describing his own work:
"The movement of his work is tactical: a matter of displacing himself,
of obstructing, as with bars, but not of conquering. Examples: the
notion of intertext? It has actually no positivity; it serves to combat
the law of context; . . . it is only a little machine for making a war
against philological law, the academic tyranny of correct meaning. This
work would therefore be defined as: *a tactics without strategy"* (1977a:
172). Opposed to literature ("writing"), the work of communication,
Barthes says, is the work of teachers standing before classes embodying,
in their voices and persons, the authority of the Law. But who stands
behind the language of literature? Who stands behind the language of
literary criticism? Or that of poetry? Or the imitated voices of Lawrence, Fowles, or even Barthes himself? "We come back to the same
problem," he says, "our sole continuing concern: the origin of a spoken
discourse does not exhaust that discourse; once set off, it is beset by
a thousand adventures, its origin becomes blurred, all its effects are
not in its cause. It is this *excess* which here concerns us" (1977: 206).
Such is the "excess" of rhetoric whose effects—and rhetoric is *all* effects—are not accountable solely by its causes.
     The lack of such accountability creates the great difficulties of lit-
erary criticism. In "On Difficulty," Steiner delineates four categories
of difficulty inhabiting modernism: *contingent* difficulties, which are
obscurities of reference that can be overcome by looking up unknown
meanings (such as the meanings of Pound's Chinese characters); *modal*
difficulties, which are obscurities in cultural assumptions that can be
overcome through scholarship and imagination; *tactical* difficulties,
which cannot be overcome but are an author's purposeful attempt to
dislocate, as Steiner says, "the inertias in the common routine of discourse" (1980: 40); and *ontological* difficulties, which also cannot be
overcome, but "in which the poet is not a *persona,* a subjectivity 'ruling
over language,' but an 'openness to,' a supreme listener to, the genius
of speech" (1980: 46). What all these difficulties (except the trivial case
of the *contingent)* have in common is that they are difficulties in reading

voices, difficulties for the second person. The rhetoric of "foreign" voices creates *modal* difficulties, the multiplication of voices creates *tactical* difficulties, and the always-possible voicelessness of discourse creates *ontological* difficulties.

This is important because clarity, univocality, and information—in a word, communication—are, as Barthes suggests, functions and aims of speech, of a subjectivity ruling over language. The "writing" of literature gives itself over to language in ways that speech never does; it more or less eschews the subject in discourse. This is why reading literature—literary criticism—is a supreme example of Barthes' sense of textuality: it seeks to hear the texts it examines, to collaborate in their making, to complete their illusion of speech. Thus Randall Jarrell says in "Some Lines from Whitman" that "to show Whitman for what he is one does not need to praise or explain or argue, one needs simply to quote" (1971: 118), and he goes on to quote Whitman at such length that he allows his reader again to hear Whitman speaking through his writing. This seems the "purest" of imitations, yet even this "reading" is at least theoretically obscure: written at different times and to different purposes by Jarrell and Whitman, it multiplies contexts and leads Jarrell to describe the "queerness" of Whitman's poetry and our resentment toward him for "having made up his own horrors, instead of sticking to ones we ourselves employ" in his achievement of what Jarrell calls "something we have no name for" (1971: 120).

This is obscure precisely because quotation displaces the instances upon which speech's naive authority rests. Such displacement, as Derrida has argued, is not an accident of particular discourses, but an aspect of language; such displacement of communication must *always* occur insofar as iterability is the distinguishing characteristic of language (see Derrida 1977; see also *Of Spirit,* esp. Ch. 5, for a discussion of what he calls "the law of quotation marks" [1989: 31]). Insofar as literature imitates "communicating" voices in a "repeatable" form, "literature" calls attention to the *shifting* at the heart of language between instance and repetition, the other and the same, the enunciatory situation of speech and the possibilities of unintended meaning. This attention is what Barthes means by the "excess" of rhetoric. In such "excess" is the rupture in the principle of reason that has led to other obscurities in postmodern criticism that are more difficult and frustrating—less "theoretical"—than that of Jarrell (or the by and large "contingent" technical difficulties of Jakobson's modernist discourse), such as those we encountered in some of Barthes' more outlandish distinctions calmly cited throughout this chapter.

What makes Barthes's distinctions—writing/speech, text/work, meaning/a meaning—so outlandish is the fact that they are simultaneously too minute and too global in their assertion: just when they seem helpful they seem to break down, "work" miraculously transforming itself into the tail of the "text," the first person into the third person, speech into writing, before (behind?) our eyes. Barthes asks, "Where is speech? In locution? In listening? In the *returns* of the one and the other? The problem is not to abolish the distinction in functions (*teacher/student*—after all, as Sade has taught us, order is one of the guarantees of pleasure) but to protect the instability and, as it were, the giddying whirl of the positions of speech" (1977: 205–6). Such a metonymic whirl of questions (Whose questions are they? Who is speaking?) distinguishes Barthes' tactical linguistic and literary discourse from the difficulties of Lacan's therapeutic and pedagogical strategies or Derrida's philosophical and ontological discourse, both of which are considered in the following chapters. The "play" of Derrida especially seems the play of ideas, more scandalous and less material (in the sense that Barthes offers us in the *recuperable* material "grain" of the voice) than Barthes' pleasures. Both Derrida and Barthes offer us, in their French polemics, the rhetoric of Steiner's *modal* difficulty. But when Barthes speaks of "the positions of speech," he is following a linguistic model: Jakobson's shifters, Benveniste's "persons." Such an "intertextual" mixing of discourses—here that of linguistics and criticism, figuring criticism in the language of linguistics—is a *tactical* difficulty, marshaled, as metaphors are marshaled (the "death" of the author, the "odor" of speech, the "discomfort" of writing, *jouissance* itself), to occasion a response, to produce an effect, to situate a second person: tactics without strategies.

When Derrida examines the iterability of speech, he is closer to Kierkegaard's repetition, Nietzsche's eternal return of the same, Heidegger's *Dasein*—not to a *tactical* difficulty, but to an *ontological* one. "I see in Derrida," Hillis Miller has noted, "a commitment to another kind of ultimate explanation which is not purely linguistic . . . , that is present in Derrida's continuous interest in Heidegger, who is fundamental to him. There is a genuine ontological dimension in Derrida which might make it possible to say . . . that his choice would not be, as you might think, for language as the ultimate grounding explanation. . . . In Derrida language does not come out clean, and that takes some explaining" (Johnson et al. 1985: 89). Derrida's difficulty is a scandal to reason different from Barthes' setting up and collapsing of binary oppositions, Barthes' "literary" difficulty of mixing and confusing voices. It is the scandal of Heidegger's unanswerable "ontolog-

ical" question: Why is there something rather than nothing? (1959: 1),
or Elizabeth Bates's questions before the physical presence of her husband's dead body: "Who am I? What have I been doing? I have been
fighting a husband who did not exist. *He* existed all the time. What
wrong have I done? What was that I have been living with?" (1961:
300). Barthes' difficulty is finally more placid, an aporia of language
and literature; it is embodied in *his* unanswerable question: Who is
speaking? Perhaps it is Barthes' "pleasure," what Culler calls his "he-
donism" (1983: 91–100), which precludes the ontological, so that he
seems to be among those who, as Miller describes them, "seem able
to live on from day to day and year to year, even as readers of literature,
without seeing religious or metaphysical questions as having any sort
of force or substance" (1985: 22).

What Barthes attempts is not the realization of the metaphysical
in the ordinary—which I take to be Heidegger's great project—but to
aestheticize the ordinary, as Nietzsche tries to do in *The Birth of Tragedy*. Such a project attempts to resist banality not with "Being"—or,
for that matter, with Derrida's explosive articulation of "being," *différance*—but with "literature," the discursive practices of art. Such
practices are rhetorical in an elemental aesthetic sense, the sense of
their (phenomenal) sensibility: Barthes attempts, as he says, to resist
the banal in a writing which "will always be a vested discourse, in
which the body will make its appearance (banality is discourse without
body)" (1977a: 137). For Barthes, language and signification are everywhere, disseminated, ongoing, not to be avoided, while for Derrida,
as for Kristeva, there is, alongside discourse, a glimmer of the horror
of meaninglessness and pure non-sense. For Lacan, as we shall see in
the next chapter, inhabiting discourse itself, metonymically there, is
the *power* of non-sense.

A great part of the rhetorical obscurity of postmodern literary readings
stems from the fact that their discourses combine *tactical* and *ontological* difficulties and that the distinction I am making between these
categories is as unstable as those Barthes presents. When Barthes asserts that such distinctions should not be abolished but protected in
the instability and the obscurity of their giddying whirl, he is describing
a tactical collaboration in literature and literary readings. Thus much
valued literary expression today is what Barthes calls "the total existence of writing: a text . . . made of multiple writings, drawn from many
cultures and entering into mutual relations of dialogue, parody, contestation" (1977: 148), and much criticism attempts to repeat this kind
of play with language. In Barthes there is a species of modernist rhetoric

that comes from a self-conscious sense (and the tactical pursuit) of collaboration in criticism between writing and speech, between listening and talking, between philosophy and literature, a sense such as he offers in *Roland Barthes,* of the critic writing in his own "person" which he simultaneously disowns, of the writer simultaneously controlling and being overwhelmed by language—the "unlimited" language of the rhapsodic "*third form,* neither Essay nor Novel" (1986: 281) he describes in the late Proust essay. Such modernist rhetoric comes, in other words, from the scandal to reason of playing with its written voices. This rhetorical play, in Barthes' discursive practice, is close to Steiner's definition of *tactical* difficulty: "There is a distinct sense," Steiner says, "in which we know and do not know, at the same time. This rich undecidability is exactly what the poet aims at. . . . It is, simultaneously, a subversion and energizing of rhetoric drawing attention, as poets such as Michelangelo, Gongora, and Wallace Stevens do persistently, to the inertias in the common routine of discourse" (1980: 40). It is an undecidability that finally leaves one (almost) speechless—not before what is ("What a world!" Nietzsche says in *The Birth of Tragedy* [1956: 65]), but before the enunciation of discourse, the play of rhetoric.

Such "inertias" are common, "correct," intentional, and what they leave out, as Steiner says, is reaching "out towards more delicate orderings of perception." These orderings, as Barthes suggests throughout his career, are really disorderings. When criticism presents the discomfort of such disorder, it offers the mixed discourses of collaboration between critic and text, critic and language, language and the body. Collaboration—listening—always produces obscurity because encounters with an other are always shocking and bewildering: "You have learnt something," Undershaft tells his daughter in *Major Barbara*; "That always feels at first as if you have lost something." It "might be helpful to us," Heidegger says, "to rid ourselves of the habit of always hearing only what we already understand" (1971: 58). Such encounters are "tactile" as well as "tactical": they produce the affect of loss, language's power to produce bodily responses—what Shoshana Felman calls the "scandal of the speaking body" (see Felman 1983). In Barthes' late terms, at best criticism is "punctuated" by such loss, punctuated by the anterior future of every photograph "of which death is the stake" (1981: 96).

Here we can see the logic, inscribed in his tactics, of the turn in Barthes' later work to "pleasure," in which, as one critic has noted, "the voice is not at all the condensation via synecdoche of a unified whole, but the movement of various parts of the body toward utter-

ance" (Ungar 1983: 74). For Barthes, the scandal of the speaking body
is the scandal of *signifiance,* materiality inscribed within the reserve
of language, the textualization of meaning. The description of *signifiance* with which I began offers a kind of Barthesian definition of
rhetoric and a version of the complexity of postmodernist rhetoric. It
is a definition that includes the opposition between the "statement"
(*énoncé*) and "enunciation"—an opposition, borrowed from Benveniste, between meaning and the instance of discourse. We have already
encountered this opposition in Bakhtin (he dismisses abstract "meaning") and it will become of great importance in the discussion of Lacan's rhetoric. Moreover, it encompasses the complexity of rhetoric—
troping and persuasion—I have described in modernism more generally. For Barthes, *signifiance* is rhetoric, a conception of language as
the play of the surface rather than the expression of depths (of meaning,
of personality, of clarity itself). In this conception, the particular "response" of the reader, like that of the writer, is the opposite of Jakobson's attempt to account for meaning-effects in the clarity of scientific
logic that seems to erase the reader. In this Barthes is describing the
tactical and tactile exploration that brings so much energy to his critical
discourse.

Rather than aspiring to clarity, language in Barthes functions like
musical dissonance. Dissonance, as Nietzsche describes it in *The Birth
of Tragedy,* combines the "need to hear and at the same time to go
beyond hearing. This forward propulsion, notwithstanding our supreme delight in a reality perceived in all its features, reminds us that
both conditions are aspects of one and the same Dionysiac phenomenon, of that spirit which playfully shatters and rebuilds the teeming
world of individuals" (1956: 143). Such "hearing" describes the aesthetic play of rhetoric. As opposed to the ontological questions of
Nietzsche's later work—the inscription of the "end" of Europe within
his late discourse—the dissonance of *The Birth of Tragedy* "hears" the
noise in harmony, the grain in the voice; doing so, it describes the
aesthetic sensibility of literature and literary studies. In fact, such dissonance—the incongruities of intention and execution, of model and
repetition, of the "enounced" and enunciation; the incongruities, finally, of rhetorical voices—constitutes the tactics of literary reading
and criticism altogether. (One such tactic, pursued by Derrida in "The
Deaths of Roland Barthes," is to use, almost unconsciously, Jakobson's
definition of "metonymy" as a species of synecdoche in the analysis
of the "countrapuntal" movement of Barthes' work [1988: esp. 294].)

This is why Barthes, like literature, offers us the rhetoric he does,
such as his strange "definition" of *signifiance*. Rhetoric, as the pejor-

ative use of the word suggests, is a form of obscurantism; instead of leading simply, clearly, self-evidently—in a word, logically—to its conclusion, it circles and plays, juxtaposes modes of discourse, presents voices without answering the question *Who is speaking?* Reason possesses what I have suggested is the authority of speech; it is grounded in its self-evident, non-contradictory axioms just as speech is grounded in the person and intention of the speaker before you, *behind* his or her words. Rhetoric—Barthes' "textuality"—is not grounded at all, but plays between idea and action, meaning and meaning, just as writing plays between writers and the writing that precedes them; it is the play of discourses, "made," as Barthes says, "of multiple writing, drawn from many cultures and entering into mutual relations of dialogue, parody, contestation" (1977: 148; see also Schleifer and Markley 1984).

Such a rhetoric of textuality is "obscure," yet it fails to engage fully the power and *threat* of obscurity in the mortality that walks beside discourse and experience, in its ghostly presence Lawrence circumscribes in his language. For Barthes, the radical metonymy of enunciation is finally idealized into "text" and "semiosis," which, even *resisting* the intelligence ("almost successfully," as Wallace Stevens describes poetry), still fail to engage, as modernism does, nothingness and pure non-sense. "Realism," Barthes writes,

> is always timid, and there is too much *surprise* in a world which mass media and the generalization of politics have made so profuse that it is no longer possible to figure it projectively: the world, as a literary object, escapes; knowledge deserts literature, which can no longer be either *Mimesis* or *Mathesis* but merely *Semiosis,* the adventure of what is impossible to language, in a word: *Text* (it is wrong to say that the notion of "text" repeats the notion of "literature"; literature *represents* a finite world, the text *figures* the infinite of language: without knowledge, without rationale, without intelligence). (1977a: 119)

For Barthes, textuality allows room for the "tactics" of literature, the playfulness of a combination of seriousness and parody, of philosophy and literature, of doing the police, as Dickens says, "in different voices." Barthes' reading and writing do different voices, sometimes obscurely, always excessively, in a single word (*signifiance),* in fanciful etymologies and neologisms, in prefixes, in distended sentences, in the articulation of a philosophy in a book review, in the obscurity and morass of a constant excessive cacophony of voices that drowns the critic and seemingly destroys reason (though often one voice is the voice of reason itself). Yet they always do so with a kind of superficial cheerfulness that maintains its faith, if not in a particular meaning, then in meaning in general. Near the end of his life, when he sought a *"third form,* neither Essay nor Novel" (1986: 281) beyond the intelligence of his career, he discovered, like Lawrence, that literature "coincides absolutely with an emotional landslide, a 'cry' "; then he discovered "in the body of the reader who suffers, by memory or anticipation, the remote separation of the beloved person, [that] a transcendence is posited: What Lucifer created *at the same time* love and death?" (1986: 287). Even then, he found a "moment of truth," of pathos, of what, following Rousseau, he calls "pity" (1986: 288). Such pity is half of Aristotle's response to the world, half of the enunciated power of literature.

In asking about love and death in a voice of pity rather than voiceless terror, Barthes articulates his final question: *What Lucifer created love and death?* This question focuses on the obscurity of literature and discourse while maintaining itself, like the studies of Jakobson, within the *reserve* of textuality. In this he remains closer to Yeatsian modernism than to Lawrentian, to a sense of the complicity of love and death rather than resisting, as Derrida says, that intelligible opposition. "Whenever literature becomes powerful," Yeats wrote,

> the priest, whose forerunner imagined Saint Patrick driving his chariot-wheels over his own erring sister, has to acknowledge, or see others acknowledge, that there is no evil that men and women may not be driven into by their virtues all but as readily as by their vices, and the politician, that it is not always clean hands that serve a country or foul hands that ruin it. . . . And if the priest or politician should say to the man of letters, "Into how dangerous a state of mind are you not bringing us?" the man of letters can but answer, "It is dangerous, indeed," and say, like my Seanchan, "When did we promise safety?" (1962: 121)

Like modernism itself, Yeats gives us different voices, quotations and questions, the stagings of rhetoric, even if his stagings, unlike Lawrence's, do not quite encompass the terrifying otherness of materiality, the impossibility of even an apocalyptic ending to "the roaring vast space" that darkens Tom Brangwen's eyes. Such Yeatsian stagings, as Barthes teaches us (and as Jakobson does, in his way), are our linguistic and literary tactics for overcoming the inertias that dull experience and destroy living language. This, finally, is what Barthes' critical writings do: they speak to and of language in metonymic voices not quite their own, and thus participate in the risks of collaboration and obscurity that make literature possible.

7

The Rhetoric of Pedagogy

Jacques Lacan and the Cure of Mortality

> He nodded a nod full of mystery and wisdom. "I tell you," he
> cried, "this man has enlarged my mind." He opened his arms
> wide, staring at me with his little blue eyes that were perfectly
> round.
>
> —Joseph Conrad, *Heart of Darkness*

In *A Portrait of the Artist* Stephen Dedalus explains to his friend
Lynch that, although Aristotle had not defined pity and terror in the
Poetics, he, Stephen, understood and could explain authoritatively
what Aristotle had meant. "Pity," Stephen says, "is the feeling which
arrests the mind in the presence of whatsoever is grave and constant
in human sufferings and unites it with the human sufferer. Terror is
the feeling which arrests the mind in the presence of whatsoever is
grave and constant in human sufferings and unites it with the secret
cause" (1969: 204). Stephen is describing the difference between the
beautiful and the sublime. Moreover, he is focusing on the opposition
I have tried to outline between Barthes' sense of textual "pleasure"—
pleasures that are, for the most part, *personal* (even under the figure
of *jouissance)*—and Lawrence's intermingling of rhetoric and death to
articulate an *impersonal* metonymic discourse of what cannot be spoken.

But as striking as Stephen's definitions of terror and pity is the
posture he assumes while speaking of such things. In his "lecture" to
Lynch, Stephen could be talking to *anyone:* his interlocutor fades before the universal truths to which he gives utterance (and repeats as
Lynch jokes and puns). That is, the manner he assumes is that of a
teacher in Barthes' description of the speech of teaching as opposed

to the textuality of writing. In teaching, Barthes notes, "a (previous) knowledge is transmitted by oral or written discourse, swathed in the flux of statements (books, manuals, lectures)" (1986: 336). Earlier he had written that the teacher, in his or her oral performance, falls into "a role of Authority, in which case it suffices to 'speak well,' in compliance with the Law present in every act of speech . . . (which is what is demanded of good pedagogic speech: clarity, authority)" (1977: 191). Even when such teaching struggles, as Barthes himself does, with "the two great *epistemes* of modernity, namely the materialist and the Freudian dialectics"—what he calls a moment later "the economy of the relations of production and . . . the economy of the subject"—in order that they "be made to intersect, to unite in the production of a new human relation" (1977: 212), it still attempts to recuperate the other to the same. This is the recuperation of "knowledge" which seemingly stands "outside" political or psychological economies and which, Barthes says, "like delight, dies with each body." Here again Barthes is *personalizing* his discourse, infusing it with pity. His example here is his beloved teacher, Paul Mazon: "when he died," Barthes says, "I never stopped regretting that so much knowledge of the Greek language would vanish with him, that another body should have to begin again the interminable trajectory of grammar, starting from the conjugation of *deiknumi*" (1986: 338).

Beyond such pity for the human sufferer remains the secret cause of such suffering, the terror of that suffering that so often shimmers with brightness in Lawrence: as Longinus says, "just as all dim lights are extinguished in the blaze of the sun, so do the artifices of rhetoric fade from view when bathed in the pervading splendor of sublimity" (cited by O'Hara 1987: 352). Stephen, however, unlike Lawrence, fails to explode his rhetoric in his terror. Instead, he speaks like the teacher Barthes describes who comes "unstuck piecemeal in front of everybody" (1977: 194), an object of pity, not terror. "The end of all theorizing the sublime," Daniel O'Hara asserts, "always reveals a scene of instruction, personal or communal in scope, like that which concludes Joyce's major texts"—a scene that is a "comically hollow affirmation of an annihilating prospect" of a " 'purely' literary conception of the sublime" (1987: 359). In other words, if the sublime is the experience of "terrible," as Heidegger says, "in the sense of the overpowering power which compels panic fear, true fear" (1959: 149)—if it is woven into the very experience of modernism in the sense that the modern world presented to its inhabitants the experience of decentering and loss of control examined in the first chapters of this book—then the examination of such experience in the classroom ludicrously transforms it, as Lionel Trilling said of the experience of the "force and terror" of modernist literature, to something to be studied and "learned" as an "official version of terror" (1968: 12, 27).

Still, it is possible to discover in the crisis of modernism, the "end" of Europe, a situation of learning that is more than "just" literary, in which the sublime comes to inhabit the scene of instruction and the rhetoric of pedagogy—if not in the classroom, then on the analytical couch. Freudian discourse itself, like that of modernism more generally, is one of terror and pity, articulating meaninglessness and loss at the same time it articulates what is most meaningful. It does so by forcing us to resituate its interpersonal signification—its pedagogical discourse—sublimely in relation to death.

Near the beginning of "The Resistance to Theory," Paul de Man makes a claim about the nature of teaching—a claim very close to Barthes' definition of teaching when he contrasts it to writing—that the subsequent rhetorical strategies of his essay in many ways disclaim. "Overfacile opinion notwithstanding," he writes, "teaching is not primarily an intersubjective relationship between people but a cognitive process in which self and other are only tangentially and contiguously involved. The only teaching worthy of the name is scholarly, not personal; analogies between teaching and various aspects of show business or guidance counseling are more often than not excuses for having abdicated the task" (1986: 4). Such a description of teaching as purely *cognitive*— Barthes' "pure instrument of transmission" (1985: 139), the "transference" of preexisting objects of knowledge from teacher to student— is very close to Jakobson's constative scientific critical project. It precludes any relationship between teaching and psychology, disdainfully described here as "guidance counseling." Teaching, in this definition, is not interested in how knowledge is effectively conveyed from teacher to student in the classroom. It concerns itself only with cognition, rather than including strategies to effect cognition—strategies that take into account the particular and *material* situation of the "transference" of knowledge, what de Man himself calls the "pragmatic moment" of teaching (1986: 8). In Bakhtin's terms, this pedagogy enjoins students to recite by heart, rather than to retell in their own words; it aspires to the "resurrection" of Absolute (nonmaterial) Knowledge. In this description, the teacher does not speak to any particular person; like Stephen's lecture to Lynch and like Kurtz's death-bed "pronouncement" in *Heart of Darkness,* the teacher ignores the particular situation of discourse and addresses "the whole universe" (Conrad 1971: 72).

Still, the pragmatics of teaching—its material situation—cannot be as facilely defined and dismissed as de Man's argument suggests. The situation of teaching is better figured by the child's acquisition of language—what de Man calls "a didactic assignment that no human being can bypass" (1986: 13)—whilis is not "a cognitive process in which self and other are only tangentially and contiguously involved" (1986: 4). Rather, language acquisition is a learning process of trial and error, guidance, and working through where the intersubjective functions as forcefully as the cognitive, and in which both teacher and student (parent and child) are not wholly conscious of or fully intending that the education—the "transference"—take place. Such "teaching" entails Barthes' "tactics without strategy" (1977a: 172), which is essentially *discursive* rather than cognitive; it entails the discourse (or discourses) of "enunciation," of language conceived as a *rhetorical* activity, rather than as solely the cognitive process of signification.

In these terms, the relationship between cognition and discourse—what de Man calls the relationship between grammar and rhetoric—is simultaneously essential for teaching and a problem of teaching. Teaching "transfers" knowledge conceived as situated within a cognitive schema that is grammatical, logical, and ahistorical; as such, it is, like representation conceived as *Vorstellung,* a kind of "anatomy" of what is. But because teaching is also situated at a particular material moment that locates its knowledge beyond cognition, its "transference" is something beyond simply a cognitive process, something that approaches the experience of the sublime. In a striking rhetorical figure de Man brings together these conceptions of pedagogy. After arguing that there is "a resistance inherent in the theoretical enterprise itself," he adds that "to claim that this would be a sufficient reason not to envisage doing literary theory would be like rejecting anatomy because it has failed to cure mortality" (1986: 12).

The "cure of mortality" may or may not be the aim of cognitive ("anatomical") pedagogy. In Jakobson, and even in Barthes, cognition functions as a "cure" precisely in its studied avoidance of the terror resonating within its articulations. Yet the rhetorical inclusion of the "cure" of mortality as a negated possibility in this discourse shifts de Man's discussion to another plane of conception, one that is both social and material, a kind of "pragmatic moment" of enunciation that redefines pedagogy rhetorically. In the same way, talk of death at Clarissa Dalloway's party redefines that social event in terms of a larger vision of ongoing life that includes death, that makes the haunting presence of death somehow a constituting element of human social life. The climax of *Mrs. Dalloway,* Hillis Miller argues, is the irruption of death into the life of Clarissa's party that resituates the party itself as the intersection of life and death, what Miller describes as an All Soul's Day inhabited by the dead (1982: 196). Yet the return of a dead past—the return of the repressed—exists on the surface of the present and realizes its power as fundamental to the dynamics of human feeling by conditioning, above all, the present sense and possibility of a future. In the same way, the seemingly marginal *figurative* example de Man uses in his attempt to justify the study of theory betrays the logic of its situation as marginal, as *simply* an example, *simply* rhetoric. It is, instead, a "present" enactment of enunciation, a rhetorical flourish that undermines the opposition between rhetoric and grammar, discourse and cognition, governing de Man's definition of teaching and Barthes' definition of textuality. Such an irruption in de Man's discourse creates the possibility, beyond his initial definition of teaching, of the rhetorical articulation *(Darstellung)* of pedagogy and psychology, of a sublime teaching.

The term "enunciation" recurs throughout the work of Jacques Lacan. Enunciation is symmetrically balanced with its opposite in French, *énoncé,* which has been variously translated as "statement" (as we have seen in Barthes' work) and "utterance." "Utterance" has become the more widely chosen translation for *énoncé,* although it is the less felicitous: *énoncé* is the statement, the abstract, constative "sense" of discourse. Enunciation, on the other hand, is the *act* of utterance, the performance of discourse, what Benveniste calls the "instance of discourse" (1971: 217), the linguistic gesture. But, as I suggested in Chapter 4, enunciation is not a "pure" event without relationship to anything that precedes or follows it. Rather, it is a meaning-event always connected, as Benveniste says, to something else. In fact, the concept of enunciation itself arises at the particular historical moment of modernism when coded binary oppositions came to articulate its experience. It arose (as did psychoanalysis itself, Lacan has argued) at a moment "which is historically defined by the elaboration of the notion of the subject. It poses this notion in a new way, by leading the subject back to his signifying dependence" (Lacan 1978: 77). In this, the distinction between enunciation and utterance is analogous to the distinction between discourse and cognition and to Baudrillard's larger distinction between simulation and production. It is also analogous to the speech-act distinction between the performative and constative aspects of language. Shoshana Felman, in fact, uses this analogy to bring together Lacanian psychoanalysis and Austinian ordinary language philosophy in *The Literary Speech Act* (1983).

Although *énoncé* is univocal in its meaning, there is, as my allusion to Benveniste suggests, a vital ambiguity in the concept of enunciation, one that governs Lacan's global reinterpretation of—what he calls his "return" to—Freud. On one hand, enunciation is defined as "the non-linguistic (referential) structure which underlines linguistic communication" (Greimas and Courtés 1982: 103; see also Ducrot and Todorov 1979: 323). On the other hand, enunciation is the site of signification, the place where competence and performance are joined, where accidental material objects—ink, particular sounds or gestures, colors—are integrated into a structure that signifies. In Saussurean terms, the *énoncé* is the *signified,* while *enunciation* is variously the material *signifier*—the non-linguistic element arbitrarily appropriated by language for the sake of meaning—and the *signifying,* the particular act of appropriation, the particular act of signification.

Enunciation, then, is not a simple concept. Like de Man's conception of rhetoric, it is irreducibly complex. In fact, enunciation encompasses the material conception of rhetoric that I have been developing throughout this book—the materialist dialectic that Barthes joins with the Freudian dialectic at the heart of modernity. In the complex ambiguity of "enunciation" can be seen the ambiguity of Saussure's inaugurating concept of the arbitrary nature of the sign (Culler 1976: 19–23). The linguistic sign is *arbitrary*—any material signifier can be appropriated, and the structure of language allows various distinct pronunciations of words (from a whisper to a shout) to be arbitrarily understood as equivalent, as the "same." At the same time, the sign is apparently *necessary* (or "motivated"), fully determined by the structure in which it is inscribed (Benveniste 1971: 43–49). The complexity of this concept can be seen in the common use of the word: "enunciation" is both interchangeable with "pronunciation" ("Enunciate your words!") and interchangeable with "pronouncement" ("The enunciation of policy"). In the former case, enunciation deals with the (arbitrary) signifiers of language—as Barthes says, with phonetics rather than with phonology—while in the latter case, as the *OED* says, it is "the action of declaring or asserting," the *act* of signification. In terms of the complex definition of rhetoric, enunciation as pronunciation is that aspect of rhetoric concerned with the material and seemingly trivial ornamentation of discourse, the work of show business or guidance counseling: Barthes' "tactile" rhetoric that conditions the study of phenomenological structuralism. Enunciation as pronouncement, on the other hand, is rhetoric conceived in terms of discourse's linguistic and extralinguistic ends, the (arbitrary) pronouncements of signification.

Here, then, the distinction between rhetoric and cognition should be clear. Cognition deals with the signifieds of language, the *énoncés*. Rhetoric, on the other hand, deals with enunciation in its full complexity: it encompasses the *nonlinguistic* site of *linguistic* signification, its very historicity, the pragmatic moment of language (including de Man's "intersubjective relationship between people"). Rhetoric redeems the world from nonsense, but in ways that are arbitrary without seeming so. Rhetoric is signification as pronouncement. But hovering behind discourse, resonating within it, is its own arbitrariness, its own variable pronunciations. This is why both Lacan and Freud make material nonsense so important to their understandings: "when you don't understand what you are being told," Lacan writes, "don't immediately assume that you are to blame; say to yourselves—the fact that I don't understand must itself have a meaning" (cited in Tavor Bannet 1989: 12).

The relationship between enunciation and *énoncé* is vitally important to Freudian and Lacanian psychoanalysis. Psychoanalysis seeks to discover unconscious impulses in patterns of enunciatory behavior, patterns of rhetoric. The so-called accidents of enunciation—Kurtz's whisper, Mynheer Peeperkorn's gesture, Joyce's multivalent style, even the remarkable syntactic and semantic difficulties of Lacan himself—form their own significatory patterns, just as Barthes notices that the rolled *r* of certain French dialects is a simple accident of enunciation, but that in certain contexts, "in the speech of the theatre, for instance, it signals a country accent and therefore is a part of a code, without which the message of 'ruralness' could not be either emitted or perceived" (1968: 20). Depth psychology attends to such patterns of enunciation in an attempt to discover messages of which the speaker of discourse is unaware. For this reason Peter Brooks asserts that Freud "is not only a man of great literary culture . . . , he is also—in a sense that may legitimate the somewhat pretentious word—a semiotician, intent to read all the signs produced by humans, as individuals and as a culture, and attentive to all behavior as semiotic, as coded text that can be deciphered, as ultimately charged with meaning" (1984: 322).

Such attention to all behavior as semiotic situates Freud and his project within the larger project of modernism itself. Not only does Freud mark the relationship between "production" and "simulation" by situating the subject of psychoanalysis, as Lacan says, in the historically defined moment when that subject is led "back to his signifying dependence" (1978: 77). More strikingly, he describes within his very lucidity a "sublime" sense of material mortality. In *Civilization and Its Discontents,* for instance—a book George Steiner describes as "an attempt to devise a myth of reason with which to contain the terror of history" (1971: 23)—Freud attempts to understand "happiness," "aggression," "love," "death," "satisfaction," "guilt"—each of which, according to de Man, "confers the illusion of proper meaning to a suspended open semantic structure" (1979: 198)—within a discourse and a structure of understanding which, like Jakobson's structure of understanding, will account for everything, will find meaning in every accident and danger to which human life is subject. In this text, as in Derrida's description of *Beyond the Pleasure Principle,* "everything is very constructed, very propped up, dominated by a system of rules and compensations, by an economy" (1987: 308).

Yet in *Civilization and Its Discontents* Freud multiplies the dangers to which human life is heir without offering synecdochical hierarchies to understand those dangers. "We are threatened with suffering from three directions," he writes: "from our own body, which is doomed to decay and dissolution and which cannot even do without pain and anxiety as warning signals; from the external world, which may rage against us with overwhelming and merciless forces of destruction; and finally from our relations to other men" (1961: 24). The "secret cause" of such suffering is the (non-sensical) materiality of life itself, and throughout this text Freud repeatedly describes, within the precisions of his lucidity, the failure of the "economy" of these forces (1961: 33, 76), the lack of relationship and correspondence between "civilization," the "individual," and the *material* "secret of organic life in general" (1961: 86). Such a failure governing *Civilization and Its Discontents* as a whole can be seen in the multiplication of metaphors for mind that Freud develops from these "three directions" to describe the ego in terms of biological evolution and archaeology (1961: 15–17).

The importance of this "economic" failure—what Freud calls the spinning of an "unimaginable and even absurd" fantasy (1961: 17)—is the way in which it is a failure of intelligibility. It marks how Freudian determinations of beginnings and ends, the bedrock of materiality he describes in *Beyond the Pleasure Principle* and elsewhere, disrupt semiosis and signification itself in the metonymic play of their multiplying figures. Like modernism more generally—like that of Thomas Mann and even of Conrad—Freud is articulating the "end" of European civilization by inscribing the occult sublimity of overwhelming nonsense within the measured logic of his analyses, alongside the drama of recognition that his discourse presents. He does so, not like Lawrence

through the description of experience in terms of its metonymic elements—the officer's "white hand" clenching the mug, the orderly's wrist
seemingly acting on its own in "The Prussian Officer"—but like Conrad
through the articulation of thought and understanding which, locally
lucid, nevertheless in its multiplication of figures to make sense of
experience enunciates a world in which noise and silence, truth and
lie no longer fit within a (cognitively apprehensible) economy of opposition.

In *Reading for the Plot* Brooks describes Lacan as the follower who
best understood the local lucidity of Freud's "semiotic" message (1984:
322). While this is certainly so, it is so only if we add that Lacan's
conceptions of "understanding" and "lucidity," though tutored by
Freud, are different from the master's. Freud's conception of understanding, as Brooks has described it, is, "like melodrama, . . . the drama
of recognition" (1976: 202), a cognitive enterprise. What are recognized
are depths below surfaces and preexisting causes below effects, articulated in the purely cognitive process of what de Man calls linguistic
allegory's "emphatic clarity of representation" (1981: 1). Freud seeks
such clarity of representation to describe the unconscious, what Brooks
calls "the moral occult." "The signs of the world," Brooks writes, "are
symptoms, never interpretable in themselves, but only in terms of a
behind. If melodrama can reach through to this abyss behind, bring
its overt irruption into existence, it has accomplished part of the work
of psychoanalysis" (1976: 202). Part of the work of psychoanalysis,
then, like part of the work of modernism, is *cognitive:* it interprets
phenomena in terms of what is behind them, their secret and occult
causes, to make sense of accidents, to make sense of nonsense (including the nonsense of Eliot's panorama of the futility and anarchy
that is contemporary history).

Another part of psychoanalysis, as Brooks says here also, is to
provoke abysmal nonsense—hysteria, free-floating anxiety, acting out.
Here we can find a notion of understanding, a "postmodern" notion,
different from Freud's struggle to rethink the economy of causal explanation. Instead of seeking an *énoncé* behind enunciation, psychoanalysis can instead focus on enunciation as the rhetorical play of
signifiers, what Brooks (describing Flaubert) calls "the plane of representation as pure surface" (1976: 198–99). That is, psychoanalysis
can locate the unconscious, as Lacan does, not behind or below consciousness as an agent of impulses we do not recognize (but which is
always susceptible to cognition), but inhabiting enunciation itself, a
function, not a *cause,* of discourse: its metonymic rhetorical *effect.*
Psychoanalysis can locate as unconscious the arbitrary transformation

of nonlinguistic phenomena into signifiers, into acts of signification. "What the structure of the signifying chain discloses," Lacan asserts, "is the possibility I have ... to use it in order to signify *something quite other* than what it says" (1977: 155). Language can function this way because its signifiers are arbitrary and can be appropriated to other signifying contexts. The arbitrary signifier, like Barthes' *r*, can always signify beyond its *énoncé,* beyond its usual place in the hierarchy of language (Schleifer 1987a: 392–93): this is what Lacan means by the "sliding" signifier. Moreover, because language is communal and consequently antedates any particular language user, any particular enunciation of language can also always signify more than its speaker's conscious intentional meaning; it can always leave the speaker unconscious of his or her own signification. The unconscious is acted out on the (rhetorical) surface of discourse.

While this notion of the unconscious is clearly indebted to Freud, it focuses significantly more attention on the signifier than on the signified. That is, its conception of what constitutes understanding is clearly different from Freud's (and de Man's) "cognitive" understanding. This is an example of Greimas's description of the "epistemological attitude" of "the human sciences in the twentieth century in general" (1983: 7) mentioned in Chapter 3, the replacement of depths of metaphysical constructs for a sense of the rhetorical surfaces of things and the "play" of those surfaces. As I mentioned, Greimas cites the "particularly striking" example "the psychology of manners and behavior substituted for the psychology of 'faculties' and introspection" (1983: 7), and while I do not mean to suggest that Lacan is a behavioral psychologist, the shift in focus from *énoncé* to enunciation is nevertheless a shift from seeking faculties behind behavior to exploring the rhetoric of behavior itself. It is an attempt to reconceive understanding as an act beyond mere cognition and beyond pure event. Such a "reconception" *resituates* understanding itself as a historically situated activity that is complexly rhetorical in a rhetoric whose lineaments become clear in focusing, as Barthes and Bakhtin do, on pedagogy.

A short narrative will clarify my point. A friend described to me her experience in psychoanalysis with a Lacanian analyst. At each session she would pay her fifty-dollar fee and lie down and talk. The analyst rarely responded, and my friend found herself becoming more and more anxious. In each session, expensive as they were, she tried harder and harder to get a response. In retrospect, it became clear to her that her discourse was directed not at making some statement but at making her interlocutor hear her. That is, her discourse primarily sought to achieve an intersubjective relationship, rather than a cognitive process; it eschewed *énoncé* for enunciation. And more: finally, as she and her discourse became more and more hysterical in pursuing this aim of personal recognition by the analyst, she discovered herself doing all the things her father had taught her to do as a child to gain *his* attention.

Here, then, is the psychoanalytic transference. It is not the transference of preexisting feelings from one object to another—"the transference is not," Lacan says, ". . . the shadow of something that was once alive" (1978: 254)—but the transference of discursive strategies from one situation to another. More important, here is the psychoanalytic recognition: not the re-cognition of preexisting unconscious impulses governing behavior, but the recognition, the *acknowledgment,* of what is unconscious yet inscribed in the rhetoric of behavior itself, the arbitrary nature of the sign. Such acknowledgment has far-reaching consequences, for the arbitrary nature of the sign suggests not simply that signifiers are arbitrary, but more radically that signifieds—*énoncés,* the objects of cognition—are arbitrary (Culler 1976: 23). Acknowledgment, as Stanley Cavell has suggested, has an important place in the articulation of modernist rhetoric precisely because it theatricalizes the arbitrary nature of the sign and the act of signification. "A 'failure to know,' " Cavell writes, "might just mean a piece of ignorance, an absence of something, a blank. A 'failure to acknowledge,' " he adds, "is the presence of something, a confusion, an indifference, a callousness, an exhaustion, a coldness" (1976: 254). Acknowledgment "theatricalizes" experience by *situating* it: it removes the subject of experience—the one who knows, the one who feels, the one, like my friend in psychotherapy, who imagines that she is ignorant and lacks something—from a special or "primary" relationship to his or her own seemingly "deep," "first-person" experience. It transforms the "primary" personal empathies of pity to an impersonal, metonymic series of events. In fact, acknowledgment makes cognition itself an intersubjective relationship that always takes place as a relational "event" in the present, the event of a dialogic relationship in which participants do not bring "knowledge" to their encounter so much as find themselves in a position to "acknowledge" that it is taking place.

Like Cavell, Stephen Melville has used the reorientation implicit in "acknowledgment" and "theatricality"—both of which are conceptions (though he doesn't use the term) of the "superficial" materiality of experience and significance—to define modernism itself. Modernism, Melville writes, is haunted by the idea of the rupture of continuity (1986: Ch. 1); it is haunted by the sense of both "deep" meaning and superficial futility, what I called in Chapter 3 the tension between the old conception of meaning and the new conception of function. The conception of function is that of situating and theatricalizing experience: it makes art into "mere decoration," it makes meaning into the arbitrary play of significance; it makes the future (and the past) into mere *functions* of the present.

Conrad articulates this tension in the play throughout his work—but especially in *Heart of Darkness*—between surface and depth, what Marlow calls "deep truths" and "surface truths." The deep truths are synecdochical: they are best represented by the "heart" beating in the darkness that Conrad narrates. But such a "heart" spreads, metonymically, across the African landscape to articulate Conrad's sense of being overwhelmed by experience, even while it seems to present a "cognitive" understanding of that experience. In fact, the narrative itself articulates this opposition between synecdochical understanding and metonymic experience as functional in *Heart of Darkness* by describing Marlow's narrative as one in which "the meaning of an episode was not inside like a kernel but outside, enveloping the tale which brought it out only as a glow brings out a haze" (1971: 5). In the same way, the horror of Africa for Marlow is not its secret buried significance, but the fact that Africa is too materially full: it overwhelms by its freedom, its silence, its "featureless . . . monotonous grimness" (1971: 13), so that its significance might be only a local material illusion within its "economic" chaos.

The modernist landscape of Africa is a version of what Lacan calls the "real," which he describes in the same way that Benveniste describes the "simple" nature of physiological and biological data. "The real," Lacan says, "whatever upheaval we subject it to, is always in its place" (1972: 55). Africa, like the real, simply does not respond to the human: for all the shelling, for all the work on the railroad, for all of Kurtz's appalling behavior, "no change appeared" (1971: 16). As Marlow says at the end of the novel, "the heavens do not fall for such a trifle" as his lie to Kurtz's beloved or any particular human meaning (1971: 79). In other words, what is appalling about Africa to Marlow and Kurtz is its overwhelming materiality—the overwhelming substantiveness of the landscape, like the random wastefulness of a pomegranate or the terrible sense de Man takes away from *The Triumph of Life*. "All this," Marlow says of the landscape, "was great, expectant, mute, while the man jabbered about himself" (1971: 27).

Lacan focuses precisely upon the "jabbering" in the talking cure of psychoanalysis. If the semiotician, like Jakobson and Freud, discovers that enunciations form messages, that they structure themselves into signifying patterns, into signs that signify *énoncés,* then my friend's experience in psychotherapy was precisely the opposite. The silence of the analyst forced her to acknowledge that what her childish world presented to her as the structure of language, the way to say something to her father, was only particular enunciations—particular material pronunciations—that her father appropriated as a meaning-structure to create a meaning-effect, an effect of *énoncé.* That silence forced her to acknowledge and *situate* what she could not even recognize as an object of cognition, what she was literally *unconscious of:* namely, her rhetorical act, the act of signification itself.

My friend unconsciously assumed that the way she spoke to her father in order to get a response—her enunciation in a particular material context—defined the mode of human relationships and human cognition. In this way, her experience was the reverse of what we think of as ordinary communication. Instead of using signs to signify a preexisting meaning to someone else, her speech acts suddenly became a material object that she had to acknowledge, just as Cavell argues that pain—whether one's own or another's—is something that has to be acknowledged (even in the withholding of acknowledgment [1976: 266]). In this way, her "meaning" was (or had to be acknowledged as) something different from what she would regard as the ordinary meaning of her words, something of which she had been unconscious precisely because her words were (also) meaningful. Her "understanding," at this point, is more than mere cognition, more than the analyst could have conveyed to her as information, along with, say, information about her bill or about some historical event, certainly more than "communication." Here language, as Colin MacCabe says, "is not only the instrument of communication . . . but also the instrument of noncommunication" (1985: 102), the instrument of acknowledgment, of an intersubjective relationship between people, of a historical situation. In this, language is enunciatory in the double sense of rhetoric that I have described, both an act of signification and the nonlinguistic site of an event. In fact, if the semiotician discovers that enunciations form messages, here messages are analyzed into situated enunciations, into rhetoric.

Such a recognition is effected by what I might call the affective aspect of discourse, the metonymic force that exists alongside its synecdochic understandings. In taking her father's enunciations as *énoncés,* my friend had situated her father as what Lacan calls "the subject who is supposed to know" (*sujet supposé savoir*); in the transference she situates the analyst in the same position (1978: 232). What the subject is supposed to know, as Lacan says, is "that from which no one can escape, as soon as he formulates it—quite simply, signification" (1978: 254). The object of psychoanalytic transference (who is always, Lacan says, the object of love [1978: 254]) is assumed (supposed) to possess meaning, to possess *cognition* as such. Psychoanalytic recognition does not destroy that assumption—it does not (necessarily) destroy love—but *situates* it as an effect of a particular material context. What analysis taught my friend is not how to stop repeating, positively and negatively, her father's enunciations within her interpersonal relationships, but how to recognize and avoid those situations in which such transferential responses unconsciously and destructively determined her behavior.

Modernist literature presents readers with the same kinds of *situated* discourse as analysis does: it *enacts* transferential relationships within the wider context of cultural disruption described in Part One. In *Heart of Darkness* Marlow situates Kurtz as the subject supposed to know. Like the analyst, Kurtz rarely speaks in the novel, yet he is continuously invested by Marlow as the possessor of signification, figured as the voice of the knowing subject. Even before he meets Kurtz, Marlow asserts that his one gift "that stood out pre-eminently, that carried with it a sense of real presence, was his ability to talk, his words" (1971: 48; see Brooks 1984: 246–47). And after Kurtz dies he remembers him as one who "discoursed. A voice! a voice! It rang deep to the very last. It survived his strength to hide in the magnificent folds of eloquence the barren darkness of his heart" (1971: 69). The subject supposed to know is invested with speech and discourse, with signification itself.

That subject is invested with the *knowledge* of what to say. "I was within a hair's-breadth of the last opportunity for pronouncement," Marlow notes, "and I found with humiliation that probably I would have nothing to say. This is the reason why I affirm that Kurtz was a remarkable man. He had something to say. He said it. . . . it had candour, it had conviction, . . . it had the appalling face of a glimpsed truth" (1971: 72). Such a knowing subject, like the teacher, is invested with voice and meaning, because otherwise meaning itself—"truth" itself—would seem arbitrary and meaningless: "my speech or my silence, indeed any action of mine," Marlow says, "would be a mere futility" (1971: 39). Such an investment makes the future seem possible—just as our parents ratify our futures for us, one way or another—in a world like Marlow's Africa, too full and appallingly determined by random material accident to leave room for what Marlow calls the "redeeming" idea—a synecdochical "idea"—behind the robbery, violence, and murder of imperialism (1971: 7). Without such an "idea," born of the investment of knowledge in a subject who is supposed to know, "it would," as Marlow says at the end of *Heart of Darkness,* "have been too dark—too dark altogether" (1971: 79).

The supposition that another subject knows—that the other subject is master of meaning, the way Kurtz's eloquence seems to Marlow to master the darkness of Africa—is the ground and condition for cognition, the very motor of pedagogy. In Barthes' terms, it upholds the Law (1977: 191). Besides filling up the time until the tide turns, Marlow's auditors want to acquire knowledge from "the only man of us who still 'followed the sea' " (Conrad 1971: 5); two of them, at least, silently sit through the narration of another of his "inconclusive experiences" (1971: 7). In the same way, many students study subjects like anatomy or literary theory, which are not self-evidently "useful," because someone else's knowing them simply substantiates the existence of an object of cognition. Since the discursive strategies of the subject supposed to know give rise to the possibility of signification—the possibility of cognition—they create a positivist definition of knowledge as something that can be possessed and exchanged. Thus, while our language—and our enunciatory acquisition of language in childhood—arbitrarily defines the possibilities of our world, such possibilities are "substantified" into certainties by the very fact they are articulated (Schleifer 1987: 206–9).

Nevertheless, language acquisition offers an alternative, less positivistic conception of knowledge and learning—one belonging to Lacanian "enunciatory" psychoanalysis and, more generally, to modernist postmodern rhetoric. Language acquisition is a learning—and a *teaching*—that is significantly intersubjective and substantially *unconscious.* "Linguistics," Gregory Ulmer has noted, "has no social basis as an activity except in the university" (1985: 203); it lacks such a basis precisely because of its radical difference from language acquisition. Linguistics is a purely cognitive object that by definition, in de Man's words, takes for granted "the distinction between the message and the means of communication" (1981: 15), the distinction between *énoncé* and enunciation. Linguistics is a pure metalanguage, a logical or "grammatical" description of language that does not question its own status as a language (see Greimas 1983: 80); it is a glimpse of universal truth which, like Jakobson's criticism, makes the unique object of study invisible.

Language acquisition, on the other hand, does not depend upon the exchange or transference of articulate knowledge, of a message subordinating the means of communication; it is not knowledge that can be acquired and subsequently applied. Language acquisition, as MacCabe notes, "must be understood as constant, as interminable" (1985: 101). That is, language acquisition is an activity beyond the conscious intention of either teacher or student. The child always learns language not simply as a cognitive process but as an activity within relations with his or her environment—relationships, as Felman notes in another context, that *have to do with reality* (1983: 77; see also 1982: 30). Learning language is not learning—"cognition" of—some "thing"; rather, it is the development of a strategy (or rather, a context-specific tactic) for dealing with the world in particular *instances* of world dealing, instances always charged with need, desire, demand. Felman gives a pedagogical example of such an instance when she insists on the difference between the "explicit *statements* about pedagogy" of Freud and Lacan and "the illocutionary force, the didactic function of their *utterance*," their rhetorical (enunciatory) practice. This is, "in other words, the pedagogical situation—the pedagogical dynamic in which statements function not as simple truths but as performative speech-*acts*" (1982: 24).

Infantile instances of world dealing make this most clear. Infants are helpless in relation to the world—they are, as Lacan says, anatomically incomplete due to the *"prematurity of birth"* (1977: 4). The infant is so asymmetrically *situated* within a world of needs that its acquisition of language is enunciatory, situated as demand, inhabited by desire. (Here again are the "three directions" of Freud's metonymic "economy.") Language acquisition is beyond cognition. Or rather, it is *before* cognition, what Blanchot calls (following Winnicott) the "uncertain death, always anterior . . . [which] is never individual" (1986: 66). "I shudder," Barthes writes, "like Winnicott's psychotic patient, *over a catastrophe which has already occurred*" (1981: 96). Lacanian psychoanalysis suggests that the necessary "catastrophe" of language acquisition is the (unconscious) condition of cognition. That is, like the analysand and like the student, the infant is asymmetrically situated in relation to the subject who is supposed to know—the object of transference—whose rhetoric, whose "instances" of discourse, seem overwhelmingly inhabited by signification. "The subject is supposed to know," Lacan notes, "simply by virtue of being a subject of desire" (1978: 253). Here Lacan's rhetoric functions on the margins of cognition: the subject supposed to know—parent, analyst, teacher—both possesses desire and provokes desire. In the first case, desire—like love, or guilt, or knowledge itself—is a metaphysical cause, a "depth" below the surface. In the second, desire is a function of speech, what de Man calls the "figure" of speech, a rhetorical effect.

In the second case, the subject who is supposed to know is a *position* defined in relation to the infant (analysand, student), a position *through which* individuals pass. The child acquires language by using it in relation to the parent (who is supposed to know), just as the analysand achieves recognition in a discursive relation to the analyst. Analytic recognition is not simply a cognitive process but a self-acknowledgment, as Cavell describes it, a situating of the subject in a social (intersubjective) relationship to another subject supposed to know. In the same way, the student acquires "knowledge" in class through the intersubjective linguistic functioning of knowledge, of the class, of the student himself or herself, as well as through a cognitive process. Like the child—and like the analysand—the student acquires language for dealing with the world and for situating himself or herself within the world (including in relation to cognitive knowledge).

This is not to say that *all* language is simply an act or event: language gives rise to its effects—as palpable as love, or transference, or cognition itself—and it conditions causal explanations, just as enunciation, as both the nonlinguistic aspect of discourse and the act of signification, gives rise to the abstract, constative "sense" (*énoncé*) of discourse. That is, the knowledge of language comprises the *knowable* (articulated, already enunciated) object of cognition as well as the *situated* activity of acquisition. Both come together, metonymically, in modernist responses to the cultural crisis of the twentieth century. The first arises in anxiety and allows Eliot to conceive of discourse as substantial, monumental "fragments" that can be "shored against ruin." The second also arises in anxiety, but focuses on the *activity* of signification, of making meaning. For Marlow in *Heart of Darkness,* Kurtz's last words, "The horror! The horror!" (1971: 71) make him "remarkable" because they constitute knowledge; they sum up experience: "He had summed up—he had judged. 'The horror!' He was a remarkable man. After all, this was the expression of some sort of belief. . . . It was an affirmation, a moral victory paid for by innumerable defeats, by abominable terrors, by abominable satisfactions. But it was a victory!" (1971: 72). In Conrad's narrative Kurtz's words are not so clear, not so clearly enunciated, as Marlow describes them. They are not even as clear as what the thunder says in *The Waste Land.* At the moment of death, as Marlow describes it, Kurtz "cried in a whisper at some image, at some vision—he cried out twice, a cry that was no more than a breath: 'The horror! The horror!' " (1971: 71). Kurtz's last words are his last breath, aspirated in a whisper that, *materially* in its liquid aspirants, is indistinguishable from breath, indistinguishable from the noisy nonsense of stertorous breathing (see

Mergler and Schleifer 1985: 177–83). That is, his "words" may not be enunciated words at all, but simply noise that Marlow hears—*arbitrarily*—as words.

Here Conrad narrates a cognitive process, but he situates it so it can also be understood as simply Marlow's own arbitrary rhetorical act, his act of signification: *Darstellung* apprehended as *Vorstellung*. In this, we can help define the modernist moment in what Marlow himself describes as Conrad's "telegraphic" style: Conrad's narrative, like Eliot's fragments, and like the zero degree of Joyce's quasi-indirect discourse, is shored up against the materialist ruin of theatricalization, the rhetoricity of functional surfaces. But more: in *Heart of Darkness* it is shored up against the ruin of Europe in terms of the elaboration of the subject in "his signifying dependence" (Lacan 1978: 77), in terms of acts of signification. The fact that such "universal" experience—of the subject, of culture, of the "secret of organic life in general"—is historically, and thus materially, determined is a constant acknowledged threat in modernism. Marlow selects the nightmare of his choice in his faithfulness to Kurtz, even while his narrative shows Kurtz to be the "same" as the other "flabby devils" of Africa and this choice to be no choice at all, his "eloquence" another form of European imperialism. Like Barthes, but on a different scale, Conrad is personalizing experience, synecdochically reducing "the two great *epistemes* of modernity" that Barthes describes simply to "the economy of the subject" (1977: 212). In *Heart of Darkness* European imperialism is reduced to African noisiness, the material situation of meaning to forms of rhetoric.

The conflation of *Darstellung* and *Vorstellung* in this modernist rhetoric sheds light on the dialogics of psychoanalysis and teaching. In the pedagogical situation, as in Marlow's, the "knowledge" of language is always also an act of enunciation for both teacher and student (Schleifer 1987: 202–6). Knowledge is not simply an object of exchange—the "transference" of "all the wisdom, all truth, and all sincerity" that Marlow thinks he hears at Kurtz's death (1971: 72)—but an affective relationship, what Marlow repeatedly calls, in reference to Kurtz, the "nightmare" of his choice. This is what Felman calls the "passion" of teaching. Teaching, she argues, "is not the transmission of ready-made knowledge, it is rather the creation of a new *condition* of knowledge" (1982: 30, 31). But the language of teaching, like all language, constantly implies "underlying" substances *(énoncés)* to be known. As soon as a material object (such as the sound of breathing) is appropriated as a signifier, it creates the "sense" of a related signified. In this way the object of cognition to be learned arises in the discursive strategies posited by the interhuman world in which the infant acquires language or the patient comes to hear her own enunciation or the student locates the conditions of knowledge. Such an *enunciatory* understanding of pedagogy is one in which the student, like the child, retells knowledge ("enunciates" it) in his or her own words. In this, it obviates the distinction that even a critic as sensitive as Felman draws between Lacan's pedagogical critique, which "is focused on grown-up training," and Freud's critique, which "is mainly concerned with children's education and the ways it handles and structures repression." In this understanding, as Felman herself notes citing Lacan, teaching involves "the relationship of the individual to language" (1982: 23).

In this examination of enunciation and rhetoric I am, perhaps, simply returning to Freud (who stands, synecdochically, for modernism more generally), but with this difference: in seeking the motive behind seeming accidents, Freud, like Marlow, wants to show that human behavior is semiotically motivated and cognitively understandable; Lacan emphasizes another aspect of Freudian semiotics (one also inscribed, without emphasis, in Conrad's modernist text), namely the arbitrary nature of its signs. The moment of anxiety, the hysterical symptom, and the enunciatory aspect of discourse are all both motivated and arbitrary, grammatical and rhetorical, a signifier connected to a signified and a sliding signifier: they are all objects of cognition and objects to be acknowledged. But if this is true, then why shouldn't the teacher, as de Man says, eschew the role of counselor or therapist? Why shouldn't he or she conceive of teaching as impersonal, scholarly, a solely cognitive process without any traffic with the sublime? Why shouldn't teaching *assume* that the "conditions" of knowledge have already been fulfilled?

One answer has to do with the energy of the enterprise, the "desire" for knowledge. The desire for knowledge outside the "pragmatic moment" of the classroom is not a self-evident motive of activity. It might well be that, were anatomy to develop a cure for mortality, we would all want to study anatomy. But what good reason is there to study anatomy in the absence of such a "pragmatics" of cure? One answer, then, is the affective power of transference I described earlier, the power of supposing another *knows*. Transference creates love—not only Lacan, but even Janet Malcolm has eloquently defined transference this way in more traditional psychoanalytic terms (1982: 6–22). Such love and admiration are legitimate and, in any case, unavoidable pedagogical tools.

But the modernist discourse of *Heart of Darkness* suggests another, more radical answer: the complex relationship between the double sense of enunciation that I have described. Enunciation is both nonsense and sense, the noise of breath and the act of signification. *Heart of Darkness* enacts the act of signification in Marlow's understanding—his interpretation—of Kurtz's last words: it enacts meaning in relation to death. In the same way, the therapist faces the patient with death—with silence, like the silence of Marlow's Africa, "great, expectant mute, while the man jabbered about himself" (1971: 27), or with sounds to be understood, finally, as meaningless noise. That is, the therapist, as Lacan says, "cadaverizes" his position, and in the analytic situation "he makes death present" (1977: 141). The presence of death is effected by the transformation or the reconception of the *énoncé*, the immaterial significance, as enunciation, as material and arbitrary acts of signification whose meanings are equally arbitrary.

Lacan's own rhetoric is arbitrary in this way. He has described it as a writing "not-to-be read," but as "a demand for interpretation" (cited in Felman 1985: 132), just as Kurtz's last sounds demand interpretation. Maimonides, Lacan has written, "deliberately organises his discourse in such a way that what he wants to say, which is unsayable . . . can nevertheless be revealed. It is by means of a certain disorder, of certain ruptures and certain intentional discords that he says what cannot or must not be said" (cited in Tavor Bannet 1989: 32). What Lacan himself wants to say, as Eve Tavor Bannet has argued, is the discourse of the Other (1989: 30), what Lacan calls "the voice of the subject outside the subject who structures the dream" (cited by Tavor Bannet 1989: 27). Such a subject is not a positive entity, but precisely the negative materiality I have discussed in earlier chapters. In *The Four Fundamental Concepts of Psycho-Analysis,* Lacan puns on the "*un*" of Freud's "unconscious" and the French "*un*" (one) to allow such negativity to emerge as a "positive" material force: "the limit of the *Unbewusste* [unconscious] is the *Unbegriff* [lack; i.e., the positive lack of consciousness]—not the non-concept, but the concept of lack." "Where is the background?" Lacan continues, "Is it absent? No. Rupture, split, the stroke of the opening makes absence emerge—just as the cry does not stand out against a background of silence, but on the contrary makes the silence emerge as silence" (1978: 26). The discourse of the Other, emerging in its negative materiality within the analytic situation—the scene of instruction—as *parole pleine,* the "full speech" Lacan describes as opposed to the "empty speech," achieves what Tavor Bannet calls a "genuine encounter" for the analysand (1989: 30).

What such speech is "full" of, however, is not meaning, but the activity of signification; it is "full" of "the fact that it is a word which has been uttered by the subject" (Tavor Bannet 1989: 27). "But," Tavor Bannet adds, "in Lacan this experience [of full speech] has few implications for interpersonal relations outside the analytic situation, for Lacan believes that such disalienating encounters are possible only between an analyst and analysand" (1989: 30). Such encounters, then, are "unsayable," materially rhetorical, the sublimity of psychoanalytical pedagogy. "Lacan writes about the oppressive rule of meaning," Jane Gallop has noted, "and in his style he imitates that oppression. . . . The unconscious or the signifier becomes not only the subject matter but, in the grammatical sense, the subject, the speaker of his discourse" (1985: 37). In this way, the subject of Lacan's discourse, in both senses of "subject," is enunciation, rhetoric: it is how he speaks, how we all speak. But unlike my friend both in her therapy and in her dealings with the world that led her to therapy, it is also that about which he speaks.

The therapist, like Conrad, makes the act of signification central and the fact that such signification is not necessary, that it could just as well not be, equally central. The therapist inscribes within the very (arbitrary) *position* of the therapist Heidegger's question: Why is there something rather than nothing? In this, psychoanalysis is the "cure of mortality": it is not the cure of the condition or "object" of mortality assimilated as the object of a cognitive proposition; it does not objectify and then "cure" or "end" death (see Davis 1985: 136–43). Rather, it is a cure *effected* by acknowledging the always present possibility of death, just as my friend recognized the possible death of her father in recognizing the arbitrary nature of his signs—which were *her own* enunciated signs.

In *Heart of Darkness* Marlow, like the teacher de Man describes (and Jakobson and, more anxiously, Samuel Johnson), is a kind of hero of cognition. "You know," he says, "I hate, detest, and can't bear a lie, not because I am straighter than the rest of us, but simply because it appalls me. There is a taint of death, a flavour of mortality in lies— which is exactly what I hate and detest in the world—what I want to forget" (1971: 27). He hates lies because, like death itself, they betray the "presence" (as in Barthes) that voice seemingly conveys; they betray acts of signification with futility. Yet in the end Marlow lies by telling Kurtz's Intended that his last words were her name (1971: 79). That rhetorical act of signification repeats and betrays his "cognitive" action of understanding Kurtz's last sounds. In the end Marlow presents cognition as an enunciatory response to death and darkness not very different from the patient's anxious response to silence: like Jakobson, Marlow responds to death with transcendental knowledge, and his speech remains "empty." The silence of those listening to Marlow does not provoke recognition and acknowledgment in him beyond his cognitive understanding of their inability to understand. He does not question or examine their ignorance. Thus he does not achieve, as Lacan claims psychoanalysis does, the "full" word, the *motivated* word, in its very "hermetic, enigmatic character" (Tavor Bannet 1989: 27–28) somehow beyond the rhetoricity of rhetoric.

Death, then, is the motor of signification in Marlow as well as in Lacan; as Jacques Derrida has written, "nothingness and pure nonsense" (1978: 130) are the occasion for "the bursting forth, the very raising up of speech" (1978: 103). Moreover, death is the motor of transference, the motor of love and of desire itself. For Lacan, desire itself is an act of signification, and the desire for death, the Freudian death-wish, "is not in fact a perversion of the instinct, but rather that desperate affirmation of life that is the purest form in which we recognize the death instinct" (1977: 104). It is the purest form of the affirmation of life because it appropriates death itself—the seemingly inarticulable and radically arbitrary violence of death as discontent, as aggression, as "nothingness and pure non-sense"—as a signifier in the human act of signification. In this, the death-wish seems to produce "*true death*" comparable to the "*true mourning*" that Derrida discusses as impossible precisely because, like the nonsense of death, it undermines "the whole rhetoricity of the true" (1986: 31). The death-wish possesses an irreducible impurity: it is the bursting forth of signification in the face of death, in the face of unintelligibility itself. If the analyst makes death present, it is because it was present all the time, on the very surface of discourse—like Marlow's lies and the "surface-truths" (1971: 34, 37) of Conrad's and Joyce's and Eliot's discourse—enunciated *there,* in the fact that the *énoncé* has to be constructed, realized, shored up by *material* other than itself. In short, it has to be enunciated.

Such enunciations always leave something over, something unconscious, other, material, solitary. The figures Lacan multiplies to represent such remainders are taken from a host of disparate reference systems. More self-consciously than in Freud's metonymic discourse, Lacan empties them of their usual sense "by using key words to mean something other than what they would normally mean within the reference system in question" (Tavor Bannet 1989: 33). In "The Discourse of Rome" from which I have been quoting, Lacan uses the discourse of mathematical topology—"an annulus," "the three-dimensional form of a torus," and so forth—and he enunciates such arcane figures (of which his interlocutors *must* be ignorant) to express, as he says, "the endless circularity of the dialectical process that is produced when the subject brings his solitude to realization" (1977: 105). Such enunciations—of ignorance, of death—give rise to the act of signification that Lacan calls desire. "Desire," Lacan writes, "is neither the appetite for satisfaction [of a need], nor the demand for love, but the difference that results from the subtraction of the first from the second, the phenomenon of their splitting" (1977: 287). Such desire, objectless, barred from a signified, creating a split discourse struggling with itself between enunciation and *énoncé* is, as Lacan says, "situated on the level of enunciation; whatever . . . any enunciation speaks of belongs to desire" (1978: 141). Desire resides between the objects of cognition (such as human needs) and the material nonsense of death. It is an act of signification, the intersubjective enunciation of a particular demand in a particular situation.

As such, desire obviates the difference between cognition and intersubjective relationships. "Death destroys a man: the idea of Death saves him," Helen Schlegel says in E. M. Forster's *Howards End* (1908: 239). While the cognitive "idea" of death doesn't save a person from mortality itself (neither does psychoanalysis), it creates the *condition* of intersubjective relationships—scenes of instruction—in which the subject comes into being. "We can never get back to man separate from language," Benveniste has written, "and we shall never see him inventing it. We shall never get back to man reduced to himself and exercising his wits to conceive of the existence of another." Rather, "it is through language that man constitutes himself as a *subject*" (1971: 224). Benveniste is articulating the terrible fact that no one exists in himself or herself; like Freud and Lacan, he is articulating this fact at the historically defined moment when the subject (of European history) finds itself most arbitrarily alone. This is the condition of intersubjective relationships, and it includes cognition as an act of intersubjective enunciation. As de Man says, even cognitive "*proof*" is a mode "of persuasion . . . no less rhetorical and no less at work in literary texts . . . than persuasion by seduction" (1986: 18). The condition of intersubjective relationships is the condition of desire itself, which *answers* non-sense and death with the rhetoric of language: with subjects brought together with and in discourse, with acts of signification, with cognition. All are brought together in the face of death, which, as Jakobson's African interlocutor says, is "everywhere."

In this way the enunciations of psychoanalysis help define the dialogics of teaching that Bakhtin described in his discussion of the radically rhetorical nature of discourse. The value of Lacanian enunciatory psychoanalysis to teaching is that it helps to situate it as a rhetorical human activity. The teacher, of course, does not aim to make death present— although sometimes he or she may—and neither does the teacher pursue a hysterical discourse. Rather, the teacher aims, as Felman says, to create a "passion" for learning, the possible *occasion* in students for the energy and motive to see around the received ideas of acquired enunciatory strategies, or at least to recognize them not as neutral "truths" but as rhetorical strategies inhabited by unconscious desire, by another's desire. Such an occasion is *enunciatory.* It erases the opposition between "knowledge" and "ignorance" (as Felman demonstrates), just as Lacanian analysis erases the opposition Barthes articulates between love and death. It does so by making the negativity of "ignorance" carry as much pedagogical weight as the positivity of "knowledge." "The truly revolutionary *pedagogy* discovered by Freud . . . consists in showing the ways in which, however irreducible, *ignorance itself can teach us something*" (Felman 1982: 30). Such teaching, however, is only an *occasion* for learning. Just as the analyst "cadaverizes" his position and makes death present, the teacher makes ignorance present on the very surface of discourse, in order to effect an interplay of meanings *(énoncés)* constructed, formed, realized, somewhere else—in students, in silence, in the fact that the received ideas of students are different from those of the teacher. Just as analysis allows the subject to acknowledge his or her own desire—and, perhaps, to become cognitively aware of it—so teaching makes ignorance its object, something to be understood.

In these terms, de Man's opposition between cognition and intersubjective relationships, like Barthes' opposition between writing and teaching, clearly does not exhaust the discursive possibilities of pedagogy. There is also the complex notion of enunciation, which creates the possibility of cognition in its acts of signification and the necessity of (interpersonal) desire in its arbitrary motives for such acts. That is, while teaching cannot (and should not) sustain transference's hysterical play of love and death with its aim of acknowledgment and self-awareness, it should (and can) find a way to sustain the desire inhabiting transference, the desire to create both the condition of knowledge and knowledge itself. Such *pedagogical* desire may be a kind of hysteria without its symptoms: *The Waste Land,* for instance, articulated in the zero-degree language of Mailer's *Executioner's Song.*

Stuart Schneiderman has noted that Lacan once said "he was a perfect hysteric" (1983: 16), and reading Lacan's prose one often gets a sense that he was right in this judgment. But Schneiderman goes on to say that, for Lacan, a perfect hysteric is one without symptoms. In this, Lacan was describing himself as a teacher and describing pedagogical desire. For hysteria without symptoms is like language playing between its status as the transparent medium for a cognitive process and its status as an intersubjective situation and activity. That is, if the symptoms of hysteria are rhetorical enunciatory patterns that form unconscious messages *(énoncés)* readable by the traditional analyst, then a nonsymptomatic hysteria is a true "education"—a kind of Lacanian "education"—a drawing forth, rather than a laying on, of signification. This is an *occasion* for signification—"the bursting forth, the very raising up of speech" (Derrida 1978: 103)—that is subject to cognitive (semiotic) analysis even while it enunciates an intersubjective relationship. Answering nothingness and pure non-sense, it is, as it were, the "cure of mortality," the condition of cognitive desire.

Late in life Freud himself related an anecdotal example of what Constance Penley calls "the unconscious and total respect that we accord our teachers":

> As you walked through the streets of Vienna—already a greybeard and weighed down by all the cares of family life—you might come unexpectedly on some well-preserved, elderly gentleman, and would greet him humbly almost, because you had recognized him as one of your former schoolmasters. But afterwards you would stop and reflect: "Was that really he? or only someone deceptively like him? How youthful he looks! And how old you yourself have grown! *Can it be possible that the men who used to stand for us as types of adulthood were so little older than we were?*" (cited in Penley 1986: 131)

For Penley, this passage is an example of the *effect of transference* that inhabits pedagogy. But it marks as well the objectification of desire that inhabits students' ignorance when they recite another's words without hearing—without acknowledging—their own enunciated retelling. In this way, the ignorance of students is not only what they do not know; it is also their *supposing* that their teachers *do* know. Teachers are supposed to be typical and, more than that, like Kurtz, the masters of desire and need. That supposition supports the pedagogical enterprise by supposing the teacher to be the subject of enunciation's desire—even though teachers, as Freud's story suggests, are not different from their students.

In this anecdote, the measure of the student's ignorance is the measure of death, which in *its* seeming repetitious materiality makes all human beings seem the same old men. The ignorance of students is the enunciation of difference in a world where all things seem to come to the same material end. It is the ignorance inscribed in the distinction that Marlow—and Conrad—make between Kurtz's savage black woman, an "image" of the "tenebrous and passionate soul" of the wilderness who carries herself "like the wilderness itself, with an air of brooding over an inscrutable purpose" (1971: 62), and his civilized Intended, whose face shines with "the great and saving illusion" of faith (1971: 77). This racist and sexist distinction allows Marlow to lie to the Intended at the end of the novel and allows Conrad to lie to himself about an "unselfish belief in the idea" that can redeem imperialism (1971: 7). Such ignorance, like the desire for death that chooses its own end in Lacan (1977: 104–5), and like Lacan's own distinction between empty and full speech, inhabits meaning as a desire. In Marlow's case, it is a desire for light and truth, for possible preexisting objects of cognition. In Freud's case, it is the student's desire that someone know, that someone master, if only cognitively, this mysterious world. In Lacan's case, it is the desire that psychoanalysis, the talking cure, actually cure. This transferential desire is the motor of pedagogy, and it is what psychoanalysis can teach us about teaching, for teaching, like modernism and criticism, is rhetorical and enunciatory. Beyond the *énoncé* inhabiting books and lectures—the cognitive process of pedagogy inhabiting "the person who says *I*," as Barthes says, ". . . *setting out* a body of knowledge, . . . *never knowing how that discourse is being received*"(1977: 194)—is a *situation* of teaching that provokes desire and occasions signification.

Enunciated pedagogy—psychoanalytic pedagogy—is a kind of cure of mortality. As a pure cognitive process, it forgets death, erases it, in the same way that Marlow wants to forget mortality and that anatomy does "forget" the mortality of the body it studies. As an intersubjective counseling, a scene of transference, it is the cure of received ideas effected by the confrontation of mortality and the desire to which mortality gives rise. But most of all, as a social institution, the pedagogical cure of mortality, like the "cure" of a priest, is the "parish" of mortality, where life goes on, language is taken up, and teachers, as in Freud's anecdote, become fellow citizens and fellow mortals growing old with their students.

8

The Rhetoric of Mourning

Jacques Derrida and the Scene of Rhetoric

But was it Ulysses? Or was it only the warmth of the sun
On her pillow? The thought kept beating in her like her heart.
The two kept beating together.

> —Wallace Stevens, "The World
> as Meditation"

In an essay entitled "Domesticating the Foreign Devils," Nancy Armstrong addresses the question of the clashing rhetorics of contemporary literary studies, a question that takes in the larger issue of the possibilities of the "translations," as Jakobson might call them ("transference," Derrida says [1987: 383; 1979: 87]), of postmodern discourse theory altogether. Armstrong is specifically addressing the viability of the interdisciplinary rhetorics I have been examining in relation to contemporary rhetorical practices. She begins by asking, "What . . . is the nature of the transformation necessary to domesticate structuralism so that it no longer estranges readers who have traditional literary training? Can a linguistics-based theory undergo such transformation and still remain what it is?" (1982: 248). Armstrong is questioning whether cross-cultural and interdisciplinary studies are possible, whether rhetoric can speak across disciplines, and, if so, under what circumstances and at what cost. In the most radical way, she is asking if the "negative" materialism of death can, in fact, inhabit the "cure"—the parish—of discourse and understanding.

This, in fact, is the question that Jacques Derrida asks of psychoanalysis generally and of Lacan most specifically. Lacan, he says, has taken the "theses" of *Beyond the Pleasure Principle* describing the death drive most seriously and has "constructed an entire discourse" around this seriousness (1987: 377). Derrida asks whether in such a discourse the immanence of death,

> as an internal necessity of life, the "proper path toward death".... were nothing but a consoling belief? And if it were an illusion destined to help us, as the Poet once more says, "to bear the burden of existence" ...? To make it more bearable as *Ananke* than it would be as accident or chance? Let us translate: and if the authenticity proper to *Dasein* as *Sein zum Tode* [Heidegger's "being-in-the-world" as "being-towards-death"], if its *Eigentlichkeit* [authenticity] were but the lure of a proximity, of a self-presence *(Da)* of the proper, even if in a form which would no longer be that of the subject, of consciousness, of the person, of man, of living substance? (1987: 373)

Is such consolation, he is asking, the "consolation" of death itself, the "authenticity" of death, the intelligence that recognizes death in its "authenticity," simply a "great narrative poem, the only story that one always tells oneself, that one addresses to oneself, the poetics of the proper as reconciliation, consolation, serenity?" (1987: 363). With these questions Derrida is asking whether death can be domesticated, diverted, brought back, reduced, and incorporated, if not into "humanism" (for these are Sartre's words, cited in Chapter 4), then into the "endless circularity of the dialectical process" that Lacan describes, which is produced "when the subject brings his solitude to realization" in relation to the "death instinct" (1977: 105, 104).

Derrida, like Armstrong, is asking to what extent the foreignness of death, its *otherness,* will allow death to make itself at home in language, in modernism, in even what I have called the "resonations" of discourse. Can the "other" of Europe—which is to say, the foreign "other," neither white nor male, and not, as Westerners were learning at the turn of the century, simply a more or less debased "version" of the European—what Derrida calls the "utterly *other*" (1979: 100), somehow be thought? Reading Blanchot's *L'arrêt de mort (Death Sentence* [but also "reprieve," the "arrest" of death]), Derrida attempts to examine the narrator's relationship to two absolutely separate women in the narrative (which might, in fact, be two absolutely separate—*metonymically* separate—narratives). The narrator's "double signature" on an *arrêt de mort,* Derrida writes, "binds him to each of the two dead women ..., each of these two revenants, living on as ghostly fiancées—this bond is double.... It signifies, desires, *arrête* life death, the life the death of the other so that the other lives *and* dies, the other of the other—who *is* without being the *same*. For there is an other of the other, and it is not the same: this is what the order of the symbol seeks desperately to deny" (1979: 165–66). The order of the symbol is the order of binarism Jakobson describes, the order of the "persons" of discourse in Barthes, even the discourse of the Other in Lacan. Derrida's question concerns whether there is something *beyond* the symbol, *beyond* Jakobson's intelligence or Barthes' pleasure principle or the solitude of Lacan's subject.

To speak in figures, Derrida is asking whether Stephen Dedalus and Leopold Bloom can and finally do meet. "Jewgreek is greekjew," says Stephen's cap in the *Circe* episode, "Extremes meet" (Joyce 1961: 504). But the question remains: Do Greek and Jew meet only in dreams—in Lacan's terms, do father and daughter meet only in the imaginary—or is another meeting, say on Eccles Street, possible? "Encounter *is* separation," Derrida writes in his early essay on Edmond Jabès. "Such a proposition, which contradicts 'logic,' breaks the unity of Being—which resides in the fragile link of the 'is'—by welcoming the other and difference into the source of meaning" (1978: 74). The modernist rhetoric of contemporary discourse theory that I have been describing throughout this book attempts to create at least this ambiguous "welcome," this modest "encounter," this seeming meeting-place for extremes. Philosophy, psychoanalysis, theology, linguistics, semiotics, all have met literature under the rubric of "rhetoric," a rubric that Terry Eagleton explicitly describes as "discourse theory" (1983: 206).

But the question remains whether such a rhetoric of the heterogeneous is possible. Can the returning Odysseus be *compared* to the exiled Abraham? "Are we Jews? Are we Greeks?" asks Derrida; and he answers, "We live in the difference between the Jew and the Greek, which is perhaps the unity of what is called history" (1978: 153). In an essay entitled "Jewish Oedipus," Jean-François Lyotard also confronts Greek and Jew: "Oedipus fulfills his fate of desire; the fate of Hamlet is the non-fulfillment of desire: this chiasmus is the one that extends between what is Greek and what is Jewish, between the tragic and the ethical" (1977: 401). Lyotard goes on to describe this opposition in terms close to the opposition between interpersonal persuasion and material configuration, the two conceptions of rhetoric with which I began this study.

In Hebraic ethics representation is forbidden, the eye closes, the ear opens in order to hear the father's spoken word. . . .

"Hearing," writes Rudolf Bultmann, "is the way to perceive God. . . . Hearing is the knowledge—abolishing all distance— of knowing oneself encountered, of recognizing the claim of him who speaks." Thus one does not *speculate,* one does not ontologize, as Emmanuel Levinas would say. . . . Yet the ethical subject knows himself possessed by an Other who has spoken; he knows himself . . . elected in "a passivity . . . [which] does not become eros, nothing suppresses in this passivity the trace of the Other in his virility in order to bring the Other back to the Same. . . ." (1977: 402–3)

For the Jew there is no return because there is no reconciliation. The Other remains outside, heterogeneous, not so much the incomprehensible barbarian as simply another nation *(Goyim),* in what Derrida calls the "violence" of nonassimilation, discontinuity, otherness.

Lyotard contrasts the speculation of the Hellenic, Apollonian eye, which takes in all in its "thing-bound and gestaltist perception" (1977: 397), to the Jewish ear. Against the eye, which, even if it takes in all, can be closed, is faced the ear that *cannot* close, "so that the cry or the lapsus or the silence coming from somewhere else may be heard" (1977: 401). This "facing" of eye and ear is what Armstrong calls the "clash of discourses." It suggests what, living in our time, we have been taught to listen and look for: that within language might be inscribed an Other discourse, one not heard above or below the vision of the text but "resonating" against it, as one figure of an optical illusion is inscribed against the other. Such resonation is articulated in Stevens's poetry. It can be heard, for instance, in "Waving Adieu, Adieu, Adieu," where Stevens asserts that "just to be there and to behold" is a form of "saying farewell, repeating farewell" (1954: 127). Such an assertion presents a discourse in which, as Derrida says, "the 'same' words suddenly [change] their sense, overflowing with sense or exceeding it altogether, and nevertheless impassive, imperturbable, identical to themselves, allowing you still to read in the new code of this anasemic translation what belonged to the other word, the same one, before . . ." (1979a: 5). Similarly, it can be seen in Stevens's clashing figure from the epigraph to this chapter, "The World as Meditation," where thought and heart beat together (1954: 521) in an enunciatory gesture both significatory and physical, marking, I shall argue, negative materiality, the locus of discursive violence, the rhetoric of mourning.

In *The Post Card* as well as in his study of Blanchot, Derrida describes this "facing"—this clash of discourses—in the simple juxtaposition *"life death,"* in which "death is not opposable, does not differ, in the sense of opposition, from the two principles [the "road" to death and life's "detour" Freud describes in *Beyond the Pleasure Principle*] and their *différance.*" Rather, death "is inscribed, although non-inscribable, in the process of this structure. . . . If death is not opposable it is, already, *life death*" (1987: 285). Such a figure, "life death," presents the radical metonymy of modernist rhetoric that I have been describing, "without causality, without absolute synchrony, without order." It presents "seriality without paradigm . . . . [whose elements are] at once analogous (hence the series) and utterly different, offering no guarantee of analogy" (1979: 165, 130). In this, discourse presents the "mute word," the "*ghost* effect," and the basic "psychoanalytic problematic" Derrida describes in the work of Nicolas Abraham: "How can we include in a discourse," Abraham asks, "*any* discourse, that which, being the very condition of discourse, would by its very essence *escape* discourse?" (cited in Derrida 1977a: 77, 91, 93).

In the terms I have been developing in this book, how can the *materiality* of discourse, inscribed and traversed (as all materiality is) by death, by the metonymic historicity of death, be "included" in discourse? An "analysis" resulting in the paradox of this "superimprinting of texts"—the superimprinting of "relationships of cryptic haunting from mark to mark" (1979: 137), which is neither inclusion nor exclusion and which "surpasses negativity," as Derrida says (1979: 107)—would speak "*like* an unconscious, in the manner of the unconscious, *Wo Ich war soll Es werden*" (1977a: 76): where I (the ego) was, there shall it (the id) come to be. Here Derrida is proceeding in the manner of Lacanian analysis, reversing Freud's great semiotic project of replacing the nonsense of "it" with human meanings. Where meaning, sense, "life" is, so shall the nonsensical materiality of meaning, of sense, of "death" also, non-opposably, resonate. Where the triumph of life is articulated, so too shall resonate what Derrida, following Freud, calls the "triumph" of mourning (1979: 108–10).

Throughout his work Derrida has focused upon and made the materiality resonating in discourse a theme in his work. He describes that theme as the violence of and in language, what he specifically calls "the original violence of discourse" in "Violence and Metaphysics" (1978: 133). Moreover, he has done so in ways that parallel what I am describing as the violence effected by rhetoric when it is conceived not only as simply ornamenting what could have been said in a different way, but also "superimprinting" on this conception another conceiving of rhetoric as determining meaning and experience. This violence is articulated in Greimas's figure of the "explosion" of meaning in language (see Mergler and Schleifer 1985), but throughout his work Derrida extensively describes the violence inscribed in language and figures it, significantly, in terms of what I am calling the negative materiality of death. Thus he argues that writing "obeys the principle of discontinuity," the negative materiality of spacing. "The caesura does not simply finish and fix meaning," he writes. Rather, "primarily, the caesura makes meaning emerge. It does not do so alone, of course; but without interruption—between letters, words, sentences, books—no signification could be awakened. *Assuming* that Nature refuses the *leap,* one can understand why Scripture will never be Nature. It proceeds by leaps alone. Which makes it perilous. Death strolls between letters" (1978: 71).

The violence of language, Derrida argues, is a function of the self-contradictory senses of "writing" resonating in language: "writing in the common sense is the dead letter, it is the carrier of death. It exhausts life. On the other hand, . . . writing in the metaphoric sense, natural, divine, and living writing, is venerated" (1976: 17). "Natural writing," he says, "is immediately united to the voice and to breath" (1976: 17); in it the accidental materiality of language—the acoustical image, the marks on the page, the *sound* of Kurtz's breathing—becomes a transparency for thought. The violence embedded in language is the fact that its materiality cannot disappear, that it is not quite secondary and transparent, but a determination of discourse itself: "What writing itself, in its nonphonetic moment, betrays, is life. It menaces at once the breath, the spirit, and history as the spirit's relationship with itself. It is their end, their finitude, their paralysis. Cutting breath short, sterilizing or immobilizing spiritual creation in the repetition of the letter, . . . it is the principle of death and of difference in the becoming of being" (1976: 25). Writing cuts life short by creating the illusion of summing up, of judging—with candor, conviction, and the vibrating note of revolt—within what Derrida calls its "long metonymy." Unlike the Greek, who elects "Being," the Jew, he writes, "elects writing which elects the Jew, in an exchange responsible for truth's thorough suffusion with historicity and for history's *assignment* of itself to its empiricity" (1978: 65; see also Handelman 1983: 104).

In this, as Susan Handelman has written, "Derrida's specific form of Jewish heresy is not metonymy become metaphor but metonymy run amok, metonymy declaring itself to be independent of all foundations and yet claiming to be the origin and law of everything" (1983: 122). Last words, like Kurtz's last enunciation noted by Marlow, or like the "hoarse breathing" of the "death-rattle" [*râles*] Derrida describes in *L'arrêt de mort* (1979: 115), signify through a kind of violence

by virtue of their material (and liminal) situation in a world where
nothing, certainly no language, is "last." The violence of language, like
that of psychoanalysis, is the violent conjunction of materiality and
"spirituality," and its final violence is death: "it is always an *external*
constraint," writes Derrida, "that arrests a text in general, i.e. *anything,*
for example life death" (1979: 115).

Death is inscribed in language as that material "other" both addressed and invoked (dative and vocative): "the other cannot be what
it is, infinitely other, except in finitude and mortality (mine *and* its)"
(1978: 114–15). Thus Derrida writes that "the dative or vocative dimension which opens the original direction of language cannot lend
itself to inclusion in and modification by the accusative or attributive
dimension of the object without violence. Language, therefore, cannot
make its own possibility a totality and *include* within itself its own
origin or its own end" (1978: 95). Derrida is describing the distinction
between *enunciation* and *énoncé* examined in the last chapter. The
accusative or attributive dimension (the dimension of *énoncé*) is a
systematic structure (in Lévi-Strauss's terms, "an atemporal matrix
structure" [1984: 184]), while the dative or vocative dimension (the
dimension of enunciation) is an activity which, above all, articulates
itself within the materiality of what Derrida calls "the living present."

That materiality is marked by the other in which death, "although
non-inscribable" (Derrida 1987: 285), is inscribed.

> The other is given over in person *as other,* that is, as that which
> does not reveal itself, as that which cannot be made thematic.
> I could not possibly speak of the Other, make of the Other a
> theme, pronounce the Other as object, in the accusative. I can
> only, I *must* only speak to the other; that is, I must call him
> in the vocative, which is not a category, a *case* of speech, but
> rather the bursting forth, the very raising up of speech. . . . I
> can speak *of it* only by speaking *to it;* and I *may* reach it only
> as I *must* reach it. But I must only *reach* it as the inaccessible,
> the invisible, the intangible. (1978: 103)

Language violates the other by inscribing it within the same in the
same way that modernism makes the other its theme, politically, geo-
graphically, culturally. (And in the "same" way that Derrida, at least
in his early work, thematizes death. Compare the passage above, from
"Violence and Metaphysics," to the "athetic" reading of *Beyond the
Pleasure Principle* in "To Speculate—on 'Freud' " in *The Post Card.*)
Language effects its violation of the other in a violent gesture marking
the "living present," the temporality and corporality (in a word, the

materiality) of its statement. As Derrida says, "the living present is originally marked by death" (1978: 133). In this way the future is inscribed within an always present materiality. But language also marks the present with the future—it "haunts" the present from mark to mark. If the material death that awaits us is articulated in the *present* arbitrary assumption of a material signifier that language enacts, then the possibility of meaning (which is another articulation of the future, insofar as meaning—both intentional and unintentional meaning—only takes place in the future) is articulated in discourse as well.

This is why Derrida asserts that the Other is both addressed and hidden in discourse, why the death drive is both a consolation and an anxiety (1987: 363). Like the double time and ambiguous corporality of language, like the "double bind" of a "death sentence," of "death" as symbol and death as non-inscribable negative materiality, it is both there and not there. In this assertion Derrida is subsuming the psychoanalytics of discourse examined in the last chapter under a broader understanding of rhetoric. That is, he makes the mortality inscribed in language more apparent, more explicit: it is the violence of language, addressing and veiling that other unspeakable violence of temporality, bodily decrepitude and death:

> Discourse, therefore, if it is originally violent, can only *do itself violence,* only negate itself in order to affirm itself. . . . This secondary war, as the avowal of violence, is the least possible violence, the only way to repress the worst violence, the violence of primitive and prelogical silence, of an unimaginable night which would not even be the opposite of nonviolence: nothingness or pure non-sense. Thus discourse chooses itself violently in opposition to nothingness or pure non-sense, and, in philosophy, against nihilism. (1978: 130)

It is precisely this violence of radically metonymic opposition—the opposition of what Lévi-Strauss calls the "dual periodicity" of breathing and sense (1975: 14)—that distinguishes Derrida from the *systematic* oppositions of Jakobson's structuralism and of traditional philosophy more generally.

In other words, the violence of language for Derrida is the violence of the "restricted economy" of meaning (a term Derrida borrows from Georges Bataille) that wrests from the play of language and the more terrible play of time a semantic "reserve" of the "timeless simplicity of an intelligible object" (1978: 225). The "reserve" of language, Derrida argues in a discussion of Hegel, is that ability of language and discourse to use everything in, to appropriate everything to, its signifying force "by means of which philosophy," Derrida says, ". . . could both include within itself and anticipate all the figures of its beyond" (1978: 252). The reserve of language allows it to appropriate everything to the accusative case, to make everything speakable. Everything, that is, except the sacred—in Derrida's words, "the heedless sacrifice of presence and meaning" (1978: 257)—which in this early essay he figures as laughter, though later he figures it as "mourning's mourning." Here Derrida describes the "burst of laughter," "the almost nothing into which meaning sinks" in discourse as figuring the "point" of nonreserve in language. It is "the *point*," he says, "at which destruction, suppression, death and sacrifice constitute so irreversible an expenditure, so radical a negativity—here we would have to say an expenditure and a negativity *without reserve*—that they can no longer be determined as negativity in a process of a system" (1978: 256, 259). Rather than such a determination—which, after all, is a determination of meaning— here language circumscribes the locus or "point" of the silent violence of nothingness or pure non-sense in the bursting forth of laughter, or in the enunciation of the vocative "primal cry" of mourning.

I believe Derrida is situating the possibility of the sacred—the effect of the sacred—in language. The sacred is a kind of radical negativity in language, the palpable "force" of language—whether understood as Jakobson's sense that the "truth" inhabiting language cannot be resisted, or Barthes' sense of the force of textuality, or Lacan's sense of the "full" word as a psychological and psychoanalytical force. Derrida sees this force, more explicitly than these other "postmodern" critics, as the force of our historical and mortal condition inhabiting and resonating within language as rhetoric without reserve. I use the term "resonate," but in his description of the death of Freud's daughter, Sophie—the mother of the child who plays *fort: da* in *Beyond the Pleasure Principle*—Derrida speaks of the "intonations" that could be understood in reading Freud's letters: " 'As if she had never been' can be understood according to several intonations," Derrida writes, "but it must be taken into account that one intonation always traverses the other" (1987: 329). The crisscross traversings of intonations is a constant possibility within the wealth of sensible meanings language presents to us. In this case, it is the superimprinting of "negativity" so radical that it is "non-opposable" in relation to any "positivity," to the reserved meanings of discourse: the destruction, suppression, death, and sacrifice of Sophie's life "as if she had never been." Such traversing, Derrida says, is "a procession underneath the other [discourse], and [goes] past it *in silence,* as if it did not see it, as if it had nothing to do with it, a double band, a 'double bind,' and a blindly jealous double" (1979: 78).

It is, I could say, the procession of the death drive, which, Derrida does say, "always *comes* from *leaving,* which always *has just left*" (1987: 369), like the one who walks besides Eliot in *The Waste Land.* Moreover, such negativity haunts language like a ghost—the ghostliness of negative materiality, or the repetition compulsion that is the focus of *Beyond the Pleasure Principle* and Lacan's "Seminar on 'The Purloined Letter.' " Derrida describes such compulsion as a form of the "sacred" under the negative designation of "*the return of the demonic.*" He adds, however, that "truly speaking, there is not a return *of the* demonic. The demon is that very thing which *comes back* without having been called by the [pleasure principle]. . . . Like Socrates' demon—which will have made everyone write, beginning with him who passes for never having done so—this automaton comes back without coming back to anyone, it produces effects of ventriloquism without origin, without emission, and without addressee. . . . Finality without end, the beauty of the devil" (1987: 341). Writing here seems to be discourse without a subject, the *force* of language "beyond" the intentions of meaning (which French defines in its articulation of "meaning," *vouloir dire,* "wanting to say"). Writing is ventriloquism without origin, "voicelessness" (Derrida 1979: 104), what de Man calls "the power of death" (1984: 122). Elsewhere Derrida describes death itself "as the result of the dissemination of the rhythm of life [of discourse? intonation?] with no finishing stroke, unbordered and unbounded arrhythmy" (1979: 121). In this he inscribes death within language in a way that articulates the sacred and still makes the discourse of mourning function like prayer and the "violence" of language more generally, beyond even the "reserve" of de Man's despair. Moreover, in this he is participating in a major gesture of modernist discourse, a kind of suffusing elegy in a rhetoric, like Stevens's, that attempts to articulate whatever remains sacred in the face of nothingness and non-sense, something that might suffice.

Both prayer and mourning address another who is "absent," not *there.* Prayer may address the possibility of the presence of that other—it articulates faith in that possibility—while mourning self-consciously addresses absence itself and thus starkly conceives of itself as words without an object or an interlocutor, as simply "rhetorical." Yet the vocatives of both prayer and mourning also function the way more ordinary accusative (or "referential") discourse functions. Unlike mourning and like referential discourse, prayer shapes its address to

create the effect of substantifying the objects of discourse: it creates
effects of transcendentality, knowledge, identity. However, mourning
also functions by creating such discursive effects, even if, in mourning,
they are negatively conceived as simply "rhetorical"—functions, as
Nietzsche says, of an apparatus of falsification (Stambaugh 1972: 71).
In any case, as I argued in Chapter 4, it is the referential or accusative
aspect of language that allows Samuel Johnson to understand that he
does no violence to Juvenal in "The Vanity of Human Wishes" when
he translates *dinoscere* with five nouns and verbs for seeing, because,
rather than addressing another, he is surveying the world. Johnson's
horror of madness eschews both cursing and blessing—it eschews the
sacred in language altogether, whether it manifests itself in mourning
or prayer—and it does so to avoid discontinuity with what Barthes calls
"a rhythm, a tempo, a history" (1972: 181). Wordsworth shares this
urge to continuity (see Hartman 1964; Schleifer 1977), and his impulse
to narrative—his urge to discursive signification—is a refusal of what
Derrida calls the "apocalyptic superimprinting of texts" (1979: 137).
It is a refusal of the direct address of apostrophe, an encounter with
an Other.

Still, prayer shares the urge to discursive signification in its vocative
encounters (which, as Derrida says, are also "separations" [1978: 74])
with an Other. (Mourning also possesses this urge to discourse, but
without the transcendental "reserve" of prayer.) Religious faith, like
de Man's definition of metaphor, translates mere possibility into certainty; it is the ground for an encounter with the absolutely other that
is more than the vocative yet less than the accusative. Such faith seems
to create its discourse absurdly, simply by a suspension of overwhelming disbelief. It seems to be, as de Man says of Kierkegaard, "a leap
out of language into faith" (1969: 204), a leap out of rhetoric. But this
"absurd" faith remains an effect of language, a "sacred" effect of rhetoric and its apocalyptic "traversings." In these terms, language itself,
with its "power of generalization," its accusative urge to transcendentality, makes faith itself another material and "phenomenal" effect.
Such a definition of faith as a "language-effect" even suggests the possibility of encountering an other *within* language, within what Derrida
call "*disbelief* itself" (1986: 21), faithlessly, rhetorically. Here disbelief,
along with being overwhelming—along with being a motive for
"faith"—would itself seem an effect of language in a world where vir-
tually everything—not only the toil and strife of crowded life, but linguistic activity itself—is a function of contingent materialism.

Such material "disbelief" is the breach of prayer, the opposite of
prayer. But it is not nihilism, as many have argued, even if it produces

the light, as Derrida says, "where nothingness appears" (1986: 21). Rather, it is prayer without the "reserve" of belief, the rhetoric of mourning articulated in a language that can be figured, as Derrida figures it, by "death." Its relationship to nihilism is the same as mourning's relationship to melancholia. It is, in other words, an instance of rhetoric without reserve—precisely that "sublime," neither belief nor disbelief, that the high modernism of Yeats, Eliot, Conrad, articulates and recoils from.

Such "encounters" with an Other—whether faithfully or faithlessly—might well define literary criticism, especially the rhetorical criticism I am examining here. Criticism has always attempted to suspend disbelief even when it attempted to confront not simply the elements of meaning (the imperium of the eye, for instance) but even different modes of discourse (that of eye and ear, for instance, or that of Greek and Jew). In this way it has aspired to be a kind of sacred discourse. In *Mimesis,* for instance, Erich Auerbach begins his account of the representation of reality in Western literature by comparing two modes of discourse, the specular rhetoric of Homer and another rhetoric, the sacred texts of the ancient Jews:

> It would be difficult, then, to imagine styles more contrasted than those of these two equally ancient and equally epic texts. On the one hand, externalized, uniformly illuminated phenomena, at a definite time and in a definite place, connected together without lacunae in a perpetual foreground; thoughts and feeling completely expressed; events taking place in leisurely fashion and with very little suspense. On the other hand the externalization of only so much of the phenomena as is necessary for the purpose of the narrative, all else left in obscurity; the decisive points of the narrative alone are emphasized, what lies between is nonexistent; time and place are undefined and call for interpretation; thoughts and feeling remain unexpressed, are only suggested by the silence and the fragmentary speeches; the whole, permeated with the most unrelieved suspense and directed toward a single goal (and to that extent far more of a unity), remains mysterious and "fraught with background." (1957: 9)

For Auerbach there seems to be no intersection of sacred and profane discourses. Homer's "real" world, he writes, "into which we are lured, exists for itself, contains nothing but itself; and Homeric poems conceal nothing, they contain no teaching and no secret second meaning" (1957: 11). In the story of Abraham and Isaac, however, "since the

reader knows that God is a hidden God, his effort to interpret it constantly finds something new to feed upon. . . . Far from seeking, like
Homer, merely to make us forget our own reality for a few hours, it
seeks to overcome our reality: we are to fit our own life into its world,
feel ourselves to be elements in its structure of universal history" (1957:
12).

Auerbach is comparing two radically opposed rhetorical modes of
discourse: that of the "fraught" silence of the Bible against the noisy
spectacle of Homer's world in which "everything is visible" (1957: 2).
Auerbach is describing speech and sight against silence, the accusative
against the vocative; in doing so, he is crossing literature with something else—doctrine, a sacred text, above all, as he says, "truth." What
the biblical writer "produced," Auerbach says, "was not primarily oriented toward 'realism'. . . ; it was oriented toward truth" (1957: 11–
12). This "truth" is not "knowledge" as Nietzsche described it: it cannot
be encompassed by the accusative imperium of the eye. Johnson knew
knowledge could sustain different rhetorical modes, just as it could
ignore the confusion of curse and blessing; like the Greeks, like Aristotle, he *knew* whatever was was clear, determined by form, susceptible to knowledge, the self-evidence of the eye. This seeing could be
articulated in five different words, verbs and nouns, because reality
was—it had to be—full, its elements discretely (and transcendentally)
self-identical. Johnson knew knowledge could sustain different rhetorical modes because of his faith in what is: for him, rhetoric itself was
simple, wholly tactical, but embedded within the strategic aim—the
purpose—of articulating knowledge which was in no way subject to the
play of rhetoric. For Johnson, as in Derrida's description of Heidegger,
"the thinking of the rhetoricity of rhetoric . . . is in no way a rhetoric"
(1986: 109).

The "truth" of the Bible, however—like the sacred truth of prayer—
is conceived not as referential verity but as power, overwhelming power.
Truth, Auerbach argues, did not interest Homer, because truth invokes
the other in a discourse that describes strategy without tactics: "the
Scripture stories do not, like Homer's, court our favor, they do not
flatter us that they may please us and enchant us—they seek to subject
us, and if we refuse to be subjected, we are rebels" (1957: 12). Unlike
Jakobson's rhetoric of passivity, which flatters by positioning his readings in subjects who know in an "unbiased, attentive, exhaustive, total"
way (1968: 127), Scripture seeks to overpower us with its silence, with
"indications" of "thoughts which remain unexpressed" (1957: 8). It
seeks to overpower us, as death and disbelief do, "without reserve."
Yet it does so *non-rhetorically*: Scripture offers us the impossibility—

the *violence*—of contrast without comparison, depth without surface, the horror of the sacred.

This is the work of the vocative, of apostrophe which, as Jonathan Culler has argued, is a means of articulating depth because it offers the "image of voice"—a figure that confuses eye and ear. Thus Culler writes, "Whitman says that 'I and mine'—which is to say strong poets—'do not convince by arguments, similes, rhymes. We convince by our presence.' The poet makes himself a poetic presence through an image of voice, and nothing figures voice better than the pure *O* of undifferentiated voicing" (1981: 142). The deep truth is imageless, Shelley said, and his problem, unlike Johnson's, is to plumb that depth, to attempt to articulate that truth, to "hear" what is not to be heard. (His problem is also unlike that of the "semiotic" Freud who, like Marlow at Kurtz's death, immediately and without discussion "translates" the child's sound, "o-o-o-o," into the German word *fort* [see Derrida 1987: 311–12].) Shelley offers a fine image of the discourse of the "deep truth"—it is the discourse of prayer—in "Hymn to Intellectual Beauty," in which the ghostly shadow of Intellectual Beauty nourishes thought "Like darkness to a dying flame!" (1914: 527).

Such "hidden" presence—like the hidden presence of God that Auerbach describes inhabiting language and rhetoric, and like Longinus's negative image of the sublime ("for just as all dim lights are extinguished in the blaze of the sun, so do the artifices of rhetoric fade from view when bathed in the pervading splendor of sublimity")—is a species of negativity, a voice that cannot be repeated, not simply, as Shelley's lyric implies, because language cannot approach it, but because it is a voice that calls for a response rather than proferring knowledge. "God separated himself from himself," Derrida says in the essay on Jabès, "in order to let us speak, in order to astonish and to interrogate us. He did so not by speaking but by keeping still, by letting silence interrupt his voice and his signs, by letting the Tables be broken" (1978: 67). Only faith can approach such absent presence—such deferred, radically metonymic "presence"—through prayer.

In *Fear and Trembling*, Kierkegaard, like Auerbach, attempts to articulate the situation of Abraham as one more profound than that of a Hellenic poet like Shelley seeking to "know" God.

> Abraham keeps silent—but he *cannot* speak. Therein lies the distress and anguish. For if I when I speak am unable to make myself intelligible, then I am not speaking—even though I were to talk uninterruptedly day and night. Such is the case with Abraham. He is able to utter everything, but one thing he

cannot say, i.e., say it in such a way that another understands it, and so he is not speaking. The relief of speech is that it translates me into the universal. Now Abraham is able to say the most beautiful things any language can express about how he loves Isaac. But it is not this he has at heart to say, it is the profounder thought that he would sacrifice him because it is a trial. This latter thought no one can understand, and hence everyone can only misunderstand the former. (1954: 122–23)

Abraham cannot speak the image of God's voice; he cannot repeat God's saying because, unlike Nature and Passion, which Johnson says are everywhere the same, God's sayings are never the "same." They are untranslatable into another system of signs, never to be understood.

There is no language for God's language because that language is only depth. It is a sacred text, as Barthes says, a *writing* beyond hearing, "symbolical, introverted, ostensibly turned towards an occult side of language, whereas [*speech*, Johnson's language, Homer's language] is nothing but the flow of empty signs, the movement of which alone is significant" (Barthes 1967: 19). Barthes is describing the absolute difference from the noisy spectacle of Homer's rhetoric of the silence of the sacred text. God's speech cannot be repeated because that speech is pure act, an apostrophe that cannot be imaged: like Abraham's silence, it is *immaterial.* And above all, the language that addresses God, the language of prayer, is *non-rhetorical*; it aims at avoiding at all costs the violence of language and rhetoric, the violence of death. "In the last analysis, according to Levinas," Derrida says,

> nonviolent language would be a language which would do without the verb *to be,* that is, without predication. Predication is the first violence. Since the verb *to be* and the predicative act are implied in every other verb, in every common noun, nonviolent language, in the last analysis, would be purified of all *rhetoric,* which is what Levinas explicitly desires; and purified of every *verb.* Would such a language still deserve its name? Is a language free from all rhetoric possible? The Greeks, who taught us what *Logos* meant, would never have accepted this. (1978: 147)

Language without rhetoric is the language of prayer, the language of tongues. In *The Executioner's Song* the devout Mormon, Pete Galovan, "didn't remember all the things he said in the prayer, or even if he held her hand while he prayed. One was not supposed to remember what was said in prayers. It was a sacred moment, and not really to be repeated" (Mailer 1979: 133). Such nonrepeatable moments do not allow the "same"; rather, they leap out of language toward the sacred.

Late in life Kierkegaard reevaluated the negativity and—more important—the *rhetoricity* of Socrates that he had described in his first book, *The Concept of Irony* (see Schleifer 1984: 183–200 for an examination of Kierkegaard's early thesis). "The Socratic irony," he argues in *Concluding Unscientific Postscript,* allows room for what he calls the "Socratic gaze," a way of not seeing in a world of sight, a kind of blindness, a form of silent prayer: "Socrates has understood his God-relationship in such a manner that he dared not say anything at all, from fear of indulging in foolish prattle" (1968: 83). After all the irony, all the words, all the mere rhetoric, Socrates discovered the essential secret: "when Socrates isolated himself from every external relationship by making an appeal to his *daemon,* and assumed, as I suppose, that everyone must do the same, such a view of life . . . constituted an essential secret, because it cannot be communicated directly. The most that Socrates could do was to help another negatively, by a maieutic artistry, to achieve the same view" (1968: 74). Such maieutic artistry—Kierkegaard calls it "indirect communication"—describes the indirect rhetoric of prayer.

Yet if it apprehends a silence beyond irony, the Socratic ignorance of eye is still not Kierkegaard's absolute prayer precisely because the *"non-rhetorical"* discourse of prayer does not admit even an "indirect" rhetoric: "the Socratic ignorance," Kierkegaard concludes, "is a witty jest in comparison with the earnestness of facing the absurd; and the Socratic existential inwardness is as Greek light-mindedness in comparison with the grave strenuousness of faith" (1968: 188). As the case of Abraham shows, the grave strenuousness of Hebraic faith is but a little removed from the "disbelief" of mourning that Derrida describes, from modernism's *work* of mourning. Yet that little remove is the difference—an absolute difference—between the non-rhetorical silence of prayer and the violent rhetoric, the rhetoric without reserve, of mourning.

In his pseudonymous writing Kierkegaard follows Socrates and develops a technique for contrast without comparison, the "indirect" method of irony. As Geoffrey Hartman has noted, irony achieves "the elimination of the surface/depth distinction" (1981: 167), and for Kierkegaard it achieves it in prayer through the elimination of surface—of rhetoric—in favor of depth. Derrida also performs this ironic confrontation ("encounter," "superimprinting," "traversing") in his work, yet he does so more explicitly and less faithfully than Kierkegaard's Socrates, so that the scene of this confrontation is what he calls "the concept (material of language)" (1978: 95), the scene of rhetoric. (In this, he is more the Greek than the Jew.) For Derrida, as for the literary modernism I have described, the scene of rhetoric is on the surface, enacted in an absolute theatricalization of language that is rhetoric without reserve. In some ways Derrida is a kind of Samuel Johnson gone mad: his rhetorical strategy uses elements *across* different linguistic levels—this can be seen most clearly in his neologisms, in which he presents particular figures for his effects (Schleifer 1987: 181–82)—in the same way that Johnson has the wit of his eye, so to speak, in his survey of the topologies of crowded life. Yet, unlike Johnson, Derrida multiplies these figures—"supplement," "hymen," *"différance," "arrêt de mort,"* "life death," and so on and on—taking them up and putting them down until it seems that metonymy has run amok.

Derrida's irony is thoroughly rhetorical and textual, thoroughly witty, thoroughly Greek. Even his polemical "confrontations," such as that with Searle, construct their discursive tactics, their rhetoric, by means of particular words so that his attempt to "deconstruct" Western metaphysics seems tightly bound, rhetorically bound, to texts in ways that the more serious—the more "Jewish"—Kierkegaard's is not (see Said 1983: 183–84). "Deconstruction," Christopher Norris notes, is "an activity of reading which remains closely tied to the texts it interrogates, and which can never set up independently as a self-enclosed system of operative conceptions" (1982: 31). Derrida's lack of "seriousness"—which is metonymic rather than synecdochic, a lack of faith in the "universality" of discourse rather than Kierkegaard's faith that there *must* be transcendental significance in the particular—articulates the "wittiness" of rhetoric. "Wit," Hartman argues, "the presence of mind in words, is the opposite of a failure to speak. Yet wit, pointed or periphrastic, is often felt as a wounding of language. . . . Wit is called for in moments when words might fail as meanings" (1981: 135). Johnson and Derrida (as opposed to Kierkegaard, who only "speaks" pseudonymously) are full of words, the former with a faith in the efficacy of words, the latter with the "ironic" sense that they are irreducibly complex, traversed by complexity. Both are inscribed on the "axis" of wit, the axis, finally, of rhetoric.

Derrida is fully rhetorical, tied to texts as material objects whose very effects of transcendence are rhetorical effects that remain immanently in the living present marked by death. As he says of Freud, rather than manipulating metaphors in order "to make of the known an allusion to the unknown"—clearly the rhetorical strategy of Shelley and Kierkegaard—Freud makes "through the insistence of his metaphoric investment . . . what we believe we know under the name of writing enigmatic" (1978: 199): where the ego was, there shall the id come to be. Like Lacan, Derrida insists that the arbitrary nature of the sign is not to leap out of language, as Kierkegaard does, but to reveal rhetorically

> the poetic or the ecstatic ... that *in every discourse* ... can open itself up to the absolute loss of its sense, to the (non)-base of the sacred, of nonmeaning, of un-knowledge or of play, to the swoon from which it is reawakened by a throw of the dice. What is poetic in sovereignty is announced in "the moment when poetry renounces *theme* and meaning" [in Bataille's words]. It is only announced in this renunciation, for, given over to "play without rules," poetry risks letting itself be domesticated, "subordinated," better than ever. This risk is properly *modern.* To avoid it, poetry must be ... [as] Bataille says ... "the commentary on its absence of meaning." ... The poetic image is not *subordinated* to the extent that it "leads from the known to the unknown;" but poetry is almost entirely fallen poetry in that it retains ... metaphors that it has certainly torn from the "servile domain" ... (1978: 261–62).

If Kierkegaard seeks prayer beyond language, then Derrida seeks the risk of a "*modern*" and modernist moment in language. He realizes this in his discourse as the rhetoric of mourning, just as the modernist poets, in Stephen Spender's description, made "the crisis of poetry, the necessity of criticism, the themes of their poetry" and made "the vision of what a civilization has lost" the overriding elegiac theme of their work (1965: 254). Derrida articulates a sacred vocative discourse. But unlike Kierkegaardian Romanticism, he eschews synecdoche and articulates a language that speaks "in memory of" another who is "irremediably absent, annulled to the point of knowing or receiving nothing himself of what takes place in his memory" (1986: 21). Such a discourse, like that of prayer and psychoanalysis (but unlike that of Johnson or Jakobson, or even Barthes' textualities), is sacred.

The rhetoric of Derrida can be most clearly discerned if we examine it in relation to the modernist language of Wallace Stevens. Stevens achieves a rhetoric of mourning close to that of Derrida's critical discourse, in which the violence of language is not the accusatory violence of Yeats or Eliot, but a kind of invocatory violence resonating "behind" or "alongside" language just as Derrida constantly hears "death" alongside language, hears the sacred activity of generating meaning in a world of nothingness and pure non-sense. In "The Owl in the Sarcophagus," his elegy for his friend Henry Church, Stevens describes three forms that move among the dead: "high sleep," "high peace," "And a third form, she that says / Good-by in the darkness, speaking quietly there, / To those that cannot say good-by themselves." Describing this third figure, Stevens articulates its rhetoric: "The third form speaks, because the ear repeats, / Without a voice, inventions of farewell" (1954: 432). A few lines later Stevens quotes and describes this third figure,

> she that in the syllable between life

> And death cries quickly, in a flash of voice,
> Keep you, keep you, I am gone, oh keep you as
> My memory, is the mother of us all,

> The earthly mother and the mother of
> The dead.

The rhetoric of mourning speaks for those who cannot speak for themselves. But more than this—or included within this—it speaks for the mourners themselves, who, as psychologists tell us, in the "shock" of bereavement are bereaved of voice as well as friend.

Mourning is a well-structured psychological process that people experience in a repeated pattern of ordered stages of behavior. In fact, anthropologists suggest that the stages of mourning may be invariant across cultures. The first stage is often called denial or shock, and it is often characterized by numbness, refusal to accept the loss, and a kind of speechlessness. Mourning, then, has a particular relationship to speech and discourse, just as Derrida says that the "thought of death . . . begins, like thought and like death, in the memory of language" (1988: 279). Moreover, like prayer, mourning has a curious relationship to silence. It calls upon the ear to silently repeat voice: it calls upon the ear, as Stevens often does, to "hear" what is not said, what is not there, just as mourning articulates a relationship with someone who is gone. "But O the heavy change," Milton laments in *Lycidas,* "now thou art gon, / Now thou art gon, and never must return." What can be heard in such lament is change itself in relation to meaning and ordinary experience. Maurice Blanchot narrates a related experience— the experience of mourning itself, I think—in a paragraph called "A primal scene?" which I quoted in Chapter 2. There a child looks through a window and sees "the ordinary sky, with clouds, grey light— pallid daylight without depth. What happens then: the sky, the *same* sky, suddenly open, absolutely black and absolutely empty, revealing (as though the pane had broken) such an absence that all has since always and forevermore been lost therein—so lost that therein is affirmed and dissolved the vertiginous knowledge that nothing is what there is, and first of all nothing beyond" (1986: 72). Blanchot is describing an experience of mourning, but it is also an experience that Derrida describes as "something other than a consolation, a mourning, a new well-being, a reconciliation with death," what he describes as "mourning's own mourning" (1985: 73).

The rhetoric of mourning—or what Freud calls, in a remarkably apt description, the *"work* of mourning"—attempts, among other things, the recovery of voice in the face of such experience, the recovery of rhetoric. It is, as Stevens seems to suggest, the recovery of speech—a "flash of voice"—if only in the ear's silent repetition of "farewell." Such a discourse is a rhetoric "without reserve." It seeks, as Greimas says of poetry in general, to "reachieve the 'primal cry,' " to produce the "illusory signification of a 'deep meaning,' hidden and inherent in the plane of expression" of language (1967: 279). Peter Sacks has argued that this is the work of mourning and, in literary terms, the work of elegy. "Much of the elegist's task," Sacks writes, "lies in his reluctant resubmission to the constraints of language" (1985: xiii). This task is the opposite of faith's leap out of language and rhetoric. "By a primitive form of mourning," Sacks continues, "the child not only comes to terms with the otherness and absence of his first love-object, he also learns to *represent absence,* and to make the absent present, by means of a substitutive figure accompanied by an elementary language" (1985: 11). De Man figures such represented absence as *prosopopoeia,* the rhetorical term designating, as he says, "the fiction of an apostrophe to an absent, deceased, or voiceless entity, which posits the possibility of the latter's reply and confers upon it the power of speech." Such power manifests itself by creating a face: "voice assumes mouth, eye, and finally face. . . . Prosopopoeia is the trope of autobiography by which one's name . . . is made intelligible and memorable as a face" (1984: 75–76). What is memorable about a face, however, is that it encompasses the being, the existence of an other in its ability, as Derrida says in his discussion of Levinas, to exchange glances (1978: 98).

In these terms, the work of mourning is a work of violence, and prosopopoeia articulates or reiterates what Derrida calls "the original violence of discourse" (1978: 133; see also 101): mourning articulates voice for the other and voice for the speaking subject. As Derrida says, "I could not possibly speak of the Other, . . . I *must* only speak to the other . . . in the vocative, . . . the bursting forth, the very raising up of speech" (1978: 103). The bursting of language—the violence of the vocative—is a response to the "worst" violence of death itself: nothingness or pure non-sense. In this way mourning, unlike prayer, is the language of the vocative in its very "primal cry": "the survivor," Sacks says, "leans upon the name, which takes on, by dint of repetition, a kind of substantiality, allowing it not only to refer to but almost to replace the dead" (1985: 26). Such substantification is very different from that determined by faith: it substantifies loss, not presence; it is a powerful rhetorical signifier marking absence in a "real" world in which, as Lacan says, everything is *in its place*. For this reason, I think, Stevens never mentions Henry Church's name in "The Owl in the Sarcophagus," and for this reason elegy usually finds "another" name for the object of mourning.

But in *Memoires for Paul de Man* Derrida repeats Paul de Man's name time and time again in a way, as he says, to remember and memorialize him, in what he calls "a magical incantation, uttered without many illusions, but as if, having become as one with his name in my memory, the departed friend would respond to the just call of his name as if the impossibility of distinguishing Paul de Man from the name 'Paul de Man' conferred a power of resurrection on naming itself, or better still, on the apostrophe of the call recalling 'the naked name,' as if any uttered name resuscitated resurrection: 'Lazarus, arise!'—this is what the apostrophe to the naked name would say or stage" (1986: 47). In mourning it is not the object of discourse, or even the Other who is addressed that is substantified. Rather, the very rhetoric of discourse—the material raising up (the "staging") of speech and the ability of that speech to produce "effects"—is substantified. In fact, this substantification of language is, in an important way, the "work" of mourning that Freud describes. "What are we doing," Derrida asks in his elegy for Barthes, "when we exchange these discourses? Over what are we keeping watch? Are we trying to negate death or retain it? . . . Should we convince ourselves that the death never took place or that it is irreversible, that we are protected from a return of the dead? Or should we make the dead our ally ('the dead within me'), . . . to finish him off by exalting him, to reduce him in any case to that which can still be contained by a literary or rhetorical performance . . . [within] all the ruses of the individual or collective 'labor of mourning'?" (1988: 277). The "labor" or "work" of mourning, Derrida continues, is precisely the "problem": "if mourning labors," he says, "it does so only to dialectize death, to dialectize that which Roland Barthes *called* 'undialectical' ('I could do no more than await my total, undialectical death' [Barthes 1981: 72])" (Derrida 1988: 277).

The "work" of mourning, then, is the very enunciation of speech— its literary or rhetorical performance—in protest of, but also in "deference" to, reality. The "normal outcome" of mourning, Freud says, "is that deference for reality gains the day"; nevertheless, "its behest cannot be at once obeyed" (1963: 166). The deference for reality of which Freud speaks is deference for death, for the death of the other, and more, the death inscribed in prosopopoeia—which, de Man says, "as the trope of address, is the very figure of the reader and of reading" (1986: 45). Prosopopoeia, Derrida adds in reading de Man, "remains a fictive voice, although I believe that this voice already haunts any said real or present voice" (1986: 26). It haunts it like a demon, the "ghostly" materiality of non-sense returning to discourse even though, in the very material of discourse itself—in the fact that it is "staged," "enunciated," articulated by means of material wholly other than itself and, equal to all this, addressed to another who "is given over in person *as other*" (1978: 103)—this "fictive voice" is always already *there*.

For this reason Derrida says "there can be no *true mourning*." Rather, mourning is "only a tendency: a tendency to accept incomprehension, to leave a place for it, and to enumerate coldly, almost like death itself, those modes of language which, in short, deny the whole rhetoricity of the true.... In doing so, they also deny, paradoxically, the *truth* of mourning, which consists of a certain rhetoricity—the allegorical memory which constitutes any trace as always being the trace of the other" (1986: 31). The work of mourning, then, is to say, as Stevens says, "what nothingness permits," and to say it—to invoke it—*through* some other language. Derrida's example of the rhetoricity of mourning as its "allegorical memory" remembers de Man's work on allegory, "The Rhetoric of Temporality"—but only to ears that can hear the allusion through the discussion of mourning's truth, ears that cannot help repeating Paul de Man's name when allegory is discussed. Here discourse becomes hallucinatory, just as de Man himself notes that prosopopoeia is "hallucinatory": "it is the visual shape of something that has no sensory existence" (1986: 49). A speaking ear, for instance; or a dead friend.

Throughout his poetry Stevens provides us with such hallucinatory hearing—the nothing that both is and isn't there, music beyond the genius of the sea, the mother of beauty within whose bosom we devise our sleepless mothers who wait and care. He does so, as does Derrida's discourse, in a rhetoric of mourning. Like Shelley's "Hymn to Intellectual Beauty" in which Intellectual Beauty is figured as something to be seen *through* the brightness of life, so Stevens sees death and the ear that repeats it—makes it heard—*through* the discourses of life, our "same" life, the cacophony of voices with which *A Passage to India* ends and modernism begins. Shelley's language, however, is that of prayer, which Derrida argues (significantly in the rhetoric of counterfactual subjunctives) would be "nonviolent": "without the verb *to be*," "without predication," "purified of all *rhetoric*" (1978: 147).

Stevens's language of mourning, like Derrida's, articulates that moment in modernism when discourse is contaminated by rhetoric—when it is enacted at the very scene of rhetoric. Yet this rhetoric, like Shelley's prayer, affords a kind of nourishment in its hearing. Take, for instance, Stevens's late poem, "The Plain Sense of Things":

> After the leaves have fallen, we return
> To a plain sense of things. It is as if
> We had come to an end of the imagination,
> Inanimate in an inert savoir.
>
> It is difficult even to chose the adjective
> For this blank cold, this sadness without cause.
> The great structure has become a minor house.
> No turban walks across the lessened floors.
>
> The greenhouse never so badly needed paint.
> The chimney is fifty years old and slants to one side.
> A fantastic effort has failed, a repetition
> In a repetitiousness of men and flies. (1954: 502)

Stevens figures what can be seen *through* the springtime life in winter, "the great pond and its waste of the lilies" as he says in this poem, a plain sense, a blank cold of mourning. It is seen (or heard) through the ordinary, what Herbert Schneidau calls the "sacramentalism" of modern writing using the most "humble and unremarkable" things— like the ordinary sky Blanchot describes, or the house Stevens describes—to figure the sacred (1977: 438). But here the sacred is conceived of as negative, as a kind of negative materiality. In the first stanza, for instance, "inanimate" is reduced to its material sound, *in-an-imate*, the ghostly repetition ("return") of its sound that is there all along, "in an inert": where meaning (or "spirit," or the imagination) was, there shall non-sense (or the blank cold of "matter" and the "letter") come to be.

Derrida uses and describes a similar rhetoric—"mourning's own mourning"—to articulate whatever can be called the sacred in the violence of rhetoric "without reserve." Rhetoric without reserve is the very scene of rhetoric, the place where the material of language creates effects alternating between meaning and nonmeaning—the two definitions of rhetoric I have been pursuing in this book. "If all justice begins with speech," Derrida says, "all speech is not just. Rhetoric may amount to the violence of theory, which *reduces* the other when it *leads* the other, whether through psychology, demagogy, or even pedagogy which is not instruction" (1978: 106). Here Derrida is vaguely alluding to Freud's description of psychoanalysis, education, and government as the " 'impossible' professions in which one can be quite sure of unsatisfying results" (Freud 1963a: 266). In "Freud and the Scene of Writing" Derrida adds "literature" to these rhetorical disciplines, which all correspond, also quite vaguely, to the different rhetorics examined in this book.

But more important, in "Freud and the Scene of Writing" Derrida calls for "a psychoanalysis of literature respectful of the *originality* of the literary signifier" (1978: 230), which he describes as the "textual drama" of the conflict between meaning and nonmeaning, the sacred and the profane. Such a psychoanalysis of the signifier focuses on that side of language which is not "reserved," the noise of laughter or the silence inscribed in the rhetoric of mourning in which nonreserve, *disbelief* itself, rises up from or is enunciated within meaningful language. Each time we speak or act "in memory of" a dead friend, Derrida says in *Memoires for Paul de Man,* "we know our friend to be gone forever, irremediably absent, annulled to the point of knowing or receiving nothing himself of what takes place in his memory. In this terrifying lucidity, in the light of this incinerating blaze where nothingness appears, we remain in *disbelief* itself. For never will we believe either in death or immortality" (1986: 21). The blaze where nothingness appears is the "flash of voice" of Stevens's poem and of modernism more generally, the moment of discourse (not of laughter) in which the material silence behind or resonating within language, the nothingness and non-sense language violates, rises up alongside language itself.

Like de Man, and like the psychoanalysis of Lacan in which the analyst "cadaverizes" himself to create what I believe is the scene of mourning, an occasion for the bursting forth of speech, Derrida here arrives at the *rhetorical* problem of metaphor, of figurative language. Metaphor is rhetoric as strategy, but it is also rhetoric as the material of language, "the animality of the letter" (1978: 73), the condition of language. "Before being a rhetorical procedure within language," Derrida writes, "metaphor would be the emergence of language itself" (1978: 112). If metaphor is the emergence of language, mourning is the explicit site of that emergence in which language and its opposite—the "nonreserve" of language, a radical "negativity" that cannot even be called "negativity," that "cannot be inscribed in discourse" (1978:

259)—play against one another in a blaze where nothingness appears,
nurtured as darkness nurtures a dying flame.

This emergence of language, as Stevens says, takes place in silent
repetition—the repetition of ear—in which nothing is said and heard.
Listen to this poem:

> That would be waving and that would be crying,
> Crying and shouting and meaning farewell,
> Farewell in the eyes and farewell at the center,
> Just to stand still without moving a hand.
>
> In a world without heaven to follow, the stops
> Would be endings, more poignant than partings, profounder,
> And that would be saying farewell, repeating farewell,
> Just to be there and just to behold. (1954: 127)

Here, as in so many of Stevens's poems, nothingness blazes forth. Its
violence is that of dying embedded in our lives and in our language,
inhabiting everything in the play between the accusative and vocative
forces of language, the same and the other, inhabiting every ordinary
thing in its acknowledged otherness. "To be one's singular self," Stevens
goes on,

> To despise
> The being that yielded so little, acquired
> So little, too little to care, to turn
> To the ever-jubilant weather . . .
>
> That would be bidding farewell, be bidding farewell.

In this poem poignancy comes from the stops of death hovering behind
all the smallest gestures of life—sipping a cup, sleeping, lying still—
with mourning's discourse of farewell.

In other words, death marks Stevens's discourse as it marks language for Derrida. This poem of middle age—"Waving Adieu, Adieu,
Adieu"—doesn't narrate anything; rather, it attempts to create a mood,
to reveal something within or behind language, to remark something
just as Stevens notes in old age that "Questions Are Remarks," and
that his grandson's question is "complete because it contains / His
utmost statement. It is his own array, / His own pageant and procession
and display, / As far as nothingness permits . . ." (1954: 463). Stevens's
rhetoric, like that of mourning, marks what "nothingness permits" by
invoking the nonsense and terror of death behind life while it narrates
and describes the fullness of the life of the child and of language: "In
the weed of summer comes this green sprout why." That is, Stevens

lets nothingness blaze forth by invoking its continued, speechless presence: its inaccessible, absent presence as other within the questions of "drowsy, infant, old men."

Mourning describes in its rhetoric the equally inaccessible (absent) presence of the other within language and discourse. "What is laughable," Derrida says, "is the *submission* to the self-evidence of meaning, to the force of this imperative: that there must be meaning, that nothing must be definitely lost in death, or further, that death should receive the signification [in Hegel] of 'absolute negativity' " (1978: 256–57). What is laughable—in its absurdity, in its presumption, and finally in its nurturing sustenance—is the affirmation to which language gives rise. What is laughable is that mourning can, in fact, "work"—that Stevens's poems, for instance, afford so much pleasure, even when such pleasures circulate (as they do in his early poem, "The Pleasures of Merely Circulating") around questions whose rhetoric mark and re-mark death in the world: "Is there any secrets in skulls . . . ? / Do the drummers in black hoods / Rumble anything out of their drums?" (1954: 150).

In "Freud and the Scene of Writing" Derrida describes the "originality of Freud's aim," which, among other things he suggests, includes a conception of "life which can defend itself against death only through an *economy* of death" (1978: 202). That economy is, like all economies, an economy of *reserve,* and nowhere is this reserve more fully breached in Freud than in "Mourning and Melancholia," which struggles so hard to distinguish between (to discern: *dinoscere)* normal and abnormal mourning, between the same and the other. "In analysis," Freud writes, "it often becomes evident that first one, then another memory is activated and that the laments which are perpetually the same and wearisome in their monotony nevertheless each time take their rise in some different unconscious source. . . . The character of withdrawing the libido bit by bit is therefore to be ascribed alike to mourning and to melancholia; it is probably sustained by the same economic arrangements and serves the same purposes in both" (1963: 177). Malady and health, mourning and prayer assume the same form and follow the same economy. Despite this similarity, in the economy of psychoanalysis Freud is able to *hear* the difference between mourning and melancholia. Such discernment, Derrida says, requires a "keen ear," "an ear with keen hearing, an ear that perceives differences. . . . between apparently similar things. . . . the keen ear must be able to distinguish the active from the reactive, the affirmative from the negative, even though apparently they are the same thing" (1985: 50).

The keen ear is an ear for rhetoric, an ear that can *repeat* the sacred word within the ordinary (is it the performative "farewell"? the vocative name? a primal cry?), that can distinguish between truth and rhetoricity. Derrida renames Freud's "Notes upon the Mystic Writing Pad" "The Scene of Writing," and we could equally rename "Mourning and Melancholia" "The Scene of Rhetoric." For mourning is the scene of rhetoric, the place where the "rhetoricity" of rhetoric cannot be erased, where there is nothing else between our ordinary lives and the nothingness or pure non-sense of death than the gestures of rhetoric. In the *Memoires for Paul de Man* Derrida describes the scene of rhetoric: "I can only, from now on," Derrida says, articulating that *now* which Milton speaks and which is always marked in mourning, "I can only, from now on, speak of him in the desire to speak to him, in the desire to speak with him and, finally, to leave to him the chance to speak" (1986: 126).

Mourning, unlike laughter, makes room for discourse, for the silence of a speaking ear—which Derrida elsewhere calls "the ear of the other"—in its gestures of farewell. It does so because it makes clear the *future* and the *promise* inscribed in all discourse—the "counterfactual conditionals" and "future tenses" that George Steiner asserts "are fundamental to the dynamics of human feeling" (1975: 216). With language, Steiner argues, "we can *say anything*." "This latent totality," he continues, "is awesome and should be felt as such" (1975: 216). The essence of language and discourse is not its referential power but its representational, rhetorical power (*Vorstellung* and *Darstellung*): its defining and awesome case is its ability to speak to and for the dead. Language can say anything—as Derrida says elsewhere, even "the semantic void *signifies*" (1981: 222)—and he sees *this* as the sacred inscribed in language, the aspect of language without reserve. "What is love, friendship, memory, from the moment two impossible promises are involved with them, sublimely, without any possible exchange?" he asks at the end of his *Memoires for Paul de Man*. He answers:

> These questions can be posed only after the death of a friend, and they are not limited to the question of mourning. What should we think of all of this, of love, of memory, of promise, of destination, of experience, since a promise, from the first moment that it pledges, and however possible it appears, pledges beyond death. . . .
>
> . . . A promise has meaning and gravity only on the condition of death, when the living person is one day all alone with his promise. (1986: 149–50)

Mourning, then, leaves us alone with language, with rhetoric, with both
its sustenance and its terror. It speaks with and for another, with and
for the mortality inscribed in language, in the dead, in the living. Its
rhetoric is as ordinary as a promise, as memory, as love.

It is as ordinary as the seeming passivity of perception (before it
became Jakobson's "science"), or confusion (before it became Barthes'
textual "tactics" without strategy), or conversation (before it became
Lacan's psychoanalytic "cure"), or even basic "human" life (before it
became simply "European" life). But at the scene of rhetoric enacted
in mourning these things—as Blanchot says, these *same* things—suddenly open, absolutely black and absolutely empty, language with and
without reserve. At this scene, it is as if in forgetful oblivion, as Stevens
says in "The Rock," love, promise, and memory might still find place,

> As if nothingness contained a metier,
> A vital assumption, an impermanence
> In its permanent cold, an illusion so desired
>
> That the green leaves came and covered the high rock,
> That the lilacs came and bloomed, like a blindness cleaned,
> Exclaiming bright sight. . . . (1954: 526)

By leaving us alone with language, mourning—the *recovered* voice of
mourning heard everywhere in Derrida—speaks what nothingness permits and what ears strain to repeat. With and without reserve, mourning repeats inventions of farewell.

The Farewell

Such a discourse—like the pleasures of the text that Barthes describes,
or even like Lacan's "full" speech—seeks to reachieve a "primal cry"
and to produce, as Greimas says in the mode of Jakobson's intelligence,
the "illusory signification of a 'deep meaning,' hidden and inherent in
the plane of expression" of language (1967: 279). Derrida—and with
him the modernist postmodern rhetoric I have described here—offers
a self-conscious sense of the rhetoricity of such "meaning," a sense
more "Greek," less charged, and marked by the kind of joyful elegy
that Nietzsche describes in the Greeks. Against the silence of prayer
and "the leap out of language into faith" that de Man describes in
Kierkegaard (1969: 204), Derrida offers the "burst of laughter" as "the
almost nothing into which meaning sinks" (1978: 256).

Like Stevens's description of modern poetry that "must resist the
intelligence / Almost successfully" (1954: 350), Derrida's "almost"

marks the scene of rhetoric—a "modern" scene—where language creates material effects alternating between meaning and nonmeaning: the two definitions of rhetoric within which modernism realizes itself. Derrida calls this the "textual drama" of the conflict between meaning and nonmeaning, the sacred and the profane, in which, as Richard Rorty says, "writing always leads to more writing, and more, and still more—just as history does not lead to Absolute Knowledge or the Final Struggle, but to more history, and more, and still more" (1982: 94). Such repetition is the scene of rhetoric, the metonymic play of materiality, on and on and on. Rather than the "classical" repetition Derrida describes in *The Post Card,* which "repeats something that precedes it" and in which "repetition succeeds a first thing, an original, a primary, a prior, the repeated itself which in and of itself is supposed to be foreign to what is repetitive or repeating in repetition" (1987: 351), "sometimes, according to a logic that is other, and non-classical, repetition is 'original,' and induces, through an unlimited propagation of itself, a general deconstruction" (1987: 351–52).

Such repetition is modern, metonymic, unlimited, and, like modernism itself, inscribed by death. "Force," Derrida writes,

> produces meaning (and space) through the power of "repetition" alone, which inhabits it originarily as its death. This power, that is, this lack of power, which opens and limits the labor of force, institutes translatability, makes possible what we call "language," transforms an absolute idiom into a limit which is always already transgressed: a pure idiom is not language; it becomes so only through repetition; repetition always already divides the point of departure of the first time. . . . If one limits oneself to the *datum or the effect of repetition,* to translation, to the obviousness of the distinction between force and meaning, not only does one miss the originality of Freud's aim, but one effaces the intensity of the relation to death as well. (1978: 213–14)

Here, at the scene of rhetoric, Derrida presents neither Jakobson's knowledge, nor Barthes' textual power, nor de Man's melancholic readings, nor the "full" speech of Lacanian psychoanalysis. Rather, he offers rhetoric without reserve, neither sacred nor profane; beyond Barthes' simple tactics, yet a tactics without a "future," since it articulates and enacts the sacredness of nonstrategic sacrifice.

In each of these writers, as in Derrida, the relationship to death is the mark of the rhetoric of modernism. That rhetoric—postmodern and modernist, alternatively and at the same time—is, as I have suggested, historically determined. But, for all these writers, this relationship is articulated in the impossible discrimination between meaning and force, the distinction between the two senses of rhetoric that inhabit, incompatibly, the language and "sense" of our time. Derrida, most explicitly of the writers treated here, makes this uneasy coexistence the object of his own uneasy rhetoric without offering the kinds of closure I have noticed in the other discourses examined. It is the uneasy coexistence between depth and surface, the mysterious and the ordinary, the sense and non-sense of life and death.

Works Cited

Achebe, Chinua (1988) "An Image of Africa: Racism in Conrad's *Heart of Darkness*." In *Heart of Darkness*, ed. Robert Kimbrough. Norton, New York. 251–62.

Adams, Henry (1931) *The Education of Henry Adams*. Modern Library, New York.

Anderson, Perry (1984) *In the Tracks of Historical Materialism*. University of Chicago Press, Chicago.

——— (1988) "Modernity and Revolution." In *Marxism and the Interpretation of Culture*, ed. Cary Nelson and Lawrence Grossberg. University of Illinois Press, Urbana. 317–38.

Armstrong, Nancy (1982) "Domesticating the Foreign Devil: Structuralism in English Letters a Decade Later." *Semiotica* 42: 247–77.

Attridge, Derek (1988) *Peculiar Language*. Cornell University Press, Ithaca.

Auerbach, Erich (1957) *Mimesis*. Trans. Willard Trask. Anchor Books, New York.

Austin, J. L. (1962) *How to Do Things with Words*. Harvard University Press, Cambridge.

Bakhtin, Mikhail (1981) *The Dialogic Imagination*. Trans. Caryl Emerson and Michael Holquist. University of Texas Press, Austin.

——— (1984) *Problems of Dostoevsky's Poetics*. Trans. Caryl Emerson. University of Minnesota Press, Minneapolis.

Bakhtin, M. M./P. N. Medvedev (1985) *The Formal Method in Literary Scholarship*. Trans. Albert Wehrle. Harvard University Press, Cambridge.

Bakhtin, M. M. (1986) *Speech Genres and Other Late Essays*. Trans. Vern McGee. University of Texas Press, Austin.

[Bakhtin]/Voloshinov, V. N. (1986a) *Marxism and the Philosophy of Language*. Trans. Ladislav Matejka and I. R. Titunik. Harvard University Press, Cambridge.

Barthes, Roland (1967) *Writing Degree Zero.* Trans. Annette Lavers and Colin Smith. Beacon Press, Boston.

—— (1968) *Elements of Semiology.* Trans. Annette Lavers and Colin Smith. Hill and Wang, New York.

—— (1972) *Critical Essays.* Trans. Richard Howard. Northwestern University Press, Evanston.

—— (1972a) *Mythologies.* Trans. Annette Lavers. Paladin Books, London.

—— (1974) *S/Z.* Trans. Richard Miller. Hill and Wang, New York.

—— (1975) *The Pleasure of the Text.* Trans. Richard Miller. Hill and Wang, New York.

—— (1976) *Sade/Fourier/Loyola.* Trans. Richard Miller. Hill and Wang, New York.

—— (1977) *Image-Music-Text.* Trans. and ed. Stephen Heath. Fontana, London.

—— (1977a) *Roland Barthes by Roland Barthes.* Trans. Richard Howard. Hill and Wang, New York.

—— (1981) *Camera Lucida.* Trans. Richard Howard. Hill and Wang, New York.

—— (1981a) "Theory of the Text." Trans. Ian McLeod. In *Untying the Text,* ed. Robert Young. Routledge, London. 31–47.

—— (1981b) "Textual Analysis of Poe's 'Valdemar,' " Trans. Geoff Bennington. In *Untying the Text,* ed. Robert Young. Routledge, London. 133–61.

—— (1982) "Inaugural Lecture, Collège de France." Trans. Richard Howard. In *A Barthes Reader,* ed. Susan Sontag. Hill and Wang, New York. 457–78.

—— (1985) *The Grain of the Voice: Interviews 1962–1980.* Trans. Linda Coverdale. Hill and Wang, New York.

—— (1986) *The Rustle of Language.* Trans. Richard Howard. Hill and Wang, New York.

Baudrillard, Jean (1983) *Simulations.* Trans. Paul Foss, Paul Patton, Philip Beitchman. Semiotext(e), New York. (A partial translation of *L'Echange symbolique et la mort.*)

—— (1988) "Symbolic Exchange and Death." Trans. Jacques Mourrain. In *Selected Writings,* ed. Mark Poster. Stanford University Press, Stanford. (A partial translation of *L'Echange symbolique et la mort.*)

Becker, Ernest (1973) *The Denial of Death.* Free Press, New York.

Benjamin, Walter (1969) *Illuminations.* Trans. Harry Zohn. Schocken Books, New York.

Benveniste, Emile (1971) *Problems in General Linguistics.* Trans. Mary Elizabeth Meek. University of Miami Press, Coral Gables.

Berman, Marshall (1982) *All That Is Solid Melts into Air: The Experience of Modernity.* Touchstone, New York.

Blanchot, Maurice (1986) *The Writing of the Disaster.* Trans. Ann Smock. University of Nebraska Press, Lincoln.

Bové, Paul (1984) "The Penitentiary of Reflection: Søren Kierkegaard and Critical Activity." In *Kierkegaard and Literature,* ed. Ronald Schleifer and Robert Markley. University of Oklahoma Press, Norman. 25–57.

Bradbury, Malcolm, and James McFarlane (1976) "The Name and Nature of Modernism." In *Modernism: 1890–1930,* ed. Malcolm Bradbury and James McFarlane. Penguin Books, Harmondsworth. 19–55.

Brooks, Peter (1976) *The Melodramatic Imagination.* Yale University Press, New Haven.

—— (1984) *Reading for the Plot.* Knopf, New York.

Brown, Malcolm (1972) *The Politics of Irish Literature.* Allen & Unwin, London.

Bruns, Gerald (1974) *Modern Poetry and the Idea of Language.* Yale University Press, New Haven.

Bullock, Alan (1976) "The Double Image." In *Modernism: 1890–1930,* ed. Malcolm Bradbury and James McFarlane. Penguin Books, Harmondsworth. 58–70.

Burger, Peter (1984) *Theory of the Avant-Garde.* Trans. Michael Shaw. University of Minnesota Press, Minneapolis.

Burke, Kenneth (1969) *A Rhetoric of Motives.* University of California Press, Berkeley and Los Angeles.

Cavell, Stanley (1976) *Must We Mean What We Say?* Cambridge University Press, Cambridge.

Charon, Jacques (1963) *Death and Western Thought.* Collier Books, New York.

Chekhov, Anton (1979) "The Lady with the Dog." Trans. Ivy Litvinov. In *Anton Chekhov's Short Stories,* ed. Ralph Matlaw. Norton, New York. 221–34.

Conrad, Joseph (1963) *Under Western Eyes.* Doubleday, New York.

—— (1971) *Heart of Darkness.* Ed. Robert Kinbrough. Norton, New York.

Craig, David (1974) *The Real Foundations: Literature and Social Change.* Oxford University Press, New York.

Culler, Jonathan (1974) *Structuralist Poetics.* Cornell University Press, Ithaca.

—— (1976) *Saussure.* Fontana/Collins, Glasgow.

—— (1981) *The Pursuit of Signs.* Cornell University Press, Ithaca.

—— (1982) *On Deconstruction.* Cornell University Press, Ithaca.

—— (1983) *Roland Barthes.* Oxford University Press, New York.

—— (1988) *Framing the Sign: Criticism and Its Institutions.* University of Oklahoma Press, Norman.

Davis, Robert Con (1985) "Error at Yale: Geoffrey Hartman, Psychoanalysis, and Deconstruction." In *Rhetoric and Form: Deconstruction at Yale,* ed. Robert Con Davis and Ronald Schleifer. University of Oklahoma Press, Norman. 136–56.

De Man, Paul (1969) "The Rhetoric of Temporality." In *Interpretation: Theory and Practice,* ed. Charles Singleton. Johns Hopkins University Press, Baltimore. 173–209.

—— (1971) *Blindness and Insight.* Oxford University Press, New York.

—— (1979) *Allegories of Reading: Figural Language in Rousseau, Nietzsche, Rilke, and Proust.* Yale University Press, New Haven.

—— (1981) "Pascal's Allegory of Doubt." In *Allegory and Representation,* ed. Stephen Greenblatt. Johns Hopkins University Press, Baltimore. 1–25.

—— (1984) *The Rhetoric of Romanticism.* Columbia University Press, New York.

—— (1984a) "Phenomenality and Materiality in Kant." In *Hermeneutics: Questions and Prospects,* ed. Gary Shapiro and Alan Sica. University of Massachusetts Press, Amherst. 121–44.

—— (1986) *The Resistance to Theory.* University of Minnesota Press, Minneapolis.

Derrida, Jacques (1976) *Of Grammatology.* Trans. Gayatri Spivak. Johns Hopkins University Press, Baltimore.

—— (1977) "Limited Inc." Trans. Samuel Weber. *Glyph* 2: 162–254.

—— (1977a) "Fors." Trans. Barbara Johnson. *Georgia Review* 31: 64–116.

—— (1978) *Writing and Difference.* Trans. Alan Bass. University of Chicago Press, Chicago.

—— (1979) "Living On/Border Lines." Trans. James Hulbert. In *Deconstruction and Criticism,* ed. Harold Bloom et al. Continuum Press, New York. 75–176.

—— (1979a) "Me—Psychoanalysis: An Introduction to the Translation of 'The Shell and the Kernel' by Nicolas Abraham." Trans. Richard Klein. *Diacritics* 9: 4–12.

—— (1980) "The Law of Genre." Trans. Avital Ronell. *Critical Inquiry* 7: 55–81.

—— (1981) *Dissemination.* Trans. Barbara Johnson. University of Chicago Press, Chicago.

—— (1981a) *Positions.* Trans. Alan Bass. University of Chicago Press, Chicago.

—— (1982) *Margins of Philosophy.* Trans. Alan Bass. University of Chicago Press, Chicago.

—— (1983) "The Principle of Reason: The University in the Eyes of Its Pupils." Trans. Catherine Porter and Edward P. Morris. *Diacritics* 13: 3–20.

—— (1985) *The Ear of the Other.* Trans. Peggy Kamuf et al. Schocken Books, New York.

—— (1986) *Memoires for Paul de Man.* Trans. Cecile Lindsay, Jonathan Culler, Eduardo Cadava. Columbia University Press, New York.

—— (1987) *The Post Card.* Trans. Alan Bass. University of Chicago Press, Chicago.

—— (1988) "The Deaths of Roland Barthes." Trans. Pascale-Anne Brault and Michael Naas. In *Philosophy and Non-Philosophy since Merleau-Ponty,* ed. High Silverman. Routledge, New York. 259–96.

—— (1988a) "Like the Sound of the Sea Deep within a Shell: Paul de Man's War." Trans. Peggy Kamuf. *Critical Inquiry* 14: 590–652.

—— (1989) *Of Spirit: Heidegger and the Question.* Trans. Geoffrey Bennington and Rachel Bowlby. University of Chicago Press, Chicago.

Ducrot, Oswald, and Tzvetan Todorov (1979) *Encyclopedic Dictionary of the Sciences of Language.* Trans. Catherine Porter. Johns Hopkins University Press, Baltimore.

Eagleton, Terry (1983) *Literary Theory: An Introduction.* University of Minnesota Press, Minneapolis.

Edwards, George (1938) *The Evolution of Finance Capitalism.* Longmans, New York.

Eliot, T. S. (1963) *Collected Poems.* Harcourt Brace Jovanovich, New York.

—— (1975) *Selected Prose,* ed. Frank Kermode. Harcourt Brace Jovanovich, New York.

Ellmann, Richard (1959) *James Joyce.* Oxford University Press, New York.

Erlich, Victor (1973) "Roman Jakobson: Grammar of Poetry and Poetry of Grammar." In *Approaches to Poetics,* ed. Seymore Chapman. Columbia University Press, New York. 1–27.

Felman, Shoshana (1982) "Psychoanalysis and Education: Teaching Terminable and Interminable." *Yale French Studies* 63: 21–44.

—— (1983) *The Literary Speech Act: Don Juan with J. L. Austin, or Seduction in Two Languages.* Trans. Catherine Porter. Cornell University Press, Ithaca.

—— (1985) *Writing and Madness.* Trans. Martha Noel Evans and Shoshana Felman. Cornell University Press, Ithaca.

Fish, Stanley (1980) *Is There a Text in This Class?* Harvard University Press, Cambridge.

Flaubert, Gustave (1965) *Madame Bovary.* Trans. Eleanor Marx Aveling, rev. Paul de Man. Norton, New York.

Fleishman, Avrom (1978) *Fiction and the Ways of Knowing.* University of Texas Press, Austin.

Forster, E. M. (1908) *Howards End.* Vintage Books, New York.

—— (1952) *A Passage to India.* Harcourt Brace and World, New York.

Foucault, Michel (1970) *The Order of Things.* Pantheon Books, New York.

Fowles, John (1969) *The French Lieutenant's Woman.* Little Brown, Boston.

Freud, Sigmund (1959) *Beyond the Pleasure Principle.* Trans. James Strachey. Bantam, New York.

—— (1961) *Civilization and Its Discontents.* Trans. James Strachey. Norton, New York.

—— (1963) "Mourning and Melancholia." Trans. Joan Riviere. In *General Psychological Theory,* ed. Philip Rieff. Collier Books, New York. 164–79.

—— (1963a) "Analysis Terminable and Interminable." In *Therapy and Techniques,* ed. Philip Rieff. Collier Books, New York. 233–71.

Frye, Northrop (1947) "Yeats and the Language of Symbolism." *University of Toronto Review* 17: 1–17.

Galan, F. W. (1985) *Historic Structures: The Prague School Project, 1928–1946.* University of Texas Press, Austin.

Gallop, Jane (1985) *Reading Lacan.* Cornell University Press, Ithaca.

Gide, André (1931) *The Counterfeiters.* Trans. Dorothy Bussy. Modern Library, New York.

Gilbert, Sandra, and Susan Gubar (1988) *No Man's Land: Volume 1, The War of the Words.* Yale University Press, New Haven.

Goux, Jean-Joseph (1984) *Les Monnayeurs du langage.* Galilee, Paris.

Greimas, A. J. (1962) "La Linguistique statistique et la linguistique structur-
ale." *Le Français Moderne* 30: 241–52; 31: 55–68.
—— (1967) "La linguistique structurale et la poétique." In *Du Sens*. Seuil,
Paris. 271–83.
—— (1970) "Du Sens." In *Du Sens*. Seuil, Paris. 7–17.
—— (1983) *Structural Semantics*. Trans. Daniele MacDowell, Ronald
Schleifer, and Alan Velie. University of Nebraska Press, Lincoln.
Greimas, A. J., and J. Courtés (1982) *Semiotics and Language: An Analytical
Dictionary*. Trans. Larry Crist, Daniel Patte et al. Indiana University
Press, Bloomington.
Hamacher, Werner, Neil Hertz, and Thomas Keenan, eds. (1989) *Responses:
On Paul de Man's Wartime Journalism*. University of Nebraska Press,
Lincoln.
Handelman, Susan (1983) "Jacques Derrida and the Heretic Hermeneutic."
In *Displacement: Derrida and After*, ed. Mark Krupnick. Indiana Uni-
versity Press, Bloomington. 98–129.
Hansen, F. R. (1985) *The Breakdown of Capitalism*. Routledge, London.
Harrington, Michael (1983) *The Politics at God's Funeral*. Penguin Books,
New York.
Hartman, Geoffrey (1964) *Wordsworth's Poetry 1787–1814*. Yale University
Press, New Haven.
—— (1970) "The Voice in the Shuttle: Language from the Point of View of
Literature." In *Beyond Formalism*. Yale University Press, New Haven.
337–55.
—— (1981) *Saving the Text*. Johns Hopkins University Press, Baltimore.
Heidegger, Martin (1959) *Introduction to Metaphysics*. Trans. Ralph Manheim.
Yale University Press, New Haven.
—— (1971) *On the Way to Language*. Trans. Peter Hertz. Harper Books,
New York.
Heilbroner, Robert (1953) *The Worldly Philosophers*. Simon and Schuster,
New York.
Hirschkop, Ken (1986) "A Response to the Forum on Mikhail Bakhtin." In
Bakhtin: Essays and Dialogues on His Work, ed. Gary Saul Morson. Uni-
versity of Chicago Press, Chicago. 73–80.
Holenstein, Elmar (1976) *Roman Jakobson's Approach to Language: Phenom-
enological Structuralism*. Trans. Catherine Schelbert and Tarcisius Schel-
bert. Indiana University Press, Bloomington.
Husserl, Edmund (1964) *The Phenomenology of Internal Time-Consciousness*.
Trans. James Churchill. Indiana University Press, Bloomington.
Huyssen, Andreas (1986) *After the Great Divide: Modernism, Mass Culture,
Postmodernism*. Indiana University Press, Bloomington.
Hynes, Samuel (1968) *The Edwardian Turn of Mind*. Princeton University
Press, Princeton.
Jakobson, Roman (1929) without title in *Selected Writings: Volume II, Word
and Language*. Mouton, 'S-Gravenhage, 1971. 711–12.
—— (1932) "Is the Film in Decline?" In Jakobson (1987) 458–65.

—— (1934) "What is Poetry?" In Jakobson (1987) 368–78.

—— (1939) "Observations sur le classement phonologique des consonnes." In *Selected Writings: Volume I, Phonological Studies.* Mouton, 'S-Gravenhage, 1962. 272–79.

—— (1956) "Two Aspects of Language and Two Types of Aphasic Disturbances." In Jakobson (1987) 95–114.

—— (1957) "Shifters, Verbal Categories, and the Russian Verb." In *Selected Writings: Volume II, Word and Language.* Mouton, 'S-Gravenhage, 1971. 130–47.

—— (1960) "Linguistics and Poetics." In Jakobson (1987) 62–94.

—— (1968) "Poetry of Grammar and Grammar of Poetry." In Jakobson (1987) 121–44.

—— (1977) "A Few Remarks on Peirce, Pathfinder in the Science of Language." *MLN* 92: 1026–32.

—— (1987) *Language and Literature.* Ed. Krystyna Pomorska and Stephen Rudy, Harvard University Press, Cambridge.

Jakobson, Roman, and Claude Lévi-Strauss (1962) "Charles Baudelaire's 'Les Chats.' " In Jakobson (1987) 180–97.

Jakobson, Roman, with Krystyna Pomorska (1983) *Dialogues.* MIT Press, Cambridge.

Jakobson, Roman, and Stephen Rudy (1977) Yeats' *"Sorrow of Love" through the Years.* In Jakobson (1987) 216–50.

Jameson, Fredric (1979) *Fables of Aggression: Wyndham Lewis, the Modernist as Fascist.* University of California Press, Berkeley and Los Angeles.

—— (1981) *The Political Unconscious.* Cornell University Press, Ithaca.

Janik, Alan, and Stephen Toulmin (1973) *Wittgenstein's Vienna.* Touchstone, New York.

Jarrell, Randall (1971) "Some Lines from Whitman." In *Criticism: Some Major American Writers,* ed. Lewis Leary. Macmillan, New York. 117–30.

Johnson, Barbara, Louis Mackey, and J. Hillis Miller (1985) "Marxism and Deconstruction: Symposium." In *Rhetoric and Form: Deconstruction at Yale,* ed. Robert Con Davis and Ronald Schleifer. University of Oklahoma Press, Norman. 75–97.

Johnson, Samuel (1958) *Rasselas, Poems, and Selected Prose,* ed. Bertrand Bronson. Riverside, Boston.

Jones, Ernest (1961) *The Life and Work of Sigmund Freud* (abridged). Basic Books, New York.

Joyce, James (1961) *Ulysses.* Random House, New York.

—— (1969) *A Portrait of the Artist as a Young Man.* Viking, New York.

—— (1976) *Dubliners.* Penguin Books, New York.

Juvenal (1938) *Saturae.* Ed. A. E. Housman. Cambridge University Press, London.

—— (1958) *The Satires of Juvenal.* Trans. Rolfe Humphries. Indiana University Press, Bloomington.

Kafka, Franz (1974) *The Castle.* Trans. Willa Muir and Edwin Muir. Schocken Books, New York.

Kenner, Hugh (1959) *The Invisible Poet: T. S. Eliot.* McDowel, Obolensky, New York.

—— (1971) *The Pound Era.* University of California Press, Berkeley.

—— (1973) *The Counterfeiters.* Anchor Books, New York.

—— (1973a) "Some Post-Symbolist Structures." In *Literary Theory and Structure,* ed. Frank Brady, John Palmer, and Martin Price. Yale University Press, New Haven. 379–93.

—— (1978) *Joyce's Voices.* University of California Press, Berkeley.

Kermode, Frank (1968) "Lawrence and Apocalyptic Types." *Critical Quarterly* 10: 14–38.

—— (1979) *The Genesis of Secrecy.* Harvard University Press, Cambridge.

Kern, Stephen (1983) *The Culture of Time and Space: 1880–1918.* Harvard University Press, Cambridge.

Kierkegaard, Søren (1954) *Fear and Trembling.* Trans. Walter Lowrie. Anchor Books, New York.

—— (1964) *Repetition.* Trans. Walter Lowrie. Harper Torchbooks, New York.

—— (1965) *The Concept of Irony.* Trans. Lee Capel. Indiana University Press, Bloomington.

—— (1968) *Concluding Unscientific Postscript.* Trans. D. F. Swenson and Walter Lowrie. Princeton University Press, Princeton.

Kristeva, Julia (1980) *Desire in Language.* Trans. Thomas Gora, Alice Jardine, and Leon S. Roudiez. Columbia University Press, New York.

—— (1982) *Powers of Horror.* Trans. Leon S. Roudiez. Columbia University Press, New York.

—— (1984) *Revolution in Poetic Language.* Trans. Margaret Waller. Columbia University Press, New York.

Lacan, Jacques (1972) "Seminar on 'The Purloined Letter.' " Trans. Jeffrey Mehlman. *Yale French Studies* 48: 38–72.

—— (1977) *Ecrits: A Selection.* Trans. Alan Sheridan. Norton, New York.

—— (1978) *The Four Fundamental Concepts of Psycho-Analysis.* Trans. Alan Sheridan, Penguin Books, Harmondsworth.

Lawrence, D. H. (1961) *The Complete Short Stories.* Penguin Books, New York. (Three consecutively paged volumes.)

—— (1976) *The Rainbow.* Penguin Books, New York.

—— (1982) *Women in Love.* Penguin Books, New York.

Lentricchia, Frank (1980) *After the New Criticism.* University of Chicago Press, Chicago.

Lévi-Strauss, Claude (1975) *The Raw and the Cooked.* Trans. John and Doreen Weightman. Harper, New York.

—— (1984) "Structure and Form: Reflections on a Work by Vladimir Propp." Trans. Monique Layton, rev. Anatoly Liberman. In Vladimir Propp, *Theory and History of Folklore.* University of Minnesota Press, Minneapolis. 167–89.

Lunn, Eugene (1982) *Marxism and Modernism.* University of California Press, Berkeley and Los Angeles.

Lyotard, François (1977) "The Jewish Oedipus." Trans. Susan Hansen. *Genre* 10: 395–411.

MacCabe, Colin (1979) *James Joyce and the Revolution of the Word.* Barnes and Noble, New York.

—— (1985) *Theoretical Essays: Film, Linguistics, Literature.* Manchester University Press, Manchester.

Mailer, Norman (1979) *The Executioner's Song.* Little Brown, Boston.

Malcolm, Janet (1982) *Psychoanalysis: The Impossible Profession.* Knopf, New York.

Mann, Thomas (1968) *The Magic Mountain.* Trans. H. T. Lowe-Porter. Knopf, New York.

Marcuse, Herbert (1965) "The Ideology of Death." In *The Meaning of Death,* ed. Herman Feifel. McGraw-Hill, New York. 64–76.

McGee, Patrick (1988) *Paperspace: Style as Ideology in Joyce's "Ulysses."* University of Nebraska Press, Lincoln.

Melville, Herman (1967) *The Confidence-Man.* Bobbs-Merrill, Indianapolis.

Melville, Stephen (1986) *Philosophy Beside Itself: On Deconstruction and Modernism.* University of Minnesota Press, Minneapolis.

Mergler, Nancy, and Ronald Schleifer (1985) "The Plain Sense of Things: Violence and the Discourse of the Aged." *Semiotica* 54: 177–99.

Miller, J. Hillis (1976) "Stevens' Rock and Criticism as Cure." *Georgia Review* 30: 5–33, 330–48.

—— (1982) *Fiction and Repetition.* Harvard University Press, Cambridge.

—— (1985) "The Search for Grounds in Literary Study." In *Rhetoric and Form: Deconstruction at Yale,* ed. Robert Con Davis and Ronald Schleifer. University of Oklahoma Press, Norman. 19–36.

—— (1986) *The Ethics of Reading.* Columbia University Press, New York.

Moretti, Franco (1983) *Signs Taken for Wonders.* Trans. Susan Fischer, David Forgacs, and David Miller. Verso Books, London.

—— (1988) "The Spell of Indecision." In *Marxism and the Interpretation of Culture,* ed. Cary Nelson and Lawrence Grossberg. University of Illinois Press, Urbana. 339–46.

Newman, Charles (1985) *The Post-Modern Aura.* Northwestern University Press, Evanston.

Nietzsche, Friedrich (1956) *The Birth of Tragedy and The Genealogy of Morals.* Trans. Francis Golfing. Anchor Books, New York.

—— (1957) *The Use and Abuse of History.* Trans. Adrian Collins. Bobbs-Merrill, Indianapolis.

—— (1967) *The Genealogy of Morals.* Trans. Walter Kaufmann and R. J. Hollingdale. Viking, New York.

—— (1968) *The Will to Power.* Trans. Walter Kaufmann and R. J. Hollingdale. Weidenfeld and Nicholson, London.

Norris, Christopher (1982) *Deconstruction: Theory and Practice.* Methuen, New York.

—— (1988) *Paul de Man: Deconstruction and the Critique of Aesthetic Ideology.* Methuen, New York.

O'Hara, Daniel (1987) "Yeats in Theory." In *Post-Structuralist Readings of English Poetry,* ed. Richard Machin and Christopher Norris. Cambridge University Press, Cambridge. 349–68.

Parkinson, Thomas (1951) *W. B. Yeats: Self-Critic.* University of California Press, Berkeley and Los Angeles.

—— (1964) *Yeats: The Later Poetry.* University of California Press, Berkeley and Los Angeles.

Penley, Constance (1986) "Teaching in Your Sleep: Feminism and Psychoanalysis." In *Theory in the Classroom,* ed. Cary Nelson. University of Illinois Press, Urbana. 129–49.

Perloff, Marjorie (1985) "Barthes and the Zero Degree of Writing." *World Literature Today* 59: 510–16.

Plato (1945) *The Republic.* Trans. Francis Cornford. Oxford University Press, New York.

Proust, Marcel (1934) *Remembrance of Things Past,* Vol. 1. Trans. C. K. Scott Moncrieff. Random House, New York.

Richards, I. A. (1970) "Jakobson's Shakespeare: The Subliminal Structure of a Sonnet." *TLS* 28 May: 589–90.

Ricoeur, Paul (1970) *Freud and Philosophy.* Trans. Denis Savage. Yale University Press, New Haven.

Riffaterre, Michael (1970) "Describing Poetic Structures: Two Approaches to Baudelaire's 'Les Chats.' " In *Structuralism,* ed. Jacques Ehrmann. Doubleday Anchor, New York. 188–230.

Rorty, Richard (1982) *Consequences of Pragmatism.* University of Minnesota Press, Minneapolis.

Ross, Andrew (1986) *The Failure of Modernism.* Columbia University Press, New York.

Ruwet, Nicolas (1970) "Linguistics and Poetics." In *The Structuralist Controversy,* ed. Richard Macksey and Eugenio Donato. Johns Hopkins University Press, Baltimore. 296–318.

Sacks, Peter (1985) *The English Elegy.* Johns Hopkins University Press, Baltimore.

Said, Edward (1983) *The World, the Text, and the Critic.* Harvard University Press, Cambridge.

Sartre, Jean Paul (1965) *What Is Literature?* Trans. Bernard Frechtman. Harper Torchbooks, New York.

Saussure, Ferdinand de (1959) *Course in General Linguistics.* Trans. Wade Baskin. McGraw-Hill, New York.

Schleifer, Ronald (1977) "Wordsworth's Yarrow and the Poetics of Repetition." *Modern Language Quarterly* 38: 348–66.

—— (1977a) "Public and Private Narrative in *Under Western Eyes.*" *Conradiana* 9: 237–54.

—— (1979) "The Civility of Sorrow: Yeats's Daimonic Tragedy." *Philological Quarterly* 58: 219–35.

—— (1981) "The Poison of Ink: Post-War Literary Criticism." *New Orleans Review* 8: 241–49.

—— (1984) "Irony and the Literary Past: On *The Concept of Irony* and *The Mill on the Floss.*" In *Kierkegaard and Literature,* ed. Ronald Schleifer and Robert Markley. University of Oklahoma Press, Norman. 183–216.

—— (1985) "The Pathway of *The Rose*: Yeats, the Lyric, and the Syntax of Symbolism." *Genre* 18: 375–96.

—— (1985a) "Grace Paley: Chaste Compactness." In *Contemporary American Women Writers: Narrative Strategies,* ed. Catherine Rainwater and William J. Scheick. University Press of Kentucky, Lexington.

—— (1987) *A. J. Greimas and the Nature of Meaning.* University of Nebraska Press, Lincoln.

—— (1987a) "Deconstruction and Linguistic Analysis." *College English* 49: 381–95.

—— (1988) "Enunciation and Genre: Mikhail Bakhtin and the 'Double-Voiced' Narration of *The Rape of the Lock.*" *New Orleans Review* 15 (4): 31–42.

—— (1990) "Yeats's Postmodern Rhetoric." In *Yeats and Postmodernism,* ed. Leonard Orr. Syracuse University Press, Syracuse.

Schleifer, Ronald, and Robert Markley (1984) "Editors' Introduction: Writing without Authority and the Reading of Kierkegaard." In *Kierkegaard and Literature,* ed. Ronald Schleifer and Robert Markley. University of Oklahoma Press, Norman. 3–22.

Schleifer, Ronald, and Alan Velie (1987) "Genre and Structure: Toward an Actantial Typology of Narrative Genres and Modes." *MLN* 102: 1123–50.

Schneidau, Herbert (1977) "Style and Sacrament in Modernist Writing." *Georgia Review* 31: 427–52.

Schneiderman, Stuart (1983) *Jacques Lacan: The Death of an Intellectual Hero.* Harvard University Press, Cambridge.

Sennett, Richard (1976) *The Fall of Public Man.* Vintage Books, New York.

Shell, Marc (1982) *Money, Language, and Thought.* University of California Press, Berkeley and Los Angeles.

Shelley, Percy (1914) *Poetical Works.* Clarendon, Oxford.

Spender, Stephen (1965) *The Struggle of the Modern.* University of California Press, Berkeley and Los Angeles.

Spengler, Oswald (1962) *The Decline of the West.* Trans. Charles Atkinson. Modern Library, New York.

Spivak, Gayatri (1988) "Can the Subaltern Speak?" In *Marxism and the Interpretation of Culture,* ed. Cary Nelson and Lawrence Grossberg. University of Illinois Press, Urbana. 271–313.

Staley, Thomas (1980) "A Beginning: Signification, Story, and Discourse in Joyce's 'The Sisters.' " In *The Genres of the Irish Literary Revival,* ed. Ronald Schleifer. Pilgrim Books, Norman, Okla. 121–37.

Stambaugh, Joan (1972) *Nietzsche's Thought of Eternal Return.* Johns Hopkins University Press, Baltimore.

Starobinski, Jean (1979) *Words upon Words: The Anagrams of Ferdinand de Saussure.* Trans. O. Emmet. Yale University Press, New Haven.

Staten, Henry (1984) *Wittgenstein and Derrida.* University of Nebraska Press, Lincoln.

Steiner, George (1971) *In Bluebeard's Castle.* Yale University Press, New Haven.

—— (1975) *After Babel.* Oxford University Press, New York.

—— (1980) *On Difficulty and Other Essays.* Oxford University Press, New York.

—— (1986) "Real Presences." The Leslie Stephen Memorial Lecture (pamphlet). Cambridge University Press, Cambridge.

—— (1989) *Real Presences.* University of Chicago Press, Chicago.

Steiner, Peter (1984) *Russian Formalism: A Metapoetics.* Cornell University Press, Ithaca.

Stevens, Wallace (1954) *Collected Poems.* Knopf, New York.

Stewart, Garrett (1984) *Death Sentences: Styles of Dying in British Fiction.* Harvard University Press, Cambridge.

Symons, Arthur (1958) *The Symbolist Movement in Literature.* E. P. Dutton, New York.

Tavor Bannet, Eve (1989) *Structuralism and the Logic of Dissent.* University of Illinois Press, Urbana.

Tipton, Frank, and Robert Aldrich (1987) *An Economic and Social History of Europe, 1890–1939.* Johns Hopkins University Press, Baltimore.

Todorov, Tzvetan (1982) *Theories of the Symbol.* Trans. Catherine Porter. Cornell University Press, Ithaca.

—— (1984) *Mikhail Bakhtin: The Dialogic Imagination.* Trans. Wlad Godzich. University of Minnesota Press, Minneapolis.

Trilling, Lionel (1968) "On the Teaching of Modern Literature." In *Beyond Culture.* Viking, New York. 3–30.

Ulmer, Gregory (1985) *Applied Grammatology.* Johns Hopkins University Press, Baltimore.

Ungar, Steven (1983) *Roland Barthes: The Professor of Desire.* University of Nebraska Press, Lincoln.

West, Cornel (1988) "Historicizing the Postmodern Debate: Arnold, Eliot, Trilling, and Fanon on the Crisis in Modern Culture." Unpublished lecture presented at University of Oklahoma, November 2, 1988. Videotape available.

Widmer, Kingsley (1980) *Edges of Extremity: Some Problems of Literary Modernism.* Tulsa Monograph Series, Vol. 17 University of Tulsa.

Williams, Raymond (1958) *Culture and Society: 1780–1950.* Columbia University Press, New York.

Yeats, W. B. (1954) *The Letters of W. B. Yeats,* ed. Allan Wade. Macmillan, New York.

—— (1956) *The Collected Poems.* Macmillan, New York.

—— (1962) *Explorations.* Macmillan, New York.

—— (1965) *The Autobiography of W. B. Yeats.* Collier Books, New York.

—— (1966) *A Vision.* Collier Books, New York.

—— (1968) *Essays and Introductions.* Collier Books, New York.

Index

A Note on the Author

Ronald Schleifer teaches at the University of Oklahoma, where he is editor of the quarterly *Genre* and co-editor (with Robert Con Davis) of the Oklahoma Project for Discourse and Theory, a series of scholarly books. His previous books include *A. J. Greimas and the Nature of Meaning* (1987), *Contemporary Literary Criticism* (edited with Robert Con Davis; 1989), *Kierkegaard and Literature* (edited with Robert Markley; 1984), and *The Genres of the Irish Literary Revival* (1980). He has also translated A. J. Greimas's *Structural Semantics* (with Daniele McDowell and Alan Velie; 1983).